KREMLIN WIVES

★ ★ ★ ★ ★ ★

Larissa Vasilieva

EDITED AND TRANSLATED BY

Cathy Porter

WEIDENFELD & NICOLSON

London

First published in Great Britain in 1994
by Weidenfeld & Nicolson

The Orion Publishing Group Ltd
Orion House
5 Upper Saint Martin's Lane
London WC2H 9EA

A catalogue record for this book is available
from the British Library

ISBN 0 297 81405 2

The photographs in this book are taken from the author's archive

Grateful acknowledgement is made to
HarperCollins Publishers Ltd for permission to
quote from *Commissar* by Thaddeus Wittlin

Typeset by Deltatype Ltd, Ellesmere Port, Wirral
Printed by Butler & Tanner Ltd, Frome and London

Contents

Illustrations

Vyacheslav and Paulina Zhemchuzhina-Molotova with their
  daughter, Svetlana
Zhemchuzhina after her release from prison, with her grandchild
Nina Teimurazovna Beria
Nina Petrovna Khrushcheva with her two children
Khrushchev with his family
Victoria Brezhneva
The Brezhnevs
Anna and Konstantin Chernenko
Before Perestroika: Raissa Gorbacheva with Galina Brezhneva
  (right)
Raissa and Mikhail Gorbachev
Raissa Gorbacheva

Introduction

If the lives of the Soviet leaders behind the red walls of the Kremlin are still a subject of boundless fascination and mystery, those of their wives remain a complete enigma. Who were these women? Were they merely shadows of husbands who were simultaneously terrifying and nondescript? What was their role in the historical process? These are some of the questions that prompted me to write this book.

Three main sources were available to me. First, there were scholarly volumes of memoirs and research published in Russia and abroad. (The women of the Kremlin figure fleetingly, if at all, in these predominantly male works.) Recently we have seen several memoirs written by wives of 'enemies of the people', tragic, disturbing and restrained. There are separate works on Nadezhda Krupskaya, Inessa Armand and Alexandra Kollontai, and collections of these women's own writings have also been published. However, these publications too tend to pass over in silence the personal details that interest us most.

The second route was legends and rumours – much of it insubstantial, but an invaluable source of information none the less. I had meetings with women who were still alive, and with relatives and close friends of those who were dead. From these people I discovered a wealth of fascinating, if occasionally unverifiable, information. Each new meeting set me the delicate task of speaking the truth while not insulting the dead or offending those still alive. It was to avoid becoming entangled in half-truths that I was drawn to the third source, namely archives, manuscripts, documents and letters.

A fourth route was through my own Kremlin connections as a writer. The playwright Ivan Vasilevich Popov had worked with

Lenin in exile, and in the summer of 1953 used my memory as a notebook for fear of committing his unique but potentially dangerous knowledge to paper. For this I am eternally grateful to him. I wish to thank all the surviving Kremlin wives, as well as the children, grandchildren and friends of those who are no longer alive, and all those who found time in these difficult days to share precious information about themselves and their loved ones. I must also thank all the historians and memoirists of the Soviet period: the official ones whose whitewashing of history enabled me to think the opposite, and the 'unofficial' and foreign ones for not having yet covered the subject themselves.

As I approached the end of this book I realised that I would have to visit the KGB building on Lubyanka Square, home of Bolshevik Russia's first secret police force, the *Cheka*. In the spring of 1991 the Moscow Writers' Union wrote on my behalf, requesting that I be allowed access to the files on Kremlin wives arrested during the purges of the 1930s and 1940s. For many weeks there was no reply. Then, in August 1991, three days after the statue of Dzerzhinsky, the *Cheka*'s founder, was toppled on Lubyanka Square, I received a telephone call from an official at the KGB asking me to come right away.

I was led upstairs to a large room overlooking Lubyanka Square, formerly the office of KGB chief Yury Andropov, and before him of Lavrenty Beria and Nikolai Ezhov.[1] The room contained a huge armchair beneath a portrait of Lenin, a long T-shaped table and a bust of Dzerzhinsky. Behind this room lay Dzerzhinsky's old office. Alone in the inquisitors' headquarters, gazing at the files piled on the vast gleaming table, I picked up the receiver of a telephone switchboard emblazoned with the emblem of the Union of Soviet Socialist Republics. The line had been disconnected. I was cut off from the world. The office was dead, and the fact that I was sitting there merely emphasised this. It was all so normal, so official, so unfrightening . . .

For a second I heard the creak of iron doors, the grate of prison keys, the shrieks, the sobs. I saw a solitary naked figure soaked in icy water, sitting beneath a glaring bulb. I saw the contorted faces of torturers and victims alike – for are we not all torturers and victims alike on this earth?

How many lives were held within these files? I read, and everything was both more simple and more terrifying . . .

[1] Heads of the NKVD, as the KGB was known before 1952.

Note on Russian Names

In Russia one has a first name, a patronymic (deriving from the father's first name), and a surname. With female names, both patronymic and surname generally end in 'a'. The normal term of semi-formal address is first name plus patronymic, and both this form and the form of first name plus maiden name or married name are used in this translation. To assist pronunciation, ´ is used here to indicate the stressed syllable.

Nadézhda Konstantínovna Lénina (*née* KRÚPSKAYA)
Inéssa Teodórovna ARMÁND
Alexándra Mikháilovna KOLLONTÁI
Laríssa Mikháilovna RÉISNER
Ólga Davídovna KÁMENEVA
Galína Sergéevna KÁMENEVA (*née* KRAVCHÉNKO)
Nadézhda Sergéevna STÁLINA (*née* ALLILÚYEVA)
Ekaterína Davídovna VOROSHÍLOVA (*née* Golda Davidovna
  GÓRBMAN)
Nadézhda Ivánovna BUDYÓNNAYA
Olga Stefánovna BUDYÓNNAYA (*née* MIKHÁILOVA)
María Vasílevna BUDYÓNNAYA
Galína Antónovna EGÓROVA
Ekaterína Ivánovna KALÍNINA (*née* Lórberg)
Paulína Semyónovna MÓLOTOVA (revolutionary name
  ZHEMCHÚZHINA)
Nína Teimurázovna BÉRIA (*née* GEGÉCHKORI)
Tatyána OKUNÉVSKAYA
Nína Petróvna KHRÚSHCHEVA (*née* KUKHÁRCHUK)
Victória Petróvna BRÉZHNEVA
Tatyána Fillípovna ANDRÓPOVA

Ańna Dmítrevna CHERNÉNKO (*née* LYUBÍMOVA)
Raíssa Maxímovna GORBACHÉVA (*née* TITARÉNKO)

Many names are given here in their intimate diminutive form, which can differ quite significantly from the full name.

Alexander – Sasha
Anna – Anya
Ekaterina – Katya
Galina – Galenka, Galya
Mikhail – Misha
Nadezhda – Nadya
Natalya – Natasha
Nina – Ninochka
Sergei – Seryozha
Vyacheslav – Vladislav

Honest Nadezhda

Vladimir Ilich Ulyanov (revolutionary name Lenin, 1870–1924), born in Simbirsk. Joined the revolutionary movement while studying law at Kazan University in the late 1880s. Imprisoned in 1895 for his part in establishing the Marxist League of Struggle for the Emancipation of the Working Class. Married Nadezhda Krupskaya during his subsequent exile in Siberia. For the next ten years he lived mainly in exile abroad, working for revolution in Russia and returning to Petrograd in April 1917 as its leader. After October 1917 he was President of the Soviet of People's Commissars (the Sovnarkom) until his death seven years later.

In the spring of 1918 a forty-nine-year-old woman moved into the Kremlin. Her face was plain and her lips were full – evidence of a passionate nature, though few would have dared to suggest this of her. She had protruding, widely-spaced eyes, whose heavy lids gave her face a sleepy expression. Her forehead was thoughtful, and her smooth hair was parted in the middle and drawn into a bun at the nape of her neck, with untidy wisps escaping onto her cheeks. Her figure was shapeless and devoid of female curves, her straight back and slow walk suggested that she had attended a good girls' high school, and her elegant hands but neglected nails suggested someone more interested in practical activity than in emphasising her female attributes. This was Nadezhda Konstantinovna Krupskaya, wife of Vladimir Lenin, leader of the Bolshevik revolution.

The new *tsaritsa*, as some at first called her, had spent most of the previous fourteen years out of the country, and was largely unknown in Russia before 1917. She knew the isolation of exile, and in the absence of modern communications this isolation was almost total. Yet although Russia may not have been ready for Krupskaya, Krupskaya was ready for Russia – probably more so than the German princesses who for the past two hundred years had occupied the Russian throne. Since her childhood she had set herself the noble goal of achieving happiness for the Russian people. And later, when Lenin's global strategy expanded this goal into the slogan 'Proletarians of all countries, unite!', this accorded perfectly with her desires.

Krupskaya's own definition of happiness is contained in the story of her life. Yet the official Soviet culture of the stagnant 1970s has cast its aura of sanctity around this life, and over successive generations the unctuous memoirs of those who knew her have reduced her to a figure of tedious sentimentality and thus forced one to seek the opposite.

'Krupskaya the model of a faithful wife? I should think so, with her looks! Nobody but Lenin would have wanted her!'

'Apparently he had an affair with . . .'

'What did she know about children? She never had any!'

'After the revolution she waged war on religion and banned some wonderful books from the libraries, because she said they were damaging to proletarian children.'

Born in St Petersburg in 1869, the only daughter of Elizaveta Vasilevna and Konstantin Ignatevich Krupsky, Nadezhda Krupskaya grew up surrounded by love.

When she was three years old her father was dismissed from his government post for his openly expressed sympathy with revolutionary ideas, and the Krupskys were banished to the provinces. After eight years spent moving from town to town, living in hardship and petitioning the government to rescind its decision, Konstantin Ignatevich and his family were finally allowed back to St Petersburg, where they settled in a squalid apartment in the slum quarter of the capital.

Nadezhda was just as comfortable playing with the poor children in the yard of their building as with the aristocratic daughters of her mother's friends. She was deeply affected by her father's dismissal, and she was quick to grasp that his problems transcended the family's situation to connect with the woes of Russia as a whole.

Anxious to give their daughter a good education and to develop her intellect in line with modern thinking, the Krupskys enrolled her in Princess Obolenskaya's *gimnazium*, an idealistic enterprise created by populists of the 1860s and 1870s, and one of the best private girls' schools in Russia. Nadezhda met here not only aristocrats' and merchants' daughters but the daughters of revolutionaries, many of whom dreamed of dedicating their lives to the people. These ideals were brought to life by the teachers and offered to the girls as an inspiring example, and the word 'revolution' was frequently heard in the Krupsky home.

In the second half of the nineteenth century, women in Russia had the opportunity to leave their families and seek an education. Surrounded by injustice, they longed to do something about it, but while the male rulers of the state held all in their power, they were inexorably drawn to the revolutionary movement and to those struggling to topple the government. Although, as revolutionaries, women were expected to act as men's faithful assistants, and most accepted this role, a few none the less enjoyed great authority within the movement.

Vera Zasulich (1849–1919) was one of these, a leader of various revolutionary circles before she shot and wounded St Petersburg's governor-general in 1879. After many years in prison and exile, Zasulich worked with Lenin during his years of political exile in Switzerland. Solitary and impractical, she was deeply hostile to the Bolshevik revolution and died disillusioned with life.

Vera Figner (1852–1942), a populist turned terrorist, was sentenced to death for her part in the assassination of Tsar Alexander II in 1881. The sentence was subsequently commuted to twenty years in Schlüsselberg fortress, and after her release in 1902 she lived for many years in Moscow, where she observed with a certain detachment the Bolsheviks' application of her ideas.

Sofia Perovskaya (1853–81) was hanged for her part in Alexander II's assassination – the first woman in Russia to be sentenced to death for a political crime.

These firstcomers signalled a new generation of revolutionary women, who were determined to win the fight.

Soon after Krupsky's death in 1883, his widow and daughter were visited by Nikolai Isaakovich Utin, a well-known revolutionary, who understood their difficult position and helped fourteen-year-old Nadezhda to find her first private teaching job. Nadezhda's schoolfriend Ariadna Tyrkova, who after the Revolution became a prominent anti-Bolshevik, wrote in her memoirs several years later:

She lived with her mother in the inner courtyard of the Durdins' building on Znamenskaya Street. They led a quiet, dull, old-fashioned life and their cramped three-room flat always smelled of onions, cabbage and pies. In the kitchen stood the cook's bed, spread with a red calico cover. In those days even a poor clerk's widow was unable to manage without domestic help; I know of nobody then who did not have at least one servant.

As the stagnant 1870s of Nadezhda's childhood gave way to the turbulent events of the 1880s, Elizaveta Vasilevna watched with a mixture of hope and apprehension as her daughter was taken under the wing of the revolutionaries. Ariadna Tyrkova wrote:

We were constantly talking about the failings of society . . . In many educated Russian families the more sensitive young people were infected by the microbe of social unrest. Of all my friends this had entered most deeply into Nadya Krupskaya. She had defined her views and marked out her path long before the rest of us, and far more irrevocably. She was someone who, once consumed by a feeling or idea, would surrender herself to it totally and forever.

In 1887, after graduating from Princess Obolenskaya's school with her governess's diploma, Nadezhda started coaching the other girls there for their final exams. The following testimonial, presented to the young teacher, extolled her achievements:

Domestic governess N. K. Krupskaya has for the past two years worked in the evenings with ten pupils . . . The girls' success is evidence of her outstanding pedagogical abilities, her wide-ranging knowledge, and her meticulous approach to her work.

Since no man had yet fallen in love with her daughter and Elizaveta Vasilevna's motherly dreams of a good match for Nadezhda began to fade, she saw this modest employment as the best her daughter could hope for. 'I'm like the Russian countryside – without bright colours,' Nadezhda would comfort her.
Ariadna Tyrkova recalls:

As a girl Nadya did not indulge in flirtation, amorous adventures or sexual games. She didn't go skating, dancing or boating, and she talked only to her schoolfriends and her mother's elderly women friends. I never saw any male guests at their flat.

Plain Nadya did not dream of men and marriage and 'all that

rubbish'. She did not aspire to the typical female lot, and she pitied her married friends for enslaving themselves to a man and wasting their talents. She had chosen to dedicate herself not to home and family but to the wider world outside. The first marker on this path was a newspaper appeal by Lev Tolstoy for educated girls to rewrite well-known works of literature in simple language for peasant consumption. Nadezhda wrote to Tolstoy volunteering her services:

> Respected Lev Nikolaevich! Recently I have realised more and more clearly how much toil, energy and health is wasted in my exploitation of others' labour. I have lived like this in order to acquire knowledge, in the hope that this would enable me to be useful later on. I now see that the knowledge I have gained is of no use to anyone, since I cannot apply it to my life and make any small amends for my own inactivity – and I do not know what is to be done about it . . .
>
> I know that editing books for the simple people is important work which demands much knowledge and experience, and I am only eighteen years old and know very little . . . But I am appealing to you because I think that to do work that I love may help me to overcome my ignorance and inexperience. So if possible, Lev Nikolaevich, please send me one or two of these books, and I will do what I can with them.

Tolstoy's daughter Tatyana sent her Alexander Dumas' *The Count of Monte Cristo*, and Nadya sat down to edit it. The task was ill-advised, as she realised herself in the course of doing it, but since she was not one to abandon a task half-done, especially one from the great Tolstoy, she persevered to the end.

While awaiting his response, she visited several groups of 'Tolstoyans', but her down-to-earth nature found their lofty abstractions distasteful and demanded something more practical. She began to seek out the younger revolutionaries, searching for some sign which would set her on the right path. For her there were no half-measures, as Ariadna Tyrkova observed:

> She would pore endlessly over a phrase in a textbook, grappling to understand exactly what it meant. But once she had finally done so she would absorb it forever, just as later she would absorb the teachings of Karl Marx and Ulyanov-Lenin.

It was in the spring of 1890 that Nadezhda read Marx's *Das Kapital*, describing it later as a 'drink of fresh water'. From that moment on it became clear to her that the path lay neither in isolated acts of terrorism nor in Tolstoyan self-perfection, but in the mighty workers' movement.

The year 1890 marked the transformation of the naïve girl seeking her own path into the revolutionary discovering the force which was to guide the rest of her life. Hungry for further education, Nadezhda enrolled in the prestigious Bestuzhev higher education courses for women. But in the autumn of 1890 she abandoned the courses and concentrated all her energies on teaching.

Ariadna Tyrkova's memoirs of the year 1890 describe how revolutionary work transformed her friend:

> She would shower me with radiant love, clasping my hands in hers and smiling bashfully. She had fine white skin, and a delicate pink flush would spread from her cheeks to her ears and chin. I had often pitied my Nadya her plainness; she now looked quite lovely. Yet behind this softness I sensed another Nadya. She had embarked upon the path that would lead her to her goal, and strange as this may sound in my modest Nadya, even the luxury of her life.
>
> It started with workers' evening classes outside the city gates. Her kind blue eyes would shine as she told me in a dull, monotonous tone of the importance of awakening the workers' class consciousness . . . I was happy for her and realised what a joy it must be to discover some all-consuming goal.

Seeing that her revolutionary daughter was totally inept at housework and tended to abandon chores half-way through, Elizaveta Vasilevna supervised all the cleaning and cooking in the flat. A devout woman, she was frightened by her daughter's growing atheism, and told Ariadna Tyrkova: 'You're as bad as my Nadya. You'd be wiser if you went to church and prayed for grace and forgiveness!' But the naturally tolerant Nadezhda did not try to argue with her mother, and the two women lived peacefully together.

Now all Nadezhda needed was someone to whom she could devote her revolutionary passion. Blushing, she would casually mention to Ariadna Tyrkova 'a certain comrade' who meant a lot to her. Since, at the time, she never mentioned his name, Ariadna assumed later that this must be Lenin. It was in fact four more years before Nadezhda met Lenin, and the man to whom she referred was probably a Marxist engineering student named Klasson, whose revolutionary circle she started to attend. They studied *Das Kapital* together, they read and argued, and shared ideas may have led to embraces – although Nadezhda's strict moral code and known tendency to lofty emotions makes this unlikely. Determined to live up to her revolutionary ideals, she was not one to succumb to fleeting sensations; a true Marxist could conquer everything. Monks and nuns mortified the flesh by fasting and praying; she did so with the aid of Marx and Engels, revolutionary meetings and her teaching work.

She recalled bringing in Tolstoy's *War and Peace* for a worker to read, and that he handed it back to her the next day, saying: 'It's rubbish! It's too long. It's for people to read lying on the sofa, it's no use to us!' Another worker named Zhukov wrote: 'She said something about India and the life of the Indians, then she suddenly started talking about our life.' Clever, open-minded and fascinated by new ideas, the young teacher with the pink cheeks and long, auburn plait was popular with her students, and after her lesson ended they would vie for the honour of walking her home at night. The man who generally succeeded was Ivan Vasilevich Babushkin, tall, elegant, moustached and blazing with youth and health as he took her arm in the dark side-streets of Petrograd.

In February 1894 St Petersburg's frosts were accompanied by a pink sun which ushered in the spring. Shrovetide approached, but nature held few charms for Nadezhda Krupskaya as she toiled away at her evening classes, her Marxism and her innumerable pamphlets and books. One of these was an exercise book containing an essay on Marxism and the market by a Marxist named Herman Krasin. She was about to put the book aside, when she saw that its margins were filled with neatly written notes, and, struck by the reader's originality and caustic tone, she read on. None of her comrades was capable of thinking in such global terms, certainly not Klasson.

Walking along the street to work that evening she happened to meet Klasson, who asked if she and her friend Zina would come to his room later for a Marxist debate to be held under the guise of a pancake party. She was unenthusiastic, feeling that she had outlived the circle and not wanting to waste time, but Klasson persisted. A man from the Volga would be there, he said, a strange character who had torn Krasin's views to shreds. Nadezhda remembered the notes in Krasin's exercise book, and decided to go. She recalled:

There were a great many people there. The discussion was about the way forward. Someone mentioned the importance of the literacy committee, and this provoked a dry, sarcastic laugh from the 'man from the Volga'.

Hearing the 'man from the Volga' speak was like a bolt of lightning for Nadezhda, and she suddenly realised that revolution was not only possible but imminent. That evening she made enquiries, and though she rarely told her mother about her revolutionary activities, on this occasion she told her all about the man from the Volga. His name was Vladimir Ulyanov, he was twenty-four years old (he looked older), and was descended from the minor nobility. His father, now dead, had been inspector of schools in the Siberian town of Simbirsk. His mother, née Blank, was the daughter of a former police doctor, and his elder brother was Alexander Ulyanov, a member of the terrorist People's Will party, executed in 1887 for the attempted assassination of Tsar Alexander III.

One evening, towards the end of the summer, Nadezhda and Lenin had a chance meeting on the steps of the library, and after they had walked back through the streets of St Petersburg to her apartment together, the words *the revolution is both possible and imminent* blazed in her mind.

This encounter determined her fate. The great love of her life was and always would be the revolution; for this she lived, worked and dreamed. Now Vladimir Ulyanov-Lenin had appeared as her leader, the embodiment of her dreams. She trusted him utterly, and in the name of the cause she would go with him to the ends of the earth, demanding nothing for herself, accepting whatever role he chose for her in his life of revolutionary sacrifice. Many women who dedicated themselves to the revolution chose the wrong man; Nadezhda had the good sense to choose the right one. She had been a star pupil, after all, and star pupils seldom make mistakes. By 1894 Lenin's mother, Maria Alexandrovna Ulyanova, had grown to understand revolutionaries, and from her first meeting with Nadezhda she knew that this young woman was exactly the wife she would have wished for her son. She was not pretty, but that meant he would not be distracted by jealousy. She was from a poor family, and although it would naturally have been better if she had had money, her poverty gave her a certain dignity and the strength to bear life's misfortunes.

It was common practice then for young unmarried comrades

anticipating long periods of political exile to protect themselves against loneliness by acquiring fictitious 'fiancées', who generally ended up as their real wives. Most of these 'fiancées' were appointed by the Party, but Lenin made his own choice. He and Nadezhda were unable to marry immediately, since in 1896 she was arrested and sentenced to six months in prison for her role in the St Petersburg strike, and the following February he was exiled to the Siberian village of Shushenskoe.

Historians have puzzled over her strange reply when Lenin wrote to Nadezhda in prison and asked her to be his wife. 'Your wife? Why not?' she wrote. What is clear from this is that she would have accepted anything he proposed. It would be better to be his wife than merely his comrade; with her talent and zeal, she would make him leader of the revolution. As for her mother, Elizaveta Vasilevna would accept anything just so long as Nadya was not left on the shelf. After Nadezhda received Lenin's letter declaring his love and asking her to be his wife, she petitioned to be transferred to his place of exile. Her request was granted and in 1898 she and her mother set off for Siberia.

Elizaveta Vasilevna, the poor widow of a would-be revolutionary, had visited her daughter in prison, and now followed her to Shushenskoe. Determined that her twenty-nine-year-old daughter should lead a proper married life on leaving prison, she offered the newly-weds her services as cook, washerwoman and chambermaid. She was an educated woman, and in her youth had written poetry, but she was temperamentally unattracted to politics and had little understanding of what preoccupied her daughter and son-in-law. When the two convinced atheists were forced by the authorities to be married in church, she was overjoyed. God had blessed them, whatever they might say about Him; now Lenin would have to take Nadezhda with him wherever he went.

Kind Elizaveta Vasilevna accepted her new life with fortitude – everybody in Russia had to put up with such things these days. Later on, of course, there would be children, for Nadya adored children. Elizaveta loved her son-in-law with all her heart and he reciprocated, knowing that an orderly married life was possible only with her help. Throughout his life, Lenin was surrounded by ranks of worshipful, subservient women: his mother, his wife, his sisters and their friends, his revolutionary comrades, his secretaries, maids and servants. His attitude to these women was always informed by purely political motivations, and he had an extraordinary talent for directing female energy towards the greater goal.

Nadezhda describes how revolutionary studies in exile were fired by dreams for the future: 'Ilich and I would lie awake at night dreaming of the mighty workers' demonstrations in which we would one day take part.'

Leninist hagiography has washed this couple so clean that all possible innuendo is banished. Yet it was in exile that modest Nadya discovered the powerful, passionate woman in herself, and her years in Shushenskoe, from 1898 to 1900, were two of the happiest of her life. She enjoyed all of it: love, closeness to nature, spiritual communion with the man she idolised, and the fact that she had no rivals and of all the women in Shushenskoe she was the youngest and prettiest. Her cheeks flushed, her hair she wore in a long, thick plait to show off her youth, and her slim figure and modest St Petersburg dresses provoked the village girls' longing stares. According to a revolutionary named Lepeshinsky, all who saw her in Shushenskoe were charmed by her, and men fell in love with her.

But revolutionary principles banished all narrow-minded jealousy between the Lenins.

> We were newly married, and this helped us through our exile. If I don't write about it now it doesn't mean there was no poetry or youthful passion in our life, we just couldn't bear anything *petit bourgeois*. Ilich and I met as fully-formed Marxists, and this shaped all our life and work together.

One can draw any number of conclusions from Krupskaya's artless account of their life in Siberia.

> Things were extraordinarily cheap in Shushenskoe. Vladimir Ilich's eight-rouble 'salary' bought him a clean room, food, washing, mending . . . Of course dinner and supper were very plain. Every week they would slaughter a sheep for Vladimir Ilich, and he would eat it every day until he could eat no more. They would put his week's supply of meat in the trough in which they mixed the cattle-food, and the farm-girl would chop it into cutlets for him. There was more than enough milk for Vladimir Ilich and his dog, a fine Gordon setter named Zhenka, whom he taught to fetch and carry and perform all sorts of tricks.

With the arrival of Krupskaya and her mother, Lenin's life improved still further:

We lived as a family. That summer we couldn't find anyone to help with the housework. Mother and I struggled with the Russian stove and I kept spilling dumpling soup all over the floor. In October a girl called Pasha moved in to help us. She was thirteen, scraggy and sharp-elbowed, and she took on all the housework for us. I taught her to read and write, and she adorned the walls with Mother's instructions: 'Never, never spill the tea!'

So two able-bodied women had to hand over the housework to a thirteen-year-old girl — and were guilty of exploiting child labour into the bargain, something they fiercely denounced in others.

At times a new and uncharacteristically cruel note appears in Nadezhda Krupskaya's memoirs. Most of the exiles living in the area then were either former People's Will terrorists (the 'old men') or the younger Marxist social democrats. When one of the Marxists escaped, the 'old men' were angry not to have been warned in time so they could clean their rooms in case of a search.

Vladimir Ilich said: 'There's nothing worse than these exile dramas. They're a distraction. The "old men's" nerves are shot. It's not surprising after hard labour and all they've endured, but we mustn't get involved. We have our work to do, we must save our energy.'

Left to herself, Krupskaya would happily have got involved, but as she gradually turned into Lenin's shadow she learned to agree with him on everything. She describes the meeting at which Lenin engineered the final break with the 'old men':

The decision had already been taken, and we just had to carry it through as painlessly as possible. We broke with them because it was necessary, but we did so with more regret than anger. Afterwards we had nothing more to do with them.

In exile, where people lived by respect and consideration, the episode was a mortal blow for the 'old men'. Nadya understood the cruelty of the break, but as the kindly woman standing beside her hero was transformed into a stern soldier of the revolution, she learned to deny such feelings, and, as though to bring form and content into alignment, her short-lived beauty now vanished. This was partly due to the onset of the thyroid condition which was to torment her for the rest of her life. But illness, far from distracting Nadezhda Krupskaya from the revolutionary path, merely helped to rule out any entertainments which might have lured her away from it.

*

While the name of Stalin is connected in the popular mind with something huge and terrifying, Lenin's name means little to Russians now. There is the white statue of the good, curly-headed boy, one hand resting on a pedestal, the other tucked into the belt of his trousers. And there is the image of middle-aged Lenin, bald and kindly, with his small beard and narrow eyes. By far the most interesting rumour to challenge these stereotypes of Lenin is of his love affair with his fellow revolutionary Inessa Armand.

In 1889, fifteen-year-old Inessa Teodorovna Stephane and her sister Renée, orphaned daughters of a couple of itinerant French actors, travelled from Paris to the large estate of Pushkino, outside Moscow, where their aunt taught music and French to a family of wealthy Russified French textile merchants named the Armands.

Pretty, intelligent, sweet-natured and musical, the two girls flew like exotic birds into the Armand family, whose three sons, Alexander, Vladimir and Boris, were ready to love them with all the passion of their romantic hearts. Although strict Russian etiquette made such lowly-born girls unsuitable as wives for them, the brothers held progressive views and lived their lives in a conscious attempt to undermine the merchant house of Armand.

In 1893 Inessa, then nineteen, married Alexander, and over the next eight years they had four children: Alexander, Fyodor, Inessa and Varvara. These years saw the stirrings of a new female social consciousness and a longing for activity. Inspired by Tolstoy's ideas on popular education, Inessa set up a school for peasant children on the Armands' estate. It was there too that she read Lenin's *Development of Capitalism in Russia*, and this work started her on her revolutionary path. Rejecting Tolstoy's image of woman as 'brood mare', she chose as her model the sexually and politically emancipated heroine of Nikolai Chernyshevsky's novel *What Is To Be Done?*, who sets up a women's sewing cooperative and lives in a *ménage à trois* with her husband and his best friend.

Alexander Armand's wife had no further to look than to his younger, more politically radical brother, Vladimir, who had embraced Marxism and had always been emotionally close to Inessa. In the summer of 1903, while on holiday with Vladimir, she discovered that she was pregnant again. Alexander accepted that she was in love with his brother, and she and the four children moved to Moscow to live with Vladimir. That autumn in Switzerland she gave birth to her fifth child, Andrei.

Vladimir unquestioningly accepted Inessa's revolutionary views and spent the rest of his life following her to prison, exile and emigration, while the noble Alexander continued to love and support her, bailing her out of jail, taking the children whenever she was away and doing whatever she asked of him. Some have condemned Inessa for putting a life of prison and exile above her children, yet she seized every opportunity to see them, and reunions were always a joy. In many ways she seemed in the happy position of living her life in the way that best suited her. Yet in the autumn of 1908 she wrote from exile to her friends the Asknazys:

> The conflict between personal, family interests and those of society is the most serious problem facing the intelligentsia today. One or the other invariably has to be sacrificed. All of us have to face this painful choice, and whatever we decide is always equally painful.

A few days after writing this letter, Inessa escaped from exile, and after staying for a few days in Moscow to see her children and Alexander she left Russia illegally for Finland. From there she travelled to the French Riviera, where Vladimir was in hospital receiving treatment. She wrote to the Asknazys:

> I never suspected that he was so ill, I thought he would have a minor operation to clear the abscess . . . Yet two weeks after I arrived he was dead. For me his death was an irreparable loss. All my personal happiness was bound up with him, and without personal happiness it is hard to live.

In this same letter, however, she also describes plans concerning a very different kind of happiness:

> . . . I am now in Paris, and will try to busy myself here. I want to make contact with the French socialist party. If I can do this, I shall be able to gather experience for future work.

Inessa had long been in correspondence with Lenin and worshipped him as her teacher, and it was some time in 1909, while still in deep mourning for Vladimir, that she met him in person. It is not known whether the meeting took place in the Russian library on Rue Gobelin, or at the Bolshevik printshop on the Rue d'Orléans, in a crowd of Paris social democrats at a cheap émigré canteen, or in Brussels, where Inessa was living.

Krupskaya wrote:

In 1910 Inessa Armand left Brussels for Paris with her small son and two daughters. She immediately became one of the most active members of our Paris group. She was an ardent Bolshevik, and our people in Paris quickly grew attached to her.

Krupskaya and her mother responded to Inessa with affection. Both Inessa and Elizaveta Vasilevna were cultured women, both of them smoked, and the two would sit together for hours chatting. Perhaps Elizaveta Vasilevna realised that it would be difficult for her son-in-law not to fall in love with the beautiful Inessa, and was trying to protect her daughter by befriending her. But Krupskaya had the strength to rise above *petit bourgeois* notions of marital fidelity. She was a born conspirator, capable of limitless discretion in the interests of the revolution, and it is hard to imagine her taking umbrage or dissolving into tears before a rival who was, above all else, a comrade.

Throughout 1912, when living in Poland, Krupskaya saw even more of Inessa Armand. (Krupskaya herself was suffering from her old thyroid complaint at the time; prison, exile and endless moves from town to town took a heavy toll on revolutionary women's health and were the sacrifices that had to be paid in serving the common cause.) Krupskaya wrote:

> Inessa arrived in Poronin in the middle of a meeting . . . She was already displaying symptoms of tuberculosis, but she had lost none of her energy and attended to Party matters with greater passion than ever. All of us in Krakow were overjoyed to see her . . .
>
> All of us in the Krakow group were very close to Inessa that autumn. She was brimming with joy and vitality. The house seemed warmer and more cheerful when Inessa was there. My mother was especially attached to her . . . During her visit Inessa told me a great deal about her life and her children, and she showed me their letters. There was a delightful warmth about her stories . . . She was an excellent musician and urged us to attend some Beethoven concerts. She herself played several works by Beethoven. Ilich especially loved the *Pathétique*, and he constantly asked her to play it. He loved music.

But the Krakow idyll could not last for ever. Of Inessa's sudden departure, Krupskaya writes:

> It was always assumed that she would remain in Krakow and write to Russia asking for her children to be sent out to join her. I even helped her to look for accommodation. But life in our Krakow group was very

secluded, rather like our life in exile, and there was no outlet there for her energy, which she had in such abundance then.

She decided to travel first around our overseas groups and deliver a series of reports, then to settle in Paris. Before she left we talked a great deal about women's work. Inessa insisted passionately on the widest possible propaganda amongst working women, and the publication in St Petersburg of a special women's magazine.

Is it possible that from 1909 the Leninist revolution had not only a wife but also a lover, who worked tirelessly alongside the wife, writing articles for the Bolshevik press, travelling around Europe organising conferences, translating revolutionary articles into various languages, and suffering cruelly in various European jails?

Although serving the revolution just as loyally as Krupskaya, Inessa Armand did not feel obliged to take care of Vladimir Ilich's daily needs, which were served by his clumsy wife and her able mother. She realised that any such family entanglement would be awkward, if not damaging, for the revolution, and that no spot must stain the leader's illustrious waistcoat; it was better to leave things as they were.

Both Krupskaya's and Armand's energies were controlled by the same powerful male hand. Yet Armand continued to retain much of her independence, and for this she paid an increasingly heavy price.

Long-awaited events generally happen unexpectedly. When revolution broke out on 23 February 1917 in Russia, the Lenins were in Zürich. Krupskaya describes their reactions to the news from Petrograd:

> That afternoon after dinner, while Ilich had already left for the library and I had cleared the dishes, Bronsky appeared with the words: 'Haven't you heard? There's revolution in Russia!' We hurried down to the shores of the lake, where all the newspapers were hanging up under an awning ... It was true, revolution had broken out in Russia. All Ilich's plans were being realised.

Following the news of the revolution, in April 1917, Lenin and his companions made their journey in the famous 'sealed train' across northern Europe to Petrograd. Lenin, Krupskaya and Inessa Armand shared a compartment as they travelled home to Russia, the country they had left so many years ago and for which they had lived in their thoughts, every moment of the day.

As Lenin's party was welcomed home, the two women stood a few steps behind their leader on the station platform. And as Lenin stood on an armoured car exhorting the milling crowds on the streets to support the world socialist revolution, and shouted to the crowds from the balcony of Mathilda Ksheshinskaya's palace[1], slim, elegant Inessa and bulky Krupskaya stood beneath him, throwing back their heads and listening to his words with sparkling eyes.

Yet after the speeches were over it was Krupskaya who went back with Lenin to his sisters' apartment in the north of the city.

> Ilich and I said almost nothing that night; we had not the words to express what we felt . . . Ilich gazed around the room. It was a typical Petersburg apartment, and we knew that we were home at last, and that our life in Paris, Geneva, Bern and Zürich was behind us.

Before Krupskaya lay the unknown, maybe prison, a more frightening prospect after her comparatively comfortable life in Europe. These worries were even more pressing for Lenin, however, and for the first time in many years they separated while he went into hiding, first in workers' apartments in Petrograd, then in a remote hut just across the Finnish border.

The smell of destruction brought hundreds of revolutionaries running to Russia from all over Europe, eager to seize the power sprawling at the feet of the masses. The European powers assisted their return in the hope that the power struggles in Russia would weaken the monster of revolution on their borders. And as the world meekly prostrated itself before the Bolsheviks, the knowledge that Europe itself had supported their return to Russia swelled their confidence.

Released from her role as Lenin's secretary, Krupskaya threw herself into the turmoil of Petrograd life and the part of the machine which she had reserved for herself: the ethics of the new society, and the political education of women and children in the socialist spirit. Determined that Marxism be instilled into the minds of women and children in order to ensure rich fruits in the years to come, she compiled a number of detailed amendments to the Bolsheviks' new programme on popular education, and published

---

[1] The ballerina Mathilda Ksheshinskaya had been the mistress of the Grand Prince Michael.

an appeal to the All-Russian Congress of Teachers. She wrote an article about Lenin, explaining in popular language who he was and what he wanted. She stood successfully as candidate for a place in the *Duma*, representing Petrograd's Vyborg district; she employed her teaching gifts to recruit men and women workers to Bolshevik literacy commissions; and she became secretary of the Bolshevik Central Committee in order to keep abreast of what was happening in the Party while its leader was underground.

The list of Krupskaya's activities is endless. Her life's passion, the Revolution, was finally no longer a bookish interest but had become a reality. Only a month earlier in Europe she had been a sick, prematurely-aged woman; now she was almost beautiful again. She and Lenin managed only a few brief meetings in his place of hiding, but during these meetings she kept him informed of what was happening, and as her talents blossomed he loaded her with yet more work.

Krupskaya's activities in Petrograd were mirrored by those of Inessa Armand in Moscow, where she was putting Lenin's ideas into practice with her usual passion. She made speeches, she organised groups of women workers and soviets of workers' deputies, and she was elected to the Moscow city *Duma*. She too wrote an article 'Why Does the Bourgeoisie Slander the Bolsheviks?', explaining who Lenin was and what he stood for. She started a magazine entitled *Working Woman's Life*, and in the little village of Pushkino, which years ago had welcomed her into its embrace, she organised a soviet of workers' deputies which promptly set out to undo the achievements of generations of Armands, so that she had to appeal to Lenin to intervene.

On the morning of 24 October 1917, Nadezhda Krupskaya was in Petrograd's Vyborg district when she was handed a note from Lenin informing the Bolshevik Central Committee: 'To delay the revolution is death!' She hesitated, then hurried off to the Smolny Palace, where Lenin had emerged from hiding. From that moment on she and Lenin were inseparable. People flocked to him, and he walked through the crowds followed by his wife, servant, slave and housekeeper: the workhorse of the revolution.

There were persistent rumours that Lenin wanted to live with Inessa but that the Politburo disapproved. Some say Krupskaya offered to move out of their home so that he could live with Inessa. Others say that she ordered Inessa to leave them in peace and move out to the provinces. Yet all the evidence indicates that the two women remained on friendly terms and worked well together throughout this period.

In March 1918 the Bolshevik government moved from Petrograd to Moscow, and, until the death of Stalin in the mid-1950s, the upper echelons of the Soviet state occupied the fortified centre of Moscow's Kremlin.

The Kremlin lies at the heart of the four circular roads upon which Moscow is built. The fourth, outer, ring-road was built just over twenty years ago to carry the burden of Moscow's extra traffic. The third ring, the Sadovoi or Orchard Road, dividing central Moscow from the suburbs, was once lined with apple trees, but these were destroyed in the 1930s as the volume of cars increased. The second ring, the Boulevard, divides central Moscow into its residential and business quarters. The official part of Moscow and its various institutions lies on the boundary of the innermost ring, the Kremlin itself, an uneven circle some three miles across, on top of whose high, red-brick walls and pointed battlements the Bolsheviks replaced the tsars' golden eagles with red stars.

Within the territory of the Kremlin lie the tsars' palace, the ancient theatre building (rebuilt under Khrushchev as the Palace of Congresses), three large and ancient Orthodox cathedrals, and the belfry of Ivan the Great, hitherto the highest building in Moscow. There were also numerous auxiliary buildings, where the tsars' servants lived while they were in Moscow.

From the beginning of the Revolution to the mid-1930s the Kremlin was a lively place: cars of every possible foreign make swept by, officials hurried about, mothers walked with children and grandchildren, famous leaders took a stroll.

The Bolshevik leaders moved into the old tsarist officials' houses and apartments with their wives, servants and dependants, a huge, noisy throng of people. These apartments were reached through a heavy door and along a vaulted, brightly-lit corridor laid with a red carpet with a green patterned border; at the end of the corridor hung a large mirror which made it seem longer. As the newly-elected president of the Soviet of People's Commissars, Lenin was the only Bolshevik to receive a flat directly next door to his place of work. The Lenins' flat was modestly furnished, and this modesty befitted the leader of the proletariat and was what Krupskaya wanted, although when her husband rejoiced at the proximity of their new quarters to his place of work she shook her head and said, 'It's convenient all right – no sleep, no rest, no holidays, just work!'

For the government workers and their families, living in the Kremlin, in direct contact first with Lenin, then with Stalin, required a high degree of trust. Cramped but easy-going at first, the new commissars huddled together to survive the years of havoc and civil war which followed the Revolution. As Soviet society became calmer, some spilt out from the Kremlin into the town, but this was not something of which the new government generally approved.

Common interests and experiences meant that revolutionaries tended to marry within their own circle, and most Kremlin couples were well matched. The new '*tsaritsas*' soon adjusted to their unaccustomed roles. First prison, now the Kremlin. They had earned it. Most Kremlin wives, like Krupskaya herself, were comrades and fellow-fighters and were not to be seen toiling at the stove or washing the dishes. Beyond the Kremlin walls serious matters awaited them, and they threw themselves into literacy programmes, caring for the old, sick and hungry, adopting orphans and setting up nurseries for working mothers. State nurseries quickly became popular and special ones were available for the children of the élite, yet most leaders' wives preferred to have their children looked after at home, and many Kremlin wives overcame their scruples and hired some of the unemployed nannies, cooks, maids and governesses of the former bourgeoisie who had remained in Moscow.

Soviet textbooks about the post-1917 civil war portray the tsarist White Guards as behaving like animals, slaughtering Red Guards, burning them alive in the fireboxes of trains and burying them alive in the earth. The creators of the Red Terror yielded nothing to the Whites, but they were the victors, and the victors are not judged. If Krupskaya had used her female wit to inspire her idol not to destroy his enemies but to sit them down at the table together, this would have initiated the regeneration of humanity. But it was not to be.

Throughout the ages new governments have disclosed the abuses of the previous one on taking power, before setting out to commit their own. This collection of former prisoners, exiles and émigrés, most of them no longer young, came to the Kremlin and from its heights they surveyed Russia's riches, her museums and galleries, her tsarist vaults and princely estates. The new Kremlin leaders' conduct was shaped by their experiences in prison and exile: secrecy in all things, distrust, harshness, cunning, betrayal of one's friends, self-serving lies, rigid hierarchies, and, at the core of the Party, a machine run on the principles of 'democratic centralism'. In bringing all this with them from their underground lives, the new commissars transformed Soviet life itself into a prison. But they were too intoxicated by victory to realise this as they extolled the new life and demanded that it be rigorously followed.

They had a clean record. They had not served the old regime, and had risked their lives to expose its evils and speak the truth. The workers and poor peasants, assisted by the urban intelligentsia, ensured a bright future for all mankind. This, with minor variations, was the Bolsheviks' basic theme, and as the ancient Kremlin flung open its doors to them, life gave it a fairy-tale plausibility. With them they carried all their interminable arguments about how this bright future was to be achieved. The Leninist slogan, 'Expropriate the expropriators!', could be interpreted however one wished, and from the first days of the Revolution a relentless internal power struggle raged within the Kremlin walls.

Nadezhda Krupskaya had her own part to play in this struggle. In assuming responsibility for popular education she presented herself to the world as far more than a mere female adjunct to Lenin, and it was on her initiative that religious education was banned from every school in the land.

It may have been memories of her late mother that made her justify in writing her hostility to religion:

> Why did I need religion as a child? Partly, I suppose, it was loneliness. I read and saw a lot, but could never give form to my thoughts and feelings so as to make them comprehensible to others. This was especially tormenting to me as an adolescent. I always had a lot of women friends, but we met on a completely different plane. That was why I needed God. I felt it was His job to understand what was happening in the soul of every human being. I would sit happily for hours on my own, looking at the icon lamp and thinking thoughts which could not be put into words, and knowing that there was someone close by who understood me. That is why Marxism cured me so radically of any form of religion. The elimination of the vestiges of religion was later hindered by people's ignorance of natural social phenomena.

From these contradictory and not entirely convincing words it is clear that Nadezhda Krupskaya sought to replace her religious world-view with Marxism. Yet her dogmatism is unattractive, and these views are especially unappealing when directed at children: 'Anti-religious education should start young, even before school, since children interest themselves in such questions very early these days.'

Despite her deep love of children, Krupskaya's own childlessness could not but affect her work with them, and the fact that she did not really know or understand them may account for a certain lifelessness in the educational programmes she created. Yet these programmes were a great deal more humane than most education circulars drawn up by men, and she often displayed her more gentle side to the many people who wrote to her asking for help.

One of these, a woman named Nina Kuritsyna, recently wrote to me:

> In 1937 my sister Lena was suffering from rheumatism and a heart condition and needed hospital treatment. Mother was in despair. She lived in a little village in Siberia with her six younger children. I was a student at Rybinsk, and I made up my mind to write to Krupskaya. Her reply arrived just over a week later, and the following day I was called to the Rybinsk medical centre, where they gave me a free travel pass, valid for the whole summer, for my sister to attend a sanatorium, and an extra allowance to Mother for the children . . . My sister is alive to this day, thank God, and I cannot forgive myself for not thanking Nadezhda Konstantinovna for what she did for us.

Yet despite her kindness, one cannot help thinking that had Nadezhda Konstantinovna wielded supreme power, she would have inaugurated the cultural inquisition far more effectively than Stalin, for she was better educated than he was. It was not just a matter of who ultimately led the Party machine, however, but of the machine's intrinsic cruelty. A gentle woman who loved children, Nadezhda Krupskaya regarded the Bolsheviks' shooting of the royal family in the summer of 1918 as unquestionably correct and necessary. A standard feature of Soviet life from the start was the banning of books. The émigré writer Roman Gul wrote:

> After the Revolution Lenin is known to have handed over the task of Russia's enlightenment to his wife. This spiritually and intellectually limited Party dogmatist issued three circulars in rapid succession, each remarkable for their unambiguous declaration that the bloodletting had started.

Generations were to be shielded from Russia's finest art and literature. The poetry of Sergei Esenin was banned for its 'religious-patriarchal basis and street psychology'. The works of Dostoevsky for their 'extreme conservative views and pathological images'. Blok, Bulgakov, Platonov, Akhmatova, Gumilyov, Voloshin, Tsvetaeva and later Pasternak were all outlawed. And the person behind this book-banning was none other than the kindly Nadezhda Konstantinovna Krupskaya.

As Krupskaya nurtured her precious machine to produce the new psychology, nothing old or great was allowed to filter through to the minds of its creators. In November 1923 Gorky wrote to the poet Vyacheslav Khodasevich:

> I can now inform you of the mind-numbing news that Plato, Kant, Schopenhauer, Solovyov, Taine, Racine, Nietzsche, Leskov and Lev Tolstoy have now all been banned, thanks to Nadezhda Konstantinovna Krupskaya.

Having toiled throughout her life to promote literacy in Russia, she was now destroying all that she had created. After years of forbidden books, underground leaflets and illegal strike-calls, she probably saw nothing criminal or contradictory about this; the banning of books is rooted deep in Russia's past, as evidenced by so many poets' tragic confrontations with the censors throughout the last century.

Krupskaya would have been shocked to be called an inquisitor as she laboured to purge future generations from literary pollution. She dreamed of creating a new person for the new society, someone without roots, or only a distilled version of them, and no need to hark back to the past.

Fighter, comrade, defender of everything Bolshevik, Krupskaya assumed a man's role to do a man's work. Her educational circulars were perfectly compatible with the ruling male structure, in which girls were virtually indistinguishable from boys. Other Kremlin wives had only to follow her example.

In the years that followed the Revolution, the euphoria of success was consumed by the harshness of everyday life and an endless succession of disasters: civil war, nationwide famine, the struggle with the counter-revolution, Krupskaya's chronic ill-health, Fanya Kaplan's failed assassination attempt on Lenin, the sudden death of Party secretary Yakov Sverdlov, and the death in 1920 of Inessa Armand.

That summer Inessa had exhausted herself organising the International Women's Conference in Moscow. According to

Krupskaya, 'Inessa could barely stand upright. Even her energy was not up to the colossal task she had set herself.' After the conference was over, many of Armand's friends urged her to leave Moscow for a rest. Lenin wrote to her: 'If you won't visit a sanatorium, why not go south to the Caucasus? Sergo[2] will organise rest, sun and interesting work for you there. Will you think about it? I warmly press your hand.'

She took Lenin's advice and left for the Caucasus, where she fell ill with cholera, and on 23 September 1920 she died, alone and neglected. Her body was brought back by train to Moscow for burial one damp autumn evening in late September, and Elizaveta Drabkina, member of a detachment of Bolsheviks defending the government against terrorist attack, recalled seeing a grief-stricken Lenin, propped up by Krupskaya, following two skinny black horses pulling a zinc coffin through the streets of Moscow.

The following day Armand's ashes were interred by the Kremlin wall on Red Square. Among the flowers placed there was a wreath of white lilies bearing the inscription: '*To Comrade Inessa, from V. I. Lenin.*' Bolshevik protocol did not strictly entitle Inessa Armand to this place by the Kremlin wall, but perhaps it was Lenin's way of thanking her for all that they had shared together, or making amends for robbing her of her freedom.

To this day, members of the Armand family fiercely deny any idea of a love affair between Lenin and Inessa. Yet some people, including her friend Ivan Popov, insist that she had a sixth child who died, and that the baby's father was Lenin. A certain Soviet film-maker even told Popov that he had seen the baby's grave in Switzerland.

Another great Bolshevik feminist of the time, Alexandra Kollontai, argued that Inessa Armand's death hastened the death of Lenin. It may well be that as he came to the end of his work this was the final blow. He had created the machine with which to destroy the old system, but this new machine required new people and they were already breathing down his neck, impatient to do what he himself was no longer capable of doing. Lenin's genius and energy were waning, and his aristocratic intellectual temperament could not tolerate the savagery he had unleashed.

As plots and enmities multiplied within the Party, the most

---

[2] Sergo Ordzhokonidze, an old comrade of Stalin from the Caucasus, was a leading Bolshevik in Georgia and Armenia during the 1920s.

improbable people united to grab what they could from the half-lifeless body of Russia. During the onset of Lenin's last illness the fighting on the civil war fronts was receding, but the battles within the Kremlin walls raged on. Lenin's illness frightened Krupskaya, and for the first time she worried about what would happen when he was gone. People were saying that he had done his work and must go, and discussions about his successor were already taking place within the Party. Some of this talk reached Krupskaya, but she tried to ignore it, convinced that no one but Lenin could see the true path.

For all the gossip, she and Lenin were a deeply united couple. She had given herself to him, with all her humanitarian warmth, her cynical judgements and her sincere faith in the working class, which was the driving-force of her life and which she sincerely believed herself to be serving. After twenty years of marriage passion may have receded, yet none could doubt the power of their attachment, and Lenin loved her as men love their *alter ego*.

As Lenin fell ill, Krupskaya took her place by his sick-bed. The best doctors attended the patient and prescribed complete rest. Ignorant of medical matters but duly respectful, the Central Committee entrusted the supervision of the doctors' regime to its general secretary, Comrade Stalin. More precisely, Stalin himself assumed this responsibility with the Central Committee's backing, and it served his purposes well.

Lenin's secretary had already secretly brought Stalin the 'Testament' which the sick leader had dictated to her, and in which he warned the Party machine:

> Stalin is too rude, and this defect, though quite tolerable in our midst and in dealings among us Communists, is intolerable in a general secretary. I therefore propose that comrades consider some way of removing Stalin from this post and appointing someone else.

The week after Stalin was made responsible for the leader's health, Lenin asked to be allowed to dictate his diary. Stalin, Kamenev and Bukharin held a meeting with the doctors, at which it was agreed that he should be allowed to dictate for five to ten minutes each day. Meetings were prohibited, and friends and servants were forbidden to talk politics with him, since it was feared this would agitate him.

Knowing Lenin's active nature, his doctors had not insisted that he be totally isolated, but for his anxious comrades this was absolutely vital. Krupskaya realised that only work could keep him alive, and on 21 December 1922 she wrote, at his dictation, a message to Trotsky about the foreign trade monopoly. In a telephone call to Krupskaya shortly afterwards, Stalin shouted at her in the foulest language for conniving in Lenin's correspondence with his arch-rival, and threatened to report her to the Party's Central Control Commission for disobeying the doctors' orders.

After more than twenty years of marriage, a wife knows her husband better than any doctor. Yet the Party could always prove that it knew best, for the Party was above everything. It seems to us now quite ludicrous that a mere colleague could threaten a sick man's wife and accuse her of mistreating him. For Krupskaya, whose nerves were already at breaking-point, this was the last straw. Yet she defended herself with her usual dignity, writing to the Control Commission to propose that the machine it had created should investigate this purely personal conflict.

> I am not exactly new to the Party. In thirty years I have not heard a single rude word from any of my comrades. The interests of Ilich and the Party are no less dear to me than they are to Stalin. At present I need all the self-control I can muster. I know better than any doctor, and certainly better than Stalin, what can and cannot be discussed with Lenin, since I know what agitates him.

This quarrel with Stalin took place in December 1922, as Lenin entered the last phase of his illness. Lenin learned of it only on 5 March 1923, and immediately dictated to his secretary a letter to Stalin in which he said:

> You were rude enough to swear at my wife over the telephone. Although she agreed to forget what you said, both Kamenev and Zinoviev heard about it from her. I do not easily forget slights against me, and I need not tell you that I take personally any slight against my wife. I therefore demand that you take back everything you said and that you apologise to her. Otherwise you may consider all relations between us at an end.

After dictating this letter, Lenin was observed by his secretaries and by Dr Kozhevnikov to be in an extremely agitated state. The next morning, after his secretary had read the letter through to him, he asked her to deliver it in person to Stalin and wait for his reply. Soon after she left, his condition deteriorated, his temperature rose, he lost the power of speech, and the paralysis spread to the left side of his body.

Lenin never returned to active life. Some, including Trotsky, claim that Stalin killed Lenin with a slow-acting poison. According to others, Stalin informed the Central Committee that when Lenin became ill he had asked for poison to put an end to his suffering. But Stalin had no need for poison; his treatment of Nadezhda Konstantinovna had had the required effect.

Lenin's letter to Stalin defending his wife was surely one of the most honourable things he ever did, and may well have cost him his life. After writing it he lived for less than a year. During this time Krupskaya never left his side, knowing that his departure would open a new page of history, and that the power so hastily gathered into his hand would soon be clutched in another, more terrifying fist.

Did she consider making her own bid for power, or did she wonder if the whole venture had been for nothing? Hardly. At Lenin's deathbed her belief in the victory of his ideas remained unshaken, even as they were being hijacked before her eyes by Stalin.

She was made of iron. Throughout Lenin's long illness she had learned to accept his death, and at his funeral in February 1924 she was not seen to shed a single tear. At his grave she addressed the mourners thus:

> These past few days, as I stood over Vladimir Ilich's coffin, I have been thinking about his life, and this is what I want to say to you. His heart beat with a passionate love for the workers, the oppressed. Comrades, he never said this himself, and I would probably not have done so at a less solemn moment . . . but now that our beloved, precious Vladimir Ilich is dead . . . I have one great request to make of you: do not let your grief for Ilich be diverted into superficial reverence for his personality. Do not build monuments to him, or palaces in his name, or hold grand celebrations in his memory. He attached little importance to such things when he was alive, and found them distasteful. Remember that much still has to be settled in our country.

These are the words not so much of a loving wife crushed by grief as of a revolutionary fighter who knows the path she must take; Krupskaya knew that all she could do now was to seek support.

Immediately after Lenin's death she wrote to the writer Maxim Gorky:

> Yesterday we buried V.I. He remained to the last as he had always been,

a man of enormous will, in full possession of his senses, laughing and joking and tenderly concerned for others. On Sunday evening he had a visit from Professor Auerbach, the oculist, and after he had left, V. I. called him back wanting to make sure he was getting enough to eat.

When he read in the newspaper that you were ill, he grew very upset and kept saying, 'Is it true? Is it true?'

According to Krupskaya, Lenin was fit, healthy and active to the end. Yet according to the artist Yury Annenkov, Lenin had by then entered an infantile state. He writes in his memoirs:

> Wanting me to do a last sketch of Lenin, Lev Borisovich Kamenev invited me in December 1923 to visit the little town of Gorky, where Lenin's illness had forced him to take refuge with his wife. I can see as clearly as if it were yesterday the spacious yellow house where they were staying. We were met by Krupskaya, who said there could be no question of a portrait, and indeed the man wrapped in a blanket, reclining on a chaise-longue, looking past us with the vacant smile of one who has passed into second childhood, could not possibly serve as a portrait of Lenin, only as an illustration of his terrible illness.

One can understand why Krupskaya would not wish even her old friend Gorky to see the leader of the Revolution in this condition, determined as she was for him to remain in popular memory as good, noble and powerful. Yet on that same day she wrote another, rarely mentioned letter to Lev Trotsky in the Caucasus. Just before Lenin died, Trotsky had gone south to the resort of Sukhumi for a holiday. Stalin had sent him a telegram there advising him not to return for the funeral, and Trotsky took his advice, later blaming Stalin for his absence. The fact was that he did not wish to attend the funeral, and he welcomed Stalin's advice.

In his memoirs, Trotsky described how, while in the Caucasus, he thought about on Lenin's life and death, and about Krupskaya:

> . . . who had been his friend for so many years and had seen the world through his eyes, and was now burying him and faced intolerable loneliness. I wanted to send her some words of sympathy and affection, but I could not bring myself to. All words seemed frivolous before the burden of events, and I feared they would sound hackneyed. I was therefore shaken by feelings of gratitude to receive, a few days later, a letter from Nadezhda Konstantinovna.

Without waiting for Trotsky's sympathy, Krupskaya had written to him:

Dear Lev Davidovich,

I want you to know that as Vladimir Ilich was looking through your book a month before his death, he stopped at the passage where you discuss Marx and Engels and asked me to read it aloud to him. He listened closely, then looked at it again himself.

I also want to tell you that V.I.'s feelings for you when you first visited us in London after your escape from Siberia remained with him all his life.

I wish you health and strength, Lev Davidovich, and I embrace you warmly.

If one is to believe Krupskaya, Lenin remained intellectually active to his last day and was thinking about Trotsky just before his death. Insensitive as ever to anyone but himself, Trotsky writes in his memoirs:

Krupskaya confirmed that, despite a long antipathy, Lenin retained the warmth he had felt for me in London, but now perhaps on a loftier historical plain. All the volumes of the falsificators would not outweigh, before the judgement of history, that little note of Krupskaya's, written just a few days after Lenin's death.

In fact, Krupskaya's note looks not to the past but to the future, and merely extends the hand of comradeship, solidarity and possible political alliance.

Not one to abandon herself to a widow's grief, Krupskaya knew that she must act. Fully aware that the choice between Stalin and Trotsky was the choice between two evils, she chose Trotsky, despite the fact that she must have known that he would not win. But for Trotsky's monstrous vanity, they might have confronted Stalin together, and together they might have waged an effective struggle within the Party. But as Trotsky failed to support Krupskaya and she was left without allies, she stifled her personal grief once again in the interests of the higher cause. She had not given her life to the Bolshevik Party for a mere Stalin to blunder in and destroy it.

At the Thirteenth Party Congress in May 1924, the first after Lenin's death, Krupskaya delivered a supplementary paper on work in the countryside, in which she spoke not like a grieving widow but like a robot:

There exists a conveyor-belt between the vanguard of the Communist Party and the working class, and this conveyor-belt is now securely in place. Vladimir Ilich spoke of this system of conveyor-belts from the proletarian vanguard to the working class itself, and from the working class to the middle and poor peasantry. The first of these conveyor-belts exists already. The establishment of the second, from the working class to the peasantry, has still to be developed.

Her speech was greeted with loud applause. Observing the ecstatic welcome which met Lenin's widow at factory and Party meetings, Stalin may well have realised that the people needed this old woman as a replacement for the former *tsaritsa*, whose murder in Ekaterinburg was still fresh in the popular memory.

It was widely known that Stalin had insulted Krupskaya and that no one had dared to intervene, and that he had accused her of driving Lenin to an early grave with her inept nursing. It was also known that he had accused her of insulting her beloved husband's memory by not visiting his embalmed body at the Mausoleum. In fact, distressed by Stalin's insistence on this ritualistic veneration of Lenin's remains, Krupskaya had pleaded that he be allowed to be buried. Just a step away from where she lived lay the unburied corpse of her husband, and the endless queues to visit his body were a symbol of all the other queues in her country.

The actress Galina Sergeevna Kravchenko, daughter-in-law of Commissar Lev Borisovich Kamenev, Chair of the Labour and Defence Council, recalls:

> In 1930 or 1931 Krupskaya came in tears to Lev Borisovich and begged him to protect her from Stalin's rudeness. Lev Borisovich tried to comfort her, but I don't know if he was able to do anything for her. She looked puffy and unwell, but she was a splendid, gentle woman. I soothed her and she put her head on my shoulder sobbing: 'It's so hard, Galechka, so hard!'

At the Fourteenth Party Congress in December 1925, Krupskaya voiced her fears about her beloved Party:

> The authority of the Party has arguably been weakened . . . Our Party was formed many years ago in the struggle against the Mensheviks and Socialist Revolutionaries, and we learned to shower our opponents with curses. Such language is obviously quite unacceptable for Party members to use when debating with each other.

She then invoked Lenin's name to warn the Party machine against an excessive enthusiasm for capitalism. The audience applauded her warmly and she was awarded her extra time.

More storms of applause greeted her at the Fifteenth Party Congress in 1927 when she voiced her fears about the cultural revolution and problems of re-educating society along Bolshevik lines. At the Sixteenth Congress in 1930 she greeted the collectivisation programme as 'a genuine agrarian revolution – a reconstruction of the peasant economy on socialist foundations'. She castigated Trotsky, now cast out of the USSR, for 'having misunderstood the peasant question'. She suggested that the full weight of the Party be used to promote the course of collectivisation, and she urged each Party member to employ 'unceasing Leninist vigilance, lest in struggling with every new twist and turn they forget their priorities and lose sight of the main purpose of the struggle'.

How aggressive Krupskaya was becoming in her seventieth year! Like all the other speakers at the Seventeenth Congress in January 1934, she missed no opportunity to mention Stalin's name. Yet while adopting the Stalinist rules of the game, she nevertheless managed to avoid unctuousness, and even managed to retain some of her dignity:

> At our last congress Comrade Stalin brought up the question of general education. This question is naturally of the utmost importance and something the Party has discussed from the start . . . But we knew that only when the conditions were right could we fulfil this enormous task.

In other words, Comrade Stalin, Lenin and I were discussing such things when you were still in your seminary.

Stalin was sensitive to such subtleties, and according to the caustic Karl Radek, he had said: 'If she doesn't shut her mouth the Party will appoint old Elena Stasova as Lenin's widow in her place!'[3]

On the evening of 26 February 1939, Nadezhda Krupskaya invited her friends to celebrate her seventieth birthday. Stalin did not attend the party but sent a cake. Later that evening Krupskaya was stricken with severe food poisoning and rushed to hospital. She died the following morning. Although Krupskaya was the only one of the guests to be affected, the survivors of the party insist that the cake must have been poisoned. At her funeral it was Stalin who carried the urn with her ashes.

Nadezhda Konstantinovna Krupskaya outlived Lenin by fifteen

[3] Elena Stasova, long-standing Bolshevik and Party functionary.

years. It must have been intolerable for her to see the agony of Bolshevism and its transformation into Stalinism. Her former colleagues at the Commissariat of Education spoke lovingly of her and respected her for her genuine kindness which coexisted with her harsh ideas. Despite her tormenting thyroid condition, she had worked, issued exhortations, published articles and endlessly written and rewritten her memoirs.

There is much good sense and inspiration in the eleven volumes which comprise Krupskaya's works, but they were never absorbed by the Stalinist school and are unlikely to survive the current hostility to Leninism. The vast Party machine, created partly by Krupskaya and reshaped by her successors, was finally smashed to pieces in August 1991. On both sides of the barricades in Moscow, where the uncrowned queen of the Revolution had lived for almost twenty years, the legacy of Bolshevism was played out by its children and grandchildren, who finally destroyed it.

2

The 'Woman Question' and Men's Response

One of the Bolsheviks' greatest victories was the almost immediate eradication of illiteracy in Russia. Having taught Russia to read and write, and grappled with the desperate problems of war, housing and economic reorganisation, the Party machine finally extended its reach into the more sensitive area of women's lives, family and marriage. Women such as Inessa Armand and Alexandra Kollontai devoted much attention to women's rights in the years before and after the Revolution. These women were not Kremlin wives but Kremlin comrades and lovers, and all to some extent endorsed the ideas of 'free love'.

Intelligent, beautiful, aristocratic and delicate as porcelain, Alexandra Kollontai had joined the revolutionary movement in 1896 and since the 1905 revolution had put women's sexuality at the centre of the Communist ideal. The new collective living could inspire higher forms of love and compassion, she wrote in her essay 'Make Way For Winged Eros'. 'It is irrelevant to the tasks of the working class whether love takes the form of a lengthy settled union or a passing liaison.'

People were disturbed and elated by Kollontai's ideas, and in an article entitled 'Marriage and Family Law', Krupskaya riposted: 'Monogamy is the most normal form of marriage, and corresponds most closely to human nature.' In nature, of course, there is no specific 'woman question', since every question concerning women concerns men too.

The staid Krupskaya and the flamboyant Kollontai in many ways represented polar opposites of the female principle, but merely to identify Kollontai in these terms would be to trivialise her complex and often contradictory life.

The Kremlin, in the first years after the Revolution, was the main headquarters of Soviet power, and a vast communal apartment. Ever fearful of counter-revolution, the Kremlin leaders kept close to the heart of government, and lived where they ruled. Ruled by all the laws of military subordination, the Kremlin garrison had its own army of cleaners, typists, secretaries and guards. Masters and servants lived together in comfortable proximity and shared the cooking, and Kremlin wives were expected to be discreet and modest, like Krupskaya. A very few women enjoyed the unspoken right to be different in their manners and dress, however, and Alexandra Kollontai led the way here.

In 1920 Kollontai was forty-eight, and the acknowledged leader of the women's movement in Russia. Although Kollontai and Krupskaya were temperamentally poles apart, there were no fundamental political differences between the two women, and in many ways they were in agreement about how socialism should reshape and improve family life. Krupskaya, like Kollontai, was against bourgeois forms of the family, and although she opposed Kollontai's theories of free love she magnanimously reconciled herself to Alexandra Kollontai's flamboyance. Moral Krupskaya, who had never in her life allowed herself to be tempted by another man, cannot have liked the startlingly open sexuality of Kollontai's relationship with a young sailor and former stevedore, Pavel Dybenko, but she saw no point in opposing Kollontai, knowing well how useful Kollontai's education and international connections could be to the young Soviet republic.

Kollontai was a mistress of the pen, and her writings about free, brave, revolutionary love were perhaps partly a justification of her affair with Dybenko. But the theory had a huge impact upon Soviet society as a whole throughout the twenties and thirties, becoming a subject of continual discussion, seized upon at every opportunity. In the Kremlin especially, the registration and the institution of marriage came to be regarded as a bourgeois throwback, and various Kremlin leaders, such as Lev Kamenev and Grigory Zinoviev, had second families outside the Kremlin walls.

Kollontai's role as vanguard of the new Soviet family life was challenged by events in her own life with Dybenko. By refusing to create a conventional home for him she made it increasingly hard to sustain intimacy, and in 1923, tormented by his endless affairs, she broke off the relationship. Dybenko tried to kill himself, the Party sent her away as ambassador to Norway, and when Dybenko followed her there she sent him away, writing to Stalin: 'Please do not link the names of Kollontai and Dybenko in the future.' Stalin, who liked to meddle in other people's romantic dramas, is said to have asked Dybenko, on his return to Moscow, if he had broken off with Kollontai. When the sailor replied that he had, Stalin said, 'You're a fool then!' Fifteen years later, Dybenko was arrested and Kollontai did not lift a finger to save him; she was well aware that it might have cost her her life to do so, even despite her role as Stalin's ambassador.

By 1924 Inessa Armand had died, Kollontai had stopped propagandising free love, and there was no one to challenge Krupskaya's views on the 'woman question'. It was perhaps to avoid the threatening complexities of her own sexuality that Krupskaya put the Party machine between man and woman in the resolution of sexual relations. She wrote:

> The non-Party masses see the Party as pioneering new forms of the family and of family life.

> The family will for a long time be a major factor in our life. We are still a long way from the ideal.

> We must deal mercilessly with Communist husbands discovered to have departed, under the influence of their wives, from Communist ethics.

Here are some of the leading Party ideologists' utterances aired during discussions on ethics and the family throughout 1923 and 1924:

> The Party has the right to inspect the family life of each one of us and enforce its line there ... Members of our Party do not give enough thought to individual propaganda, especially inside their own families. (Lyadov-Mandelstam)

> The Party has dealt with many disorders, and will also deal with disorders in Communists' family lives. (V. Solts)

> We have the right to demand of Party members that Communists take the spiritual lead in family matters. The Communist who cannot conduct his domestic life properly and introduce the guiding principles of Communism into the family is worth very little. (Commissar of Enlightenment, Anatoly Lunacharsky)

> The army of non-Party wives has not yet been accepted by the Party as one of its most serious problems. (Lyadov-Mandelstam)

Communism and the true liberation of women will start only with the start of a mass struggle, led by the proletariat in power, against the petty domestic economy: in other words, restructuring it on the lines of the larger socialist economy. *(B. Yaroslavsky)*

The woman of the future is being forged in our socialist plants and factories. Here we can see the slow but promising growth of a new type of woman, whose beauty has nothing in common with the eternal female beauty exalted by poets of the past. Aspects of this new type of woman are being reproduced by our new poets and writers, but since it is still in the dynamic of growth it is not yet fully amenable to artistic embodiment. *(V. Solts)*

'Women's weakness', once sung by poets along with the 'eternal feminine', must be judged by us an inevitable consequence of women's slavery as a result of historical conditions which will only be removed under Communism. *(Yaroslavsky)*

In 1924, as political power struggles were being squeezed into the fragile forms of family life, Lyadov-Mandelstam concluded:

What is needed is a radical change in the way we bring up our children. If the schools and children's homes of bourgeois society could artificially produce a bourgeois citizen, then this is where we must strike our first blow . . . Can a collective person be produced in an individual family? To this we must say a categorical No. A child with the collective mentality can be reared only in a collective environment. Even the best parents ruin their children by bringing them up at home.

These discussions resulted in 1926 in the Politburo's decree on the 'woman question', the first in the Party's history, which imposed tough new alimony requirements on divorced men and remained officially in force until 1989.

As the new regime raised the slogans of Peace, Freedom and Brotherhood on its bayonets, the collective development of Man advanced on a mass scale and the peace-loving female principle was discarded. Women were required to underpin society as equal but not different. The Bolsheviks' policy of supporting women's equal rights with men – or rather their right to do heavy work – encouraged women to enter the lower, local levels of power. As the prominent Georgian Bolshevik Abel Enukidze wrote in *Pravda* on 7 November 1932: 'We see increasing numbers of women in the rural and urban soviets. In the villages their number increased from 151,298 in 1927 to 316,697 in 1931.'

Since most of the country's men were about to be wiped out by war, collectivisation and terror, women's appearance in various branches of the socialist economy should have raised the economy, and women themselves, to limitless heights of achievement, women being naturally more conscientious than men, less competitive, and less prone to drink. What happened was that, having given woman the chance to work in all areas of the economy, Bolshevik man bombarded her with leaflets exhorting her to work like a man in education, medicine, everyday life, even art – and replaced the customs elaborated over the ages with idiotic plans and lifeless formulae. If she could not or would not conform to these, the machine would at best throw her down to the lower levels of power. Women's natural talents had no social relevance for the Bolsheviks (or for any of the other – male – parties of Europe or the rest of the world). The slave remained a slave, and went off to a corner to gnaw on the stale crust of Bolshevik equality.

Despite their exclusive position, the women chosen by the leaders were still slaves, albeit slaves with possibilities. At home in the Kremlin, almost every leader was under the female heel: Voroshilov, Kaganovich and Molotov decided nothing without their wives. Yet at the level of political power not one of these women, including Nadezhda Alliluyeva, Stalin's wife, but possibly excluding Nadezhda Krupskaya (and that only at the beginning), had any real influence on events. Those who challenged their position were arrested, but most fell into line, such as the Jewish Ekaterina Voroshilova, who regarded everything that happened as unquestionably correct, even the anti-Semitic campaigns of the 1940s.

As the claws of the machine reached into the Kremlin, crippling the human relationships within its walls, Kremlin wives were expected to be both Martha and Mary, housewife and comrade. Most were sensible women, and knowing that real life had little in common with their husbands' decrees, they held on to their commanders and commissars with Party comradeship, bourgeois comforts, family warmth and a Kremlin lifestyle which solidified over the years into a vast and immutable structure.

3

Woman of the Revolution or the Legend of Larissa

As Bolsheviks from the battleship *Aurora* were storming Petrograd's Winter Palace on the night of 25 October 1917 many people claim to have seen on board a tall, statuesque woman of superhuman beauty, with a pale, bloodless face and auburn braids wound around her head, and that it was she who gave the order to fire at the palace. The only woman known to be on the *Aurora* that night was the anti-Bolshevik Countess Panina, who led one of three delegations sent by the Petrograd *duma* to the Winter Palace, the Smolny and the *Aurora* and all of which were turned back. Yet the legend persisted, and in the years that followed, Soviet literature, film and theatre updated the image to that of the leather-coated, gun-toting woman revolutionary, standing on the bridge of a warship at the height of the battle, urging the sailors on and outdoing even the bravest of them in courage.

The image is based on the life of Bolshevik commissar Larissa Reisner, whose exploits during the civil war were first depicted in the play *An Optimistic Tragedy*, by Vsevolod Vishnevsky, a Bolshevik sailor on board the same ship as Reisner during the battles on the Volga.

Larissa Mikhailovna Reisner was not a Kremlin wife, although the men associated with her were men of the Kremlin. She was born into a cultured, Bolshevik-sympathising St Petersburg family in 1896, when Nadezhda Krupskaya had already joined the Leninist struggle for the liberation of the working class, and she died in 1926, when the widowed Krupskaya was losing support in the world she had helped to create. Poet, revolutionary and journalist, Reisner's brief life encompassed the First World War, two revolutions and civil war. She flashed across the white-hot sky of the Revolution like a comet, and her trace remained as an affirmation of women's strength. Known as the 'Woman of the Revolution', Reisner wanted to create a new type of woman to match the Woman of the French Revolution. She did so with her own life, and she was immortalised in the prose, drama and poetry of her time.

In all the articles written after her death, not one fails to mention her beauty. The poet Vsevolod Rozhdestvensky recalled his fellow students gasping as she entered the St Petersburg university auditorium in 1911 as one of its first women students:

> Tall and elegant in a modest grey suit of English cut, her thick dark hair wound around her head like a crown, there was something haughty and un-Russian in her regular, almost chiselled features, and her sharp, playful eyes.

According to Vadim Andreev, son of the poet Leonid Andreev, who lived with the Reisners as a boy:

> Walking along the street, she seemed to bear her beauty like a torch. Even the coarsest objects gained a new tenderness from her presence. Men would stand rooted to the spot as we passed, and few who knew her failed to fall desperately in love with her.

The writer Yury Libedinsky described her as a 'classical goddess or Nordic Valkyrie': 'I felt that to talk to her would be an extraordinary delight.' The British journalist Andrew Rothstein recalled entering her compartment during a train journey to Latvia, and being enchanted by 'her beauty, the charm of her language and her passionate commitment to Communism.' Even the poet Osip Mandelstam's wife Nadezhda, who was extremely sceptical about Larissa, was struck by her 'Germanic beauty'.

Larissa's poems are like her – cool and beautiful. As a schoolgirl, she immersed herself in poetry, and in 1914, with her father's help, she brought out a literary journal entitled *Rudin*. She tenderly and perhaps passionately loved the poet Alexander Blok, giving him a subscription to *Rudin* in the hope that his poetry might miraculously transform her too into a great poet. But Blok, who regarded women poets with barely disguised indifference, remained silent about her poetry.

She later had a romantic relationship with Blok's rival Nikolai Gumilyov. Gumilyov's wife, the poet Anna Akhmatova, was said to have been jealous of their relationship and made angry scenes. But Gumilyov too seems to have had little positive to say about Larissa's talent. In one of his letters to her he wrote:

You have beautiful, honest eyes, but you are blind. Strong young legs, but no wings. A powerful and elegant intellect, but with a strange emptiness at the centre. You are a princess turned into a statue.

No doubt wishing to soften the blow, he went on:

But no matter! I know that somewhere in Madagascar all will change, and that on a warm evening of buzzing beetles and blazing stars, in a thicket of red rosewood trees near a bubbling spring, you will tell me wonderful things that I have glimpsed only in my finest moments. Goodbye Leri, I shall write to you.

Although a cruel denial of her poetic sensibility, Gumilyov's words are an accurate assessment of Reisner's poetic personality. She was a strong focus of emotions, but her misfortune was that however much she longed to be a poet, poetry was merely one of life's many beautiful costumes, never its essence.

Reisner's coolness and *amour propre* contained a huge creative energy and hunger for life, and the Revolution allowed this energy to flourish. She worshipped Lenin. As she put it: 'I am not a timid soul, but when I am near Ilich I forget myself and become as shy as a little girl.' Since all the female places around Lenin were occupied, she remained outside the circle of his intimates and served him as best she could elsewhere. Shortly before October 1917 she carried out revolutionary propaganda work with sailors at the Kronstadt naval base. There she met and fell in love with Fyodor Raskolnikov, a sailor of peasant origins and leader of the Kronstadt Bolsheviks. Immediately after the Revolution she worked under Anatoly Lunacharsky, Commissar of Enlightenment, to preserve the imperial artefacts in the Winter Palace from the marauding masses. In the summer of 1918, as the civil war reached its height, she handed this work over to Lunacharsky and set off as Raskolnikov's wife, flag officer and adjutant, to fight with the Baltic sailors of the Volga flotilla.

That summer Larissa Reisner and the Volga flotilla sailed the length of the Volga, the Kama and the Belaya rivers, helping the Red Army to defend towns and villages from the White Guards and the White Czech legions. Many of the abandoned estates lining these rivers contained furniture, food and clothes, and she would appear on board dressed in a variety of expropriated ladies' costumes and girlish summer dresses. During the battle for Kazan she twice infiltrated the Whites' lines, dressed first as an aristocrat, then as a peasant, and incited the White soldiers to rebel against their commanders.

Larissa's courage determined the course of many of the battles during the Bolsheviks' victorious Volga campaign, and her pen and her personality turned them into legend. A sailor named Kartashov recalled ecstatically how she appeared on their cannon ship and ordered them to reconnoitre the White fleet. The commander objected that it would be too dangerous, but she insisted, boarded the cutter and sped off towards the Whites' ships:

> She stood smiling at the helm, happy to be going into danger, then disappeared from view, and only from the shooting of 37mm guns could we establish her whereabouts. We opened defensive fire, there were some artillery shots, and a few minutes later she manoeuvred the cutter back safe and unharmed.

This passion for life also guided her pen in her numerous essays from the civil war fronts, and later from Afghanistan. She had much in her favour: her parents' revolutionary sympathies, her own dedication to the Bolsheviks, and the naval victories of Fyodor Raskolnikov. Raskolnikov was a powerful figure, a monument to revolutionary courage and enthusiasm, who softened only before Larissa. His prospects as a naval commander were dazzling. Her beauty and courage were legendary. Everything seemed possible.

It may be hard for us now to imagine how the lice-ridden peasant sailors, exhausted by interminable wars, could appreciate Larissa's rather stilted speeches to them and her wealth of extraordinary ideas and outfits in the midst of poverty and destruction. She did not attempt to justify herself, merely saying: 'If you do your best for people, why not please the eye if you can?' It was her glorious femininity which gave the sailors courage, reminding them that they too had women waiting for them at home. She presented men with the challenge of her wide-ranging intellect, her courage and her tenderness, which she both resisted and indulged.

In August 1918, about a month after the assassination of the imperial family in Ekaterinburg, Larissa sailed down the Volga from Svyazhsk to Nizhny Novgorod on the former tsarist yacht, the *Mezhen*. According to a fellow sailor named L. Berlin:

> Larissa Mikhailovna was in high spirits. She quickly made herself at home in the quarters of the former *tsaritsa*, and on learning from the crew that the *tsaritsa* had scratched her name on the window of her

cabin, she mischievously crossed it out and scratched her own next to it with an uncut diamond.

All Larissa Mikhailovna's achievements existed against the background of hunger, family break-up and economic havoc. She never refused herself anything, whether risking death in battle or living like a queen while others starved. Yet she was honest, unlike those who said nothing or feigned poverty. She said: 'We're creating a new state. People need us. It would be hypocritical to deny ourselves the things people always acquire when they come to power.'

Nadezhda Mandelstam wrote:

> Larissa did not merely love poetry, she secretly believed in it. In the first years of the Revolution the conquerors included many lovers of poetry. I don't know how they managed to reconcile poetry with their Hottentot morality – it's good to kill, it's bad to be killed.

As a result of her dangerous game with life, Larissa Reisner contracted tropical malaria at the front. The illness took a heavy toll on her health, yet long after the civil war had ended her courage outwitted death. Hungry for experience, her gaze fell next on St Petersburg's poetry circles. According to her friend and fellow poet Lev Nikulin, the inhabitants of the islands would see Larissa and Blok riding around the city's islands on horses requisitioned from the front, indulging in long conversations about poetry and revolution, and people would roundly curse these 'Soviet strolls' at a time when the population was suffering such privation.

Vsevolod Rozhdestvensky was also struck by the unashamed luxury of Larissa's life when he visited her with Osip Mandelstam and their fellow poet Mikhail Kuzmin at the Petrograd Admiralty building, where she lived:

> The duty sailor led us down the dark, echoing corridors to her apartment. Outside the door our arrival was announced so ceremoniously that we were overcome with shyness. Larissa was waiting for us in a small room draped in exotic fabrics. Bronze and brass Buddhas, Kalmyk idols and Oriental majolica dishes glimmered in the corners. The floor was covered with a white felt Caspian nomad tent. On a low, wide sofa lay piles of English books and a thick classical Greek dictionary. A ship's signal flag was adorned with a revolver and an old cadet's cloak. On an old Oriental table gleamed innumerable cut-glass perfume bottles and highly-polished bronze boxes and bowls,

most likely acquired from the same Kalmyk settlements. Larissa wore a heavy gown embroidered with gold thread, and were it not for the thick chestnut braid around her head, she would have resembled some Buddhist idol.

The eclectic jumble of the famous commissar's quarters is surprising evidence that the iron revolutionary was also a woman of refined taste, with spiritual aspirations toward the calmness of the East.

In March 1921 Raskolnikov was appointed to head Soviet Russia's first diplomatic mission in Afghanistan, and Larissa travelled with him to Kabul, where she quickly became the centre of attention at the diplomatic mission. Here she wrote a series of sketches published in 1923 as *Afghanistan*. She had few illusions about herself as a poet now. On 24 November 1921 she wrote to Anna Akhmatova from the mountains of Afghanistan, where she was sheltered from all that was happening in Russia, including apparently the Bolsheviks' execution of Gumilyov as a White Guard, which had taken place three months earlier:

> Dear, respected Anna Andreevna,
> The newspapers have travelled nine thousand *versts* to tell us of the death of Blok, and for some reason it is only with you that I feel able to express how sad and absurd this seems. Only you, because it is as though the column standing beside you has fallen, a column just as fine, white and exquisitely moulded as you. Now that your natural spiritual brother is no longer here, your greatness is even more apparent . . . My dear, most tender poet, are you writing poetry? There is nothing greater than this. For one line of yours people would sacrifice one wretched year of their lives.

Larissa later assured people that despite her power in the corridors of the new government her absence from Moscow meant that she was unable to save Gumilyov from being shot as a counter-revolutionary. Nadezhda Mandelstam recalls in her memoirs how, when she and her husband visited Larissa, she told them that her mother had persuaded Lenin to send the Cheka a telegram cancelling the execution. The telegram must have been delayed, since the execution was carried out almost immediately. Nadezhda Mandelstam also recalled visiting Larissa's mother while she was away, and found her deeply distressed that Larissa had done nothing about Gumilyov's arrest.

After two years in Kabul, Larissa suddenly left Raskolnikov and returned to Moscow. Raskolnikov took her departure badly and begged her to return:

> I know there are many men far cleverer than me, but you will never find anyone who is so boundlessly devoted to you and loves you so passionately after seven years of marriage . . . Remember, I not only love you, I respect you infinitely.

Larissa Reisner was a tangle of contradictions. She could turn immorality into victory; Osip Mandelstam described to his wife how Larissa threw a party to enable Cheka agents to arrest the guests. Yet she also took a basket of food to Anna Akhmatova when she was ill, and what is striking is not that her ability to procure food – for everything was available to her – but her reverence before poetry, acknowledging its absence in her own work.

Worshipping the world of poetry, yet never pre-eminent in it, she gradually withdrew from poetry to prose, and worked hard to become a journalist. As she acquired a new set of clothes as a writer, those who knew her work observed a new maturity in it. Before, her writing had been filled with similes, metaphors and a tendency to artificiality. Now it displayed a new severity, a release from excessive prettiness. Behind this transformation stood the extraordinary figure of Karl Radek-Sobelsohn.

Witty and cynical, a prolific journalist and creator of numerous anecdotes of dubious Bolshevik reliability, Radek was one of a small group of Politburo members who continued to be politically effective after Lenin's death, and he won Larissa's heart as her devoted reader and adviser during her last years. In 1923 she travelled with Radek to Germany as a clandestine Comintern officer and journalist, writing about the aborted Hamburg uprising in her book *Hamburg at the Barricades*. On her return to Moscow she became a successful special correspondent for *Izvestia*, the newspaper of the Petrograd Soviet, and she published a book of essays, *Coal, Iron and Living People*, about her journey around Russia, during which she adopted a little boy.

In the name of the Revolution, Larissa fought, danced, written poetry and rejoiced in her youthful energy. Then, at the age of twenty-nine, she suddenly collapsed with typhoid fever. She refused to accept at first that she was dying. Only in the last minutes of her life did she briefly regain consciousness to say, 'Now I understand the danger I am in.'

The poet Varlam Shalamov, who worshipped Reisner from afar, described her funeral in 1926:

> A beautiful young woman, heroine of the civil war and the hope of literature, has died of typhoid fever at the age of twenty-nine. No one can believe it. We think we are dreaming. But Reisner is dead . . . Her coffin lay at the House of the Press on Nikitsky Boulevard. The courtyard was filled with people – soldiers, diplomats, writers. The coffin was borne out, and we saw her burnished chestnut hair coiled like rings around her head. Following the coffin walked Karl Radek, supported on each side by his friends.

Radek's suffering casts new light on his pathetic and public eleven-year fall from grace: his support of Trotsky, his betrayal of Trotsky, his eulogies to Stalin, his terror of prison, his false evidence against countless comrades, anything to save his skin.

It may have been as well that Larissa died before Radek and Raskolnikov were both destroyed by the machine on which they had worked together with all the energy of their passionate natures. Had she been alive in 1937 there is little doubt as to what would have happened to her, if only through her connection with these two 'enemies of the people'.

Boris Pasternak mourns her loss in his poem 'Memories of Larissa Reisner':

> In depths of legend, heroine, you walk,
> Along that path your steps will not fade.
> Tower like a mighty peak above my thoughts;
> For they are at home in your great shade.

With Larissa Reisner's loss Pasternak is also mourning the loss of a particularly female mystery, without which it is hard to survive the cruel world of men. The irony is that although Larissa wanted to be a poet, she became better known as its muse, when Pasternak gave her name several years later to the heroine of his *Doctor Zhivago*. Larissa Reisner and Lara are in many ways different, but Larissa's name was for Pasternak an abiding symbol of inspiration, hope and love.

A talented supporter of men as they went about their destructive business, Larissa Reisner was a type often encountered in Russian history: a popular actor, for whom life is a huge stage on which to display her numerous talents and costumes. She played her various roles magnificently: the spy crawling through the mud to enemy lines, the commissar summoning her soldiers to battle, the poet embroidering words, the journalist taking on the toughest assignments. She hurled her body against snow, hail and gunfire, she drank from stinking puddles, she swung into the saddle beside cavalry commanders, confident that the bullets would not harm her and that soon a completely new role would await her, and a new set of clothes. Perhaps this is why she dressed in others' clothes – because she had none of her own.

4

The Daughter-in-Law

Lev Borisovich Rosenfeld (revolutionary name Kamenev, 1883–1936), born in Moscow, the son of Russified Baltic Germans. Radicalised at an early age by his parents, he studied law at Moscow University, where he joined the revolutionary movement and spent the following years travelling around Russia as a propagandist and strike-organiser. In 1913 he followed the Lenins into exile in Poland. Returning with them to Petrograd after February 1917, he became an editor of Pravda. *After October 1917 he became chairman of the Moscow Soviet; after Lenin's death in 1924 he was elected head of the government. The year 1927 marked the end of Kamenev's career and the beginning of a long course of political capitulation to Stalin. In 1928, he denounced the Trotskyites. Four years later he was expelled from the Party. Readmitted in 1934, he was accused in January 1935 of being morally responsible for the assassination of Sergei Kirov and sentenced to five years in Siberia. The following July, at a trial where his brother was the main prosecution witness, Kamenev received an additional five-year sentence, and in August 1936 he and Zinoviev were the stars of the first Moscow show trial, the Trial of the Sixteen, which sentenced these 'mad dogs' to death for having formed a terrorist group allied to the Gestapo. In a last attempt to save his wife and children, Kamenev begged his sons to 'spend their lives defending the great Stalin'.*

There is an odd link between Larissa Reisner and the murdered royal family. When the poet Vyacheslav Khodasevich visited the Kamenevs in the Kremlin in 1919, Kamenev's wife, Olga Davidovna, Trotsky's sister, spoke tenderly to him of their fourteen-year-old son, Lyutik, who had joined the Volga flotilla and sailed on the royal yacht with Raskolnikov and Reisner. She told Khodasevich that Raskolnikov had dressed the boy in a sailor suit, with jacket, cap, shoes and striped jersey, and he had stood guard outside the door armed with a revolver. Khodasevich was disturbed by the thought that these might be the clothes of the murdered *tsarevich* Alexei.

Olga Davidovna continued unabashed:

> When Lyutik was little he was questioned by the tsarist police, but they got nothing out of him. He's only fourteen but he has already organised the Kremlin boys into a military league of young Communists.[1] Lyutik sits in on all our meetings, and when everyone's gone he says, 'Mama, don't trust Comrade so-and-so, he's a bourgeois and a traitor to the working class!' He was right about two old and trusted Communists, and now we ask his opinion about everything!

The widow of this young domestic oracle, Galina Sergeevna Kameneva, now lives in a little flat above the huge Stalinist Empire-style post office building on Begovaya Street. She does not look old, although everything would indicate that she must be, since she was once a star of the silent screen. Beautiful in old age, this living witness to our cinema history talked to me about the films she had made and the actors with whom she had worked.

Galina Sergeevna Kravchenko was born in 1904 in Kazan. Her parents, although not wealthy, took their pretty young daughter on a world tour, after which the family moved to Moscow, where she entered a girls' high school on Lubyanka Square (before the KGB had its headquarters there.) A talented dancer, she left high school to attend ballet school, then the Bolshoi Theatre school, where her teachers predicted a brilliant career for her as a ballerina.

Tall, blonde, graceful and vivacious, Galina Sergeevna had already danced in several ballets and operas when she happened to meet the film director Vsevolod Pudovkin, who persuaded her to study at film school. A beautiful ballerina, who also performed acrobatic studies, danced on a wire and excelled at swimming and horse-jumping, Galina Kravchenko was the model of Soviet girlhood. She could also shoot, drive a motorcycle and box. 'Boxing is

---

[1] Lyutik Kamenev's boy soldiers later became the Communist Youth League, the Komsomol.

like dancing,' she said. 'It's about lightning reactions, thinking first and moving fast.'

All this helped her in her highly successful film career. When she was twenty-six the beautiful star met her hero, not in a film but in real life, and he bore her off to a new and glamorous world.

One day in 1929 the film director Volodya Schneider, just back from China with his wife, telephoned Galina Sergeevna. 'Get dressed and come over!' he said. 'An interesting man is coming – you'll fall in love with him!' She remembers:

> I resisted and deliberately put on a plain cotton frock. But the man Volodya introduced me to was very handsome and elegant in his summer uniform. When it was time to leave he asked if he could take me home. A tram was crossing Theatre Square. I jumped on, waved and said I didn't like being taken home, but afterwards I couldn't forget the sight of his surprised eyes gazing after me. He began phoning me, and his voice was soft and bewitching. He told me he rode a motorcycle. I too had a passion for motorcycling but no bike. At that time people were allowed to train on the Leningrad Highway after midnight, and my new friend started taking me there on his Harley Davidson. He told me I was the first girl he had allowed to drive it.

Galina Kravchenko's new friend was a pilot, a graduate of the Zhukovsky Military Airforce Academy. His name was Alexander Lvovich, but everyone called him Lyutik, and he was the son of Olga Davidovna and Lev Kamenev.

One night Lyutik and his father followed her in their chauffeur-driven car to the nearby town of Gorky, and on the way they stopped for a picnic. The Kamenevs had brought a bottle with them (it was legal to drink while driving then), and Lev Borisovich tied the bottle to a tree and suggested that they all shoot at it. He, Lyutik and the chauffeur aimed and missed; then Galina aimed and smashed the bottle to pieces. 'What a girl!' said Lev Borisovich. A few days later he told her, 'Today you're moving in with us!'

Galina and Lyutik were married in June 1929, and for almost seven years she lived with him and his parents in their six-room flat on Manezh Square, opposite the Kremlin.

> Lev Borisovich's head was in the clouds. He was an optimist, all he ever thought about was books, art and music. He never discussed politics at home. He owned nothing, everything belonged to the state. When he went to Italy to meet Mussolini the Italians gave him a magnificent

motorcar, but he handed it straight to the Central Committee the moment he got back.

Olga Davidovna worked as head of the Society for Cultural Relations with Foreign Countries, then as head of the department for film promotion. She was always out working. She had been shot in the leg and head many years before. She was clever, and people said she had been pretty in her youth, but now she was moody and difficult. She could be cruel too. Lyutik would come home exhausted and take his boots off, and a few minutes later she would phone ordering him to pick her up – she had her own government car, she just wanted to show him off to her friends at work.

Trotsky, Olga Davidovna's brother, had been deported in 1927, two years before I arrived. Olga Davidovna never mentioned him. Trotsky's wife, Natalya Sedova, had left the country with him, but his younger son, Seryozha, had refused to accompany them. Seryozha used to visit us. He was a delightful young man, with two children. He was later shot, and his children were deported. I don't know how they ended up.

Olga Davidovna knew exactly what was happening and anticipated everything. I was shocked by her pessimism. 'Enjoy yourself while you're young, Galenka,' she used to say. 'Things are going to be bad for us.' When I asked her what she meant, she would say, 'You'll see, terrible grief awaits us.'

The Kamenevs had a younger son, Yura, who was still at school. He was a wonderful boy, noble, sweet-natured and poetic. There was also the cook and Lyutik's old nanny, Mrs Terenteva. She was very strict. She hadn't liked any of Lyutik's previous girlfriends but she loved me right away. We would come back late from the theatre or friends to find a light supper waiting for us on the table, with three kinds of vodka.

Lev Borisovich was in love with a woman named Glebova. She also had two sons, one by her first husband, the other by Lev Borisovich – there was the same sixteen-year age gap between her two as between Lyutik and Yura. Lev Borisovich's other family had almost nothing to do with us, although we all knew about them.

Lenin's sister, Anna Ilinichna, lived in the flat above us. She was a horrible woman – she was always sending her maid down to tell us to make less noise. We used to have lots of young people and artists around. Once we had a New Year's party with a hundred and fourteen guests, including the film director Sergei Eisenstein. Lev Borisovich worshipped Eisenstein. We showed all the latest Soviet and foreign films, then took turns shooting at the ceiling with an air-gun.

After moving into the Kremlin, Galina Sergeevna took responsibility for collecting the family's food. They each gave her five hundred roubles a month, and she would drive Lev Borisovich's car every day to collect dinner from the special Kremlin food store, the *Kremlyovka*, which is situated to this day across the river from the Kremlin. There were two sections to the *Kremlyovka* then, one for leading government officials, the other for Party workers and officials. The Kamenevs' meals, although intended only for Lev Borisovich and Olga Davidovna, were more than enough for nine people, and invariably contained half a kilo of butter and half a kilo of the finest black caviare. There were also unlimited supplies of 'iron rations' – prime cuts of meat, superb fish, items from the delicatessen, groceries, cakes, sweets and spirits. On Shrove Tuesday, hot pancakes in covered dishes would be rushed back to the apartment. ('The store wasn't far from the Kremlin, and Lev Borisovich's government car didn't have to stop at the lights.')

> Clothes were more of a problem. In 1932 Lev Borisovich asked me to buy him some socks when I was in town. I came back empty-handed. He was amazed when I told him there wasn't a pair of socks to be had in Moscow. I had my clothes made for me by the special dressmaker from the Commissariat of Internal Affairs on Kuznetsky Most. I used to meet Stalin's wife there during the early thirties – we used to sit together waiting for our fitting. I can't say we knew each other well. I found her grey and uninteresting, and I didn't like her taste in clothes – all her things were so drab.

In the autumn of 1931, when Galina Sergeevna was seven months' pregnant with her son Vitaly, Lyutik drove her around the Crimea in a Ford motorcar he had received as a gift from the United States. The other five couples staying at the Politburo guest-house at Mukholatka were also the children of Politburo members, but Lyutik and Galya occupied Stalin's suite, consisting of a bedroom, office and sitting-room. 'Mukholatka was so luxurious – I could never stay anywhere else after that. At first we were bothered by the guards, but soon we didn't even notice them. It was like a fairy-tale.'

In December 1934, Galina Sergeevna and the film director Mark Donskoy were returning by train together from shooting a film in the Crimea, when they learned of the murder of Sergei Kirov.[2]

---

[2] Politburo member Sergei Kirov was assassinated in Leningrad on 1 December 1934. His death served as the pretext for Stalin's subsequent campaign of terror.

Lyutik met her at the station, his face white as a sheet. On 16 December Lev Borisovich was arrested and deported to Siberia, and shortly afterwards his mistress Glebova was arrested and Lyutik lost his job. On the night of 5 March 1935, Lyutik too was arrested. Galina Sergeevna recalls:

Four soldiers, including one colonel, ransacked the flat. They went through the cupboard containing my films and the colonel pulled out reel after reel, one containing a unique shot of Lev Borisovich with Lenin. They pulled out every single film, unwound them all and looked at them in the light, then threw them on the floor, so the floor was piled with coils of unwound film and it took me a month to put them back again.

On 20 March they came for Olga Davidovna and she kissed Yura goodbye. She was sentenced to three years' exile in Gorky. My son Vitalik and I were evicted from our government flat, and Yura, Seryozha, Vitalik and I all moved into the headquarters of the Central Committee at 27 Gorky Street, which before the Revolution had been a second-class hotel.

In 1938 Yura decided to join his mother in Gorky. I tried to persuade him not to, but he insisted. He never returned. He was arrested in Gorky with his mother, and shot.

Lyutik went to prison twice, the first time in the Butyrki jail. When we visited him there Vitalik said, 'Papa's over the fence!' He looked terrible. He said, 'For God's sake write to Stalin and get me out of here!'

I wrote a letter to Stalin and posted it, and twenty-four hours later I telephoned his secretary, Alexander Poskryobyshev, a repulsive individual. His response was encouraging: 'Josif Vissarionovich has read your letter, and agrees to your request.'

Next I received a call from the prison telling me that my husband was leaving for Alma Ata at seven that evening, and to bring a leather coat, some money and a suitcase to the Kazan station.

I ran all the way, handed in the things at a special office and demanded a receipt. 'I know you're all crooks!' I said. I was young and fearless then. At the ticket office they told me the train was leaving at five past seven. I dashed along the carriages frantically looking for the barred windows. Right by the engine I saw the crimson uniforms of the railway officials, and suddenly there was Lyutik, freshly shaved and looking his usual cheerful self. He saw me, and put up three fingers to indicate three years. We said a long goodbye.

Behind me stood a man in a crimson cap. When the train had left he

said, 'Go quick. I let you say goodbye – now scram or I'll be in trouble!'
I thanked him.

The second time, Lyutik didn't come back. We loved each other very
much. We were never apart. It makes me mad when the papers say he
stood on the highway waiting for Stalin or Vishnevsky's car to pass so
he could shoot at them.

Galina Sergeevna eventually married again, and had a daughter.
In the summer of 1951, when the baby was away in Georgia for the
summer, her son Vitalik was arrested.

There were three of them. They spent the whole night rummaging
through our things looking for contacts. They were unbelievable boors.
They found two letters from Lev Borisovich to me, one written at the
Kremlin hospital on the day Vitalik was born, and enclosing as a gift a
little revolver from Alexandra Mikhailovna Kollontai. It was a real St
Bartholomew's Night – that was the night when they took all the
teenage children of the 'enemies of the people'.

They took my whole family, apart from my little daughter. All our
government acquaintances and actor friends avoided us, of course, I
don't blame them. In those days everyone was afraid for themselves.
There were a few exceptions, such as the writer Anna Antonovskaya,
the director Abram Romm and his actress wife, Olga Zhizneva. But my
career went into decline. They removed me from the picture *Happy
Flight* before it was finished, and replaced me with another actress. At a
film festival in February 1935 I wasn't even nominated for an award.
Everyone was looking at me at the Bolshoi Theatre as Abel Enukidze
read out the names of the prizewinners, but Enukidze looked away. (He
was a sweet man but he played around with little girls and dancers.)

They persecuted my second husband too. Before we lived together
several men would follow him up the street when he came to visit me,
and they would stand in the street looking up at my window until he
left. They started harassing me again in 1938, when I was summoned to
be interrogated. I was already remarried then, with another family. A
man started telephoning me to tell me that if I didn't help him he would
have me deported or sent to prison. Someone suggested that I write to a
certain General Korutsky in the NKVD secret police. Korutsky agreed
to see me and told me the man had not been authorised to telephone me
and wouldn't be bothering me again.

I acted in several more films. But the truth is that I was devastated. I
could have done so much more, creatively. I remember them all:
charming Lev Borisovich, unhappy Olga Davidovna, beautiful

Yurochka and my unforgettable Lyutik. Did they really exist or did I dream it?

Galina Sergeevna spreads out the documents relating to the murdered members of her family, and they cover the entire table.

Lev Borisovich Kamenev. Died: 25.8.1936. Age: 53. Cause of death: [word deleted]. Place of death: Moscow.

Olga Davidovna Kameneva. Died: 11.9.1941. Age: 58. Cause of death: [two words deleted]. Place of death: [word deleted].

Yury Lvovich Kamenev. Died: 30.1.1938. Age: 17. Cause of death: [word deleted]. Place of death [between these words someone has written 'registered']: Moscow.

Alexander Lvovich Kamenev. Died: 15.7.1939. Age: 33. Cause of death: [word deleted]. Place of death [word deleted].

Galina Sergeevna has two more bitter communiqués. The first, dated 11 November 1955, reads:

Regarding the case of Vitaly Alexandrovich Kravchenko, born 1931, sentenced by Special Session of the USSR Ministry of State Security on 18 August 1951, it has hereby been decreed on 5 November 1955 by the Juridical College for Criminal Affairs of the Soviet Supreme Court that the case is annulled due to absence of *corpus delicti*. *(Signature illegible)*

The second is a fifth death certificate:

Vitaly Alexandrovich Kravchenko. Died: 3.8.1966. Age: 34. Cause of death: poisoning. Place of death: Moscow.

5

The Despot and the Child

Josif Vissarionovich Dzhugashvili (revolutionary name Stalin: 1879–1953). Born near Tbilisi in Georgia, the son of a shoe-maker. Expelled from Tbilisi Seminary as a revolutionary and worked for the Bolsheviks underground and in exile until February 1917, when he returned to Petrograd and was elected to the Party Central Committee. After October 1917 he was made Commissar for Nationalities, and spent most of the civil war at the front. In 1922 he became Secretary of the Party Central Committee. Having concentrated power in his hands after Lenin's death in 1924, he embarked on his campaigns of forced industrialisation and collectivisation, which resulted in the purges and terror of the 1930s and 1940s. The Second World War elevated Stalin to the status of a myth but also isolated him, and the backlash followed quickly upon his death.

As the Soviet government prepared to leave Petrograd for Moscow at the beginning of 1918, each of the leaders had his life's companion by his side. Lenin had his Krupskaya, Trotsky had his Natalya, Kamenev had Olga Davidovna. The only one with no woman to love and care for him was Josif Stalin.

Behind Stalin lay years of exile in Siberia and Northern Russia, without home comforts or a woman's touch. Far in the distance was the faint memory of his first wife, Ekaterina Svanidze, who had died of tuberculosis in 1909, leaving him with their young son, Yakov. (Trotsky, in his memoirs, describes Ekaterina Svanidze as a 'young uneducated Georgian girl', yet we know that she was educated at home with governesses until the age of fourteen, and that her brother studied at Berlin University; Bolshevik psychology

54

determined that anyone from the country must necessarily be poor and uneducated.)

By the beginning of 1918 it had become urgent for the widowed Stalin to find himself a new wife. Since he had had nowhere to live in Petrograd, his revolutionary friend Sergei Alliluyev had offered him a room, but he could not continue indefinitely to stay at his friends' homes and be fed by their kind-hearted wives. There were those who hinted that if Stalin was unable to find a wife it was because no woman could endure his savage temper.

His mother urged him to go back to his village in Georgia, pick himself a strong, pretty girl and take her back to the Kremlin with him. Of course it would be good to find a woman with whom he could speak his own language at home, but such a plan was out of the question. He had no time to go to Georgia, and how would his comrades take it? For all their talk of the masses, professional revolutionaries were a special élite. A simple Georgian peasant girl would be no wife for the future leader of the People's Government, surrounded by powerful, intellectual, aristocratic women such as Nadezhda Krupskaya and Trotsky's wife Natalya Sedova; sarcastic Trotsky would walk all over him.

Where else was he to find the right woman for his new station in life, but in the next room, doing her homework? A sweet little girl, slender and graceful, the Alliluyevs' elder daughter, Nadezhda Sergeevna, was in many ways the image of Stalin's ideal; and as she turned before his eyes into a woman, she reminded him of a sinuous, dark-haired gypsy girl he had once seen performing at the circus.

Nadya was little more than a child. A year ago he had saved her life in Baku, when she had fallen into the water when playing on the quay and he had pulled her out. He must have saved her for himself. She was pretty, clever, young, the daughter of a true Bolshevik, unspoilt and untouched. She had not endured stinking tsarist prisons like Kamenev's wife or been degraded by exile like Voroshilov's Ekaterina Davidovna, who was said to have taken a fellow Bolshevik as a lover before her marriage. Alliluyev's wife, Olga, was highly promiscuous, and had just run off with yet another man, so that Nadya had to do all the cooking; Stalin found it incomprehensible how his friend put up with it.

Stalin had met the Alliluyevs in December 1900, the year before Nadya's birth, when they lived in the Georgian capital of Tbilisi. Shortly after Stalin's appearance, the talented Victor Kurnatovsky arrived from exile in Siberia, where he had made acquaintance with the Lenins and had evidently made a special impression on the young Nadezhda Krupskaya. Kurnatovsky immediately brought together all the Bolsheviks in Tbilisi; he also told Stalin about the Lenins and changed Stalin's life.

According to Nadya's brother Pavel Alliluyev, their mother was chasing first Stalin, then Kurnatovsky. Although Stalin worried that Nadya might prove as promiscuous as her mother, she seemed destined for him. As god-daughter of the prominent Georgian Bolshevik Abel Enukidze, she would not be out of place in Kremlin circles. She was young, but she would soon grow up. Stalin knew his time was coming: the right woman by his side was the key to his success. Nadya was a blank page on which he could write whatever he liked. She would be his princess!

Meanwhile in the next room Nadya was doing her homework. Since May 1916 she had been writing to a Bolshevik woman named Anna Ivanovna Radchenko, who had taken a motherly interest in the girl.

> Last summer I was so lazy that I have to take all my exams again. I went to take them this morning but I still don't know if I've passed or not. I think I've passed everything except Russian composition. The subject was easy, but I'm no good at it.
>
> It'll soon be the holidays and we'll probably spend Christmas here in Petrograd. It takes too long to go anywhere and it's too difficult and expensive. *(December 1916)*
>
> My worst subject is German, because we're supposed to read it, not translate it, and I don't know German at all, or French for that matter. I finally managed to get a five in Bible Studies. That's unheard of for me, but I've been working hard at it all term. I hate it . . . Papa and Mama are muddling along as usual. *(January 1917)*
>
> Instead of enjoying this lovely weather we sit in the classroom studying some boring subject like Bible Studies. I can't wait for summer. I'd like to come and stay with you and get a job. I think I'm old enough now, I'm nearly sixteen. *(January 1917)*

On 26 February 1917, the eve of Revolution, she wrote:

> We've been off school for four days because of the chaos in Petrograd, so I have some free time. Things are very, very tense here, I long to know what's happening in Moscow.

The following day she wrote:

> We're all fed up because for four days Petrograd's had no transport. But
> now at last we can celebrate – February 27th! Papa's so excited. He's
> been by the phone all day. Abel Enukidze arrived here today at the
> Nikolaev station in the middle of the celebrations, and he was amazed.

Nadya spent the summer of 1917 at the Radchenkos' dacha
outside Moscow.

For a few days that summer the Alliluyevs entertained the Lenins
at their flat, where Stalin met Lenin and Krupskaya for the second
time. (He had first met them in Krakow. Lenin had exceeded all his
expectations, but he disliked Krupskaya; he had no liking for plain,
efficient women.)

On her return to Petrograd, Nadya resumed her correspondence
with Anna Radchenko:

> We can still get food here. Eggs, milk, bread and meat are available but
> expensive. We can just scrape by, although we're in low spirits, like
> everyone else here. Sometimes you feel like crying, it's so depressing.
> You can't go out anywhere. There are rumours that the Bolsheviks are
> planning something for October 20th, but I don't expect there's
> anything in it. *(19 October 1917)*

> I'm fine, but depressed as usual. The school isn't managing too well.
> The electricity is turned off twice a week, so we only go in four days. I
> wanted to buy Ivan Ivanovich more cigarettes, but there was such a long
> queue I couldn't. You have to get up at dawn and even then they only
> give you a few . . .
>
> I had a big fight at school. They were collecting money for the civil
> servants, and all the girls were giving two or three roubles, but when
> they asked me I said, 'I'm not giving any.' There was an awful row!
> Now they all call me 'little Bolshevik', but they don't mean it unkindly,
> they're only teasing.
>
> Goodbye for now, I have to do my wretched Bible Studies. *(11
> December 1917)*

> Happy New Year! Things have completely changed here at home.
> Mama's not living with us any more, because we children are grown up
> now and want to do and think as we please and not dance to our
> parents' tune. We've become real anarchists – it drives her mad! That's
> not the main reason, though. The fact is, she has no life of her own here
> with us, and she's still a healthy young woman. So now I've had to take

over all the housework. I've grown up a lot this past year and I've become quite adult. I'm glad. The trouble is that I've become rude and irritable, but I'll probably grow out of it. *(February 1918)*

I'm glad you finally got the cigarettes I sent you. I'm sick of all this housework, but I think Mama will soon be back to take over again. She's lonely without her noisy brood, and of course we'll be delighted.

There's terrible hunger in Petrograd. We get just an eighth of a pound of bread each day, and some days there's none at all. I even cursed the Bolsheviks. But they've promised to increase our rations after February 18th. We'll see!

I've lost twenty pounds, I had to take in all my skirts and underclothes as they were falling off me. I've lost so much weight people are saying I must be in love! *(February 1918)*

This is not totally improbable, since within days of this letter to Anna Radchenko, Nadya abandoned her school, apparently without regret, and travelled to Moscow with Stalin as his personal assistant at the Commissariat of Nationalities.

Although they were not officially married, we may assume that from the first days of Nadya's life in Moscow her relations with Stalin changed from those of a child and the kindly 'uncle' who had saved her from the water. In the euphoria of the Revolution Stalin's friends were ecstatic. They all adored their dear little Nadya, who had grown up before their eyes. Now they were all one happy Bolshevik family! Not everyone regarded their relationship so lightly, however. Nadya was just sixteen, he was thirty-nine. According to the 1918 Family Code, which Stalin later endorsed, she was under-age, making their relationship illegal and him guilty of corrupting a minor. But already in 1918 Stalin evidently did not apply the same criteria to his own behaviour as he did to others.

On his arrival in the new capital, Stalin was allocated a study and living quarters in the Kremlin, but since he had no offices for his Commissariat he decided to appropriate some, and Nadya, as his secretary, had to type out a notice which read: 'These rooms taken by the People's Commissariat of Nationalities.' Stalin's colleague Yury Pestkovsky described how he and Stalin took this notice to a certain guest-house which Stalin had selected, and where they found another notice on the door, saying: 'These rooms taken by the Supreme Council of the Commissariat of State.' Stalin immediately tore it down and pinned up Nadya's. But he had not yet hit his stride, and the battle for the rooms was won by those who had arrived first.

In the last years of her life, Nadya's younger sister Anna denied that Stalin and Nadya lived as man and wife in Moscow, and insisted that in June 1918 she accompanied him to the Tsaritsyn front as his comrade, along with a huge entourage of four hundred Red Guards. Nadya's father went too, and several people shared a sleeping compartment. The train moved slowly and was held up at several stations. According to Anna, Alliluyev heard his daughter screaming one night, and he rushed into her compartment to find her sobbing that Stalin had raped her. Alliluyev threatened to shoot the rapist, but Stalin fell at his feet and asked for his daughter's hand.

Nadya, the gently-reared schoolgirl, spent her honeymoon steeped in the blood and heat of Tsaritsyn, a strategically crucial steppe town at the confluence of the Volga and Don rivers. Knowing that the fall of Tsaritsyn would open the Whites' path to Moscow, Stalin requested that the Soviet of People's Commissars grant him extraordinary powers to control the delivery of food supplies. His request was granted.

Voroshilov later called Tsaritsyn the 'Red Verdun'. The town turned into an armed camp, with streets and crossroads filled with Red soldiers and jails overflowing with prisoners. Outside town the front extended over sixty kilometres, and the rivers were patrolled by two cruisers, a destroyer and a steamship armed with artillery and machine-guns. Assisted by Executive Committee member Andrei Chervyakov, Stalin 'purged' the Red Army command by arresting almost the entire general staff and sailing them down the Volga on a barge which 'accidentally' sank.

Tsaritsyn was the turning-point of Stalin's career. As brothers and sisters, Reds and Whites, took up arms and fought to the death, his name was pronounced in whispers. Nadya had absorbed Bolshevism with her mother's milk, but nothing had prepared her for the cruel realities of that summer. Was this scorching revolutionary love in the midst of bullets and death to set the pattern for her life with Stalin?

On her return to Moscow from this front-line honeymoon, Nadezhda found work in Lenin's secretariat, and she and Stalin finally registered their marriage. One is curious to know why they did not do so before. According to Nadya's sister, she was reluctant to marry this man whom she did not love. Yet her daughter, Svetlana, in her book, *Only One Year*, asserts the contrary:

Olga Alliluyeva, Stalin's future mother-in-law, was well disposed to him but disapproved of Mama's marriage, doing her best to talk her out of it and calling her a 'silly fool'. She could never accept this alliance; she knew Mama was deeply unhappy, and that her later suicide was a result of 'all this foolishness'.

It may in part be that the Bolsheviks were simply indifferent to registering their marriages in the first decades of the Revolution. Ideas of free love, although never the norm, were having a deep influence on Soviet people, and official marriage was denounced as a *petit bourgeois* remnant of the old life. It was different when children came along, of course, because they needed both parents' names on the birth certificate.

Five months after the marriage was registered, Nadezhda gave birth to a son, Vasily, followed two years later by Svetlana. Following the Kremlin fashion then for adopting orphaned children, the Stalins also had living with them his son Yakov by his first marriage and the son of his late friend Artyom. Nadezhda preferred older children and found these children easier to relate to than her own two. With Vasily and Svetlana she was strict. Stalin, for all his harshness, could be excessively lenient with his children.

At Lenin's secretariat, Nadezhda Sergeevna proved an efficient, tireless worker, and despite her youth Lenin entrusted her with the most secret documents. Stalin was delighted at the prospect of being kept in touch with the latest developments; the only problem was that his young wife refused to share them with him. At first he applauded her loyalty, but there were times when he desperately needed to know what was happening and her stubbornness infuriated him.

An entry by Nadezhda Sergeevna in the duty secretaries' diary reads:

> Vladimir Ilich is unwell and his sister Maria Ilinichna says he must not be disturbed. If he needs to know something we are to consult the appropriate person. No one is to be admitted, and no messages are to be taken. Two parcels have come from Stalin and Zinoviev, but we mustn't say a word about them without special permission ...

Stalin was disappointed. He did everything for her. Her wish was law. She was living on a scale her parents could not have dreamed of. She had no worries about food, and although she still wore her old, plain, darned dresses out of nostalgia for her youth, Stalin's wife wanted for nothing. Against his principles he hired cooks and nannies for her. She could order anything she wanted to eat and it would be brought to her. She could get tickets for any play or film. True, he was generally too busy to accompany her and this upset her, but that could not be helped.

The fact was, Nadezhda felt closer to Lenin and Krupskaya, with their pre-Revolutionary culture and education, than she did to her rough, uncouth husband. Whenever she had problems at work – she herself admitted that her spelling and time-keeping were poor – Lenin would stand up for her. He knew she had recently had a baby and was finding it hard to cope. As for her spelling, he knew she had left school early, and was confident that it would improve.

Nadya's new independence flattered her proud, self-reliant temperament, and it seemed as though Stalin might finally have met his match. The peculiarities of his nature, later revealed to the world at large, were now turned upon his wife and children. Trotsky's wife, Natalya Sedova, recorded her indignation at his cruelty to little Yakov:

... a little boy of about twelve with a dark, gentle little face and startling black eyes with a gold glint in them. People say that his delicate, almost miniature frame resembles that of his mother. His manners are very gentle. He told our son Seryozha, with whom he has made friends, that his father punishes him cruelly and beats him for smoking. Stalin had once thrown him out of the flat because he smelt tobacco on his breath, and he had spent the night in the corridor with the doorman. 'But he won't make me give up tobacco by thrashing me!' he said.

Trotsky received a rather different account of Stalin's attitude to tobacco from Nikolai Bukharin, who arrived in a state of great indignation from visiting Stalin. According to Trotsky, Bukharin told him:

'Do you know what he does? He draws on his pipe, fills his mouth with smoke, then picks his year-old baby out of the cot and blows it in his face! The baby chokes and cries and Koba doubles up with laughter, shouting, "Never mind, it's good for him, it'll make him strong!" '[1]
'But that's barbarous!' I said.
'You don't know Koba – he's like that . . .'

[1] Koba was Stalin's Georgian nickname. The baby must have been Vasily Stalin.

These strange domestic scenes, as strange as life itself then, achieved ever more fantastic forms over the years.

Nadezhda Sergeevna was at the centre of the conflict between Stalin and Trotsky after the Bolshevik victory at Tsaritsyn, and the subsequent conflict between Lenin, Stalin and Krupskaya, and she behaved impeccably. She also knew things about her husband that no one else knew. When he had been drinking he loved to tell her that total power would soon be his. She did not like these conversations, yet she had seen all Lenin's comrades change since the Revolution; now their hostility was directed not against the tsarist regime but against one another, and Stalin was worse than the rest.

She was one of the first to hear of Lenin's 'Testament', in which he described her husband as 'rude, uncouth and often unjust'. She was forced to admit that he was right: Stalin was rude and often unjust to her. Over the 'Testament', too, she behaved in a perfectly correct Bolshevik fashion, yet Stalin found her secretive. She was bored and depressed by Kremlin life. It was like a prison. Everyone else there was in their forties and fifties, distrustful and obsessed with power. She was young, she wanted to study and enjoy herself.

In *Letters to a Friend*, Nadezhda's daughter Svetlana writes:

> This child laboured under the crushing burden of her love for a man twenty-two years her senior, a hardened revolutionary just back from exile, a man whom even his comrades found difficult to get along with. She cast in her lot with him like a tiny sailboat drawn to a giant ocean-going steamer. This is the way I see them, ploughing the turbulent ocean side by side. How long could the sailboat keep up with the liner? Could it weather the heavy seas?

A librarian at the Institute of Marxism–Leninism, inspecting Stalin's library after his death, described to me her visit to their Kremlin apartment:

> A row of rooms, their windows covered in dark maroon blinds. Sofas, tables and chairs with their covers on, and protruding everywhere the disconnected cables of Stalin's vast internal signalling system; the guards could hear every rustle he made, and knew when he passed from room to room.
>
> The apartment was divided into two halves, Stalin's and his daughter Svetlana's. She had three rooms, a few table-napkins, some toys, an embroidered cushion. His quarters were like a burial-vault – a huge

dining room, library, office and bedroom. Everything bore the mark of officialdom. The atmosphere was the same at his dacha.

Stalin's secretary, Yury Bazhanov, later recalled the four rooms and the plain furniture, the sentry standing permanently outside the door of their apartment, and Stalin's army cap and greatcoat hanging in the lobby. At first meals were brought to the house from the dining room of the Soviet of People's Commissars, but because of Stalin's fears of poisoning he later employed his own cooks to prepare his food at home.

Nadezhda clearly did not want to be a housewife and mother, and the children ran wild. Stalin hated this; he could not bear independent women. As Nadezhda's nerves became increasingly fraught, she became prone to hysterics. Stalin had it on good authority that her mother suffered from schizophrenia; Olga Evgenevna attended the Kremlin's special clinic and he had been told the diagnosis. 'You're a schizophrenic!' he would shout at his wife when they quarrelled. 'And you're paranoid!' Nadezhda would shout back. 'You have enemies everywhere!'

Stalin's mother had been right: a Georgian girl would have suited him far better. He found himself missing his first wife, Ekaterina Svanidze. 'This creature softened my stony heart,' he had said at her funeral. 'With her death my last warm feelings for people have died.' Given what we know about Stalin's stony heart this seems improbable. Cruel people are often sentimental; Stalin was sentimental in his relationship with his daughter Svetlana, and this sentimentality would clash again and again with Nadezhda Sergeevna's fiery temperament.

After Lenin's death in 1924 Nadezhda went to work for the magazine *Revolution and Culture*. Although her education did not go beyond six years at high school, plus the secretarial experience she had picked up in Lenin's office, she acquired her new editorial skills remarkably quickly. She would do anything to avoid sitting in the Kremlin with her children or at her husband's dinner table.

The children were easily dealt with; there was a nanny and a housekeeper, and Cheka guards always on hand. The evenings were more difficult. Stalin's Georgian nature revelled in the unlimited new opportunities for heavy drinking. Nadezhda did not drink and loathed drunken dinners. Someone had to give way, and since it was not her nature to resist, she lived by his rules for eight years. During these eight years, however, she was learning to fight back.

They slept separately now, she in the bedroom, he in his study or in a little room next to the dining room which contained the red government telephone. This telephone had become an essential accessory for the head of the government and the Party. Stalin made calls whenever he liked, but only his most trusted associates were allowed to call him, and only in exceptional circumstances. Stalin's former secretary Bazhanov wrote:

> With his family, Stalin was a despot. For days on end he would maintain a haughty silence, ignoring the questions of his wife and son. If he were out of sorts, as he frequently was, he would sit through dinner in silence, expecting everyone else to be silent too. After breakfast he would sit by the window with his pipe.
>
> The Kremlin's internal telephone would ring.
>
> 'Koba, it's Molotov!' Nadezhda Alliluyeva would say.
>
> 'Tell him I'm asleep!' Stalin would shout.
>
> You could tell a lot about Alliluyeva from the way she took her husband's calls. Living in an atmosphere of lies, she too was forced to lie, even though Molotov was clearly not phoning to pass the time of day. It shocked Nadezhda Sergeevna deeply; a servant of the Revolution capable of lying could not possibly be an object of respect.

She agreed with him less and less. Disagreements about how the children should be brought up turned into fights, and in the end neither brought them up properly and both failed them. There were too many people in the way – nannies, servants, guards – but that was an essential feature of the Kremlin mechanism.

Finally, in 1926, Nadezhda Sergeevna ran off with her two small children to Leningrad, hoping to find a job there and make a new life for herself. Outraged and ashamed, Stalin ordered her back. The quarrels now went underground and she dreamed of moving out permanently with the children to live with her sister and brother-in-law in the Ukraine.

When Lenin had died she knew that Stalin would win power, but it gave her no joy. She had seen blood at Tsaritsyn and wanted no more of it. Stalin's brilliantly orchestrated popularity campaign dramatically increased his influence in the Party. His portraits were carried through the streets during revolutionary holidays, and everyone loved, feared and respected him. Why could she not stand by him? Why could she not give her husband some support at home as he set about tackling his many enemies? She could not imagine what enemies he meant: Trotsky, Kamenev, Zinoviev and Bukharin were all Bolsheviks, Leninists and Party members fighting for the same cause.

Outside the Kremlin she found everything interesting, and even the hardest work appeared easy. She left her job at *Revolution and Culture* and went to work at the Industrial Academy, where she studied synthetic fibres. She attempted to remain anonymous and not to tell anyone at the Academy who she was, leaving her car at the corner and asking her guards not to follow her too closely as she walked to the building. This desire for anonymity sprang either from her innate modesty or from shame.

The autumn of 1927 was dark and heavy. Nadezhda Sergeevna was often ill and depressed in November, and Kremlin life was not conducive to joy. As Stalin entered the final phase of his struggle with Trotsky, and many oppositionists dear to her heart were expelled from the Party, she felt she understood nothing – but perhaps she understood everything.

Seizing upon rare moments of family peace to try and talk to Stalin, she would inevitably be told that these were not women's matters and be sent away to plan the evening's menu instead. She had reached her limit. Some of his insults to her over dinner were worse than a slap in the face. She would flush and jump up silently from the table. Terrible fights would follow when they were alone together, as she threw his words back in his face.

In November 1927 the distinguished diplomat Adolfe Ioffe killed himself. People knew that he had been ill, but they also knew that he was a Trotskyist, who together with Trotsky had signed the Brest Litovsk peace treaty with Germany in March 1918. Nadezhda Sergeevna had loved and respected Ioffe, and she and Trotsky were among the large crowd of mourners at the Novo-Deviche cemetery. Stalin's wife stood at the front of the crowd, listening in silence as Trotsky and Kamenev spoke at Ioffe's grave, young people sang civil war songs which invoked Trotsky's name, and Zinoviev abandoned funeral decorum to curse her husband's criminal betrayal of the Party. When the ceremony was over she and her guards walked back to her car. A young man from Trotsky's entourage yelled out to a battalion of Red soldiers who stood keeping order at the gates: 'Red soldiers! Hurrah to Comrade Trotsky, leader of the Red Army!' There was no response. Trotsky bowed his head and walked on.

During the first trials of the 1930s, several of Nadezhda Alliluyeva's former teachers were arrested in the 'Trial of the

Industrial Academy', which soon spread to all branches of Soviet industry. Psychologically torn between her own values and those of her husband, she began emotionally and intellectually to side with his enemies.

One could never imagine Krupskaya in such a situation. For her, Lenin was right even when he was wrong, and he was never wrong. Alone in the darkness of night she probably admitted a lot to herself, and she would speak of his over-emotional, exalted 'rages', about which only she knew. But she was never seen to disagree with him in public; she always made sure that any disagreements between them were kept private, protecting him from his own mistakes and explaining to herself and others the necessity of the Red Terror.

Nadezhda Alliluyeva was different, and more than thirty years younger than Krupskaya. When Stalin insulted Krupskaya, she probably sympathised with her, but she cannot have found Krupskaya easy to understand, and Krupskaya's militant atheism must have repelled her as she herself turned more and more to God. Religion brought calm to her turbulent soul, and she started attending church.[2]

Galina Kravchenko recalled:

Nadezhda Sergeevna looked old for her age. She could have been almost forty. If a young wife marries an old husband they both end up looking the same age . . .

She was deeply religious, and went to church. Everyone knew about it. She could obviously do things forbidden to other Party members; she had been in the Party since 1918. But you could see she was strange – even a bit mad.

A rather different picture of her emerges from the memoirs of Nikita Khrushchev, who worked with Nadezhda on the Moscow Party committee before entering the corridors of power. He wrote: 'I had a deep respect for Nadezhda Alliluyeva. She was so different from Stalin. I especially liked her modesty.'

During the parade marking the fifteenth anniversary of the Revolution, on 7 November 1932, the entire government, headed by Comrade Stalin, lined the tribune above Lenin's Mausoleum.

---

[2] Anyone but Stalin's wife would have been harassed, even arrested for attending church in the 1930s.

Beneath them on the lower tribune stood government officials and foreign guests. Ekaterina Lebedeva, wife of Alexei Lebedev, deputy chief of the Central Committee's military section, stood beside her husband with the usual lump in her throat as she watched the vast workers' demonstration passing beneath her on Red Square. Suddenly the whisper went up: 'There's Stalin's wife!', and her eyes wandered along the columns of demonstrators to where she saw Nadezhda Alliluyeva marching under the banner of the Industrial Academy.

> She was tall, and her coat was flung open despite the cold. She smiled and laughed and said something to her companions, then she looked up to the Mausoleum and waved, and her white, marble face was beautiful, her wave was regal, she was radiant.

As the crowds cheered and applauded Comrade Stalin, his wife crossed Red Square. Then, leaving her companions, she turned into the Spassky Gates and emerged with her guards at the lower tribune, where she took her place beside Nikita Khrushchev. It was bitterly cold, and she shivered as she pulled her coat around her. Peering up at Stalin on the Mausoleum, she told Khrushchev she was worried he would catch cold; he was so stubborn, she had begged him to dress more warmly, but he had not listened.

The following evening the Kremlin élite celebrated the holiday at a reception in the apartment of Stalin's close Politburo ally, Klim Voroshilov. Nadezhda Alliluyeva left early, Stalin left several hours later. The next morning the housekeeper found Nadezhda lying beside her bed in a pool of blood, with a little revolver which her brother Pavel had brought back for her from abroad. The terrified housekeeper called the nurse, and the two women lifted the cold body onto the bed. Afraid to wake Stalin, who was still sleeping a few yards away beside the red telephone, they phoned Abel Enukidze and Molotov's wife, Paulina Semyonovna Zhemchuzhina. When they arrived Stalin was woken, and he emerged into the dining room to hear them crying, 'Josif, Josif, Nadya's dead!'

This was how witnesses described the events of that morning to members of the Stalin household and later to his daughter Svetlana. Yet the passing years have inevitably tangled the knot of contradictions leading Nadezhda Alliluyeva to her tragic end, and her death has become surrounded by a mass of rumours, legends and myths.

The half-truths started at once. On 10 November the Party

Central Committee announced in *Pravda*: 'On the night of 9 November, active and dedicated Party member Nadezhda Sergeevna Alliluyeva died.'

This was followed by an article under the banner headlines:

TO THE DEAR MEMORY OF NADEZHDA SERGEEVNA ALLILUYEVA,
FRIEND AND COMRADE

We have lost a dear, beloved comrade with a beautiful soul. A young Bolshevik, filled with strength and boundlessly dedicated to the Party and the Revolution, is no more. Growing up in the family of a revolutionary worker, this was a person whose life was joined to the Revolution, at the civil war front and during the growth of socialist construction. Unceasingly modest and vigilant, Nadezhda Sergeevna selflessly served the cause of the Party, demanding much of herself and, in her last years, working tirelessly to become one of the most active student comrades at the Industrial Academy. The memory of Nadezhda Sergeevna, dedicated Bolshevik, close friend and faithful helper to Comrade Stalin, will remain forever dear to us.

Ekaterina Voroshilova, Paulina Zhemchuzhina, Zinaida Ordzhokonidze, Dora Khazan, Maria Kaganovich, Tatyana Postysheva, Ashkhen Mikoyan, K. Voroshilov, V. Molotov, S. Ordzhokonidze, V. Kuibyshev, M. Kalinin, L. Kaganovich, P. Postyshev, A. Andreev, S. Kirov, A Mikoyan, A. Enukidze

These clichéd official condolences present the head of state's wife as a sexless being dedicated only to Party and revolutionary work, and the only hint of her sex lies in the fact that the women's names are given first and in full.

Murder, suicide. The rumours swelled like a funeral march. Most reports of the solemn funeral ceremony imply that Stalin was there too. In fact he was not.

In the days that followed, the obituaries in *Pravda* gradually regained their senses. One, written by the head of the Industrial Academy, hints at a cause of death: '. . . poor health did not impede the Bolshevik diligence she brought to her studies.' This might be taken to mean that she was ill but continued to study, over-exerted herself and died – yet if this were the case one would expect to see the medical causes of death.

On 11 November *Pravda* wrote: 'A modest, dedicated young fighter in the great Bolshevik army has died mid-campaign, mid-journey, mid-studies . . .' The author then turns abruptly from the deceased to her 'suffering survivor', with condolences addressed personally to Comrade Stalin: 'His close friends and comrades understand the enormous burden of Stalin's loss, and the obligations which this places upon us in our relations with him.'

The stream of obituaries culminated on 16 November with a message printed in bold type from Nadezhda Konstantinovna Krupskaya:

Dear Josif Vissarionych,
I have recently been thinking of you and wish to press your hand. It is hard to lose the person one is close to. I remember a couple of conversations I had with you in Ilich's office during his illness. They gave me strength at the time. Again I press your hand.
Nadezhda Krupskaya

Each one of Krupskaya's words here has been weighed, considered, checked and rechecked. She probably had her own views about Nadezhda Alliluyeva's death, but with no other opportunities available to her she used this message to express her true attitude to Stalin. She may even have believed that Stalin poisoned Lenin, but she could deal with anything, even her husband's murderer, and she was letting Stalin know that nothing was forgotten.

'It is hard to lose the person one is close to' – here she is reminding him that *she* has lost *Lenin*. Her mention of the 'couple of conversations in Ilich's office', given her relations with Stalin shortly before Lenin's death, would surely remind him of his rudeness to her on the telephone.

Those who knew Krupskaya used to remark on the originality of her language, an appealing childishness, a slight affectation of exclusiveness suggesting that she could do what others could not. Her use of 'you', for instance, rather than the accepted capitalised 'You', is obviously intended to be insulting, as is her casual misspelling of Stalin's name as 'Vissarionych', rather than 'Vissarionovich'. Either the editor dared not correct her mistakes or she forbade any changes, but these details were eloquent. Nadezhda Konstantinovna Krupskaya knew that she alone had the right to this kind of official familiarity, and this familiarity in his hardest hour summed up her entire attitude to him, an attitude that was not merely lofty but contemptuous.

Izvestiya had less to say about Nadezhda Alliluyeva's death and funeral, but was less solemn. One issue of the paper even carried a poem dedicated to her memory by the popular poet Demyan Bedny:

Death takes its bloody toll
Sparing the old and the lame
And striking down those in their prime . . .

The court poet of the Kremlin could hardly have failed to be aware
of the two main explanations of Nadezhda Alliluyeva's death, but
his verses were written for the masses, and all they had to know was
that she had been struck down in her prime.

When I telephoned the KGB for material on Nadezhda Alliluyeva's
death, I was told that her file was missing, and that Stalin had given
orders that there were to be no criminal proceedings. Since this allows
one to think whatever one likes, I undertook my own research into the
vast body of legends, rumours and hearsay surrounding her death.

The main murder scenarios are as follows:
1) Stalin murdered her in a jealous rage because she was having an
affair with his son and her stepson, Yakov. On discovering them
together he dealt with her on the spot, promising to deal with Yakov
later; this explains why Stalin did not secure his son's release from a
German prisoner-of-war camp during the war.
2) Stalin murdered her because he considered her his political
opponent; she was horrified by his policies, especially collectivisation, and he could not tolerate it.
3) Stalin learned that she was supporting enemies of the people by
joining the opposition 'Group of 92', and, not wishing to dirty his
own hands, he ordered her killed.
4) She had joined an anti-Stalin opposition group, and her
accomplices had her removed for fear that she would betray them.
5) Stalin ordered the secret police to kill her because he was sick of
her jealous scenes; they no longer lived together as man and wife,
and she prevented him from drinking wine and sleeping with
ballerinas.
6) Nadezhda Alliluyeva lay dying. She could not be saved. As the
blood poured from her she whispered, 'It was Josif. I defended
Krupskaya and he never forgave me! He did it with his own
hands. . . !'

Marshall Budyonny's even more elaborate theory, as expounded
to Galina Kravchenko, was that Stalin walked into his room late
that night, and, noticing that the heavy maroon blind on the
window was twitching, he lunged at it like a maniac and fired at
Nadezhda Sergeevna, who had been looking out of the window into
the darkness.

The main suicide scenario is that Nadezhda Alliluyeva took her life to punish Stalin for his drunkenness and debauchery; that night she had discovered him with another woman and could not bear it.

Whatever the plausibility of these versions, Nikita Khrushchev was surely correct in writing:

> The circumstances of her death were mysterious, but it was undoubtedly caused by something Stalin did. There were even rumours that he had shot her ... Another version, which strikes me as fairly probable, is that Nadya shot herself because of some insult to her female dignity.

Nadezhda's daughter Svetlana, who was sixteen at the time and had more insight than anyone else into her mother's death, wrote in *Letters to a Friend*:

> Her self-control, her tremendous inner tension and discipline, her pent-up dissatisfaction and discontent, built up more and more pressure within until finally she was like a tightly coiled spring. And when the spring uncoiled at last it did so with ferocious force.
>
> That is what happened. What caused the spring to give, the immediate occasion, was trivial in itself, so trivial one might have said it happened for no reason at all. It was a minor quarrel at a banquet in honour of the Fifteenth Anniversary of the Revolution. He said to her: 'Hey you, drink!' And she screamed: 'Don't talk to me that way!', jumping up in front of everyone and running from the table.

For the actual details of what happened that night let us listen to Vyacheslav Molotov, Politburo member and Stalin's closest ally, speaking in the last years of his life to the poet Felix Chuev. Molotov supported his leader in everything, and one can hear his implicit condemnation of Alliluyeva. But he was at the table with them that evening and was qualified to know better than anyone else what happened:

> There was jealousy, of course, but it was probably unfounded. There was a hairdresser whom Stalin used to visit to be shaved, and his wife hated it. She was so young. After the November 7th parade a big crowd of us gathered in Voroshilov's flat and Stalin was rolling lumps of bread into balls and throwing them at Egorov's wife. Alliluyeva was a bit crazy in those days, and she couldn't bear it. She left the party with my wife, Paulina Semyonovna, and they walked around the Kremlin together. It was late at night, and she complained to my wife about the

business with the hairdresser, and the way Stalin had been flirting that evening. It didn't mean anything, he was just a bit drunk, but she took it very hard. She was terribly jealous of him – it was the gypsy blood in her. Paulina Semyonovna criticised her, and said it was wrong of her to abandon him at such a difficult time . . .

Maria Vasilevna, Marshall Budyonny's widow, was equally critical, describing to me how her husband had commiserated with Stalin after Alliluyeva's death:

My husband told me Nadezhda Sergeevna was a bit mad. She was always nagging and humiliating Stalin in front of other people. 'I don't know how he puts up with it!' my husband used to say. 'What normal mother would leave her children as orphans?'

Those more sympathetic to Nadezhda Alliluyeva emphasise her profound disillusionment with the politics that had at first so attracted her, and the terrible affect this had upon her. According to Galina Kravchenko: 'The evening before her death, she shouted, "I hate you all! Look at this table, and the people are starving!" '

Trotsky, in his Mexican hiding-place, had his own interpretation of the tragedy:

With collectivisation at its height and mass shootings and starvation in the villages, Alliluyeva apparently came under pressure from her father to persuade Stalin to change his rural policies. Her mother too, who was from the countryside, was constantly telling her of the horrors being inflicted on the peasants. When Alliluyeva spoke of this to Stalin he forbade her to see her mother or to receive her in the Kremlin. But Alliluyeva would meet her in town, and this strengthened her resolve.

During the party at Voroshilov's apartment she dared to criticise Stalin. He showered her with obscenities in front of all the guests, and when she got home she killed herself.

Anna Larina, wife of Politburo member Nikolai Bukharin, recalls in her memoirs, *This I Shall Not Forget*:

In November 1932 I came home from the Institute and found N.I.[3] there. He had just been at the funeral of Nadezhda Sergeevna Alliluyeva. He looked pale and agitated. N.I. and Nadezhda Sergeevna had had a warm regard for each other; she had secretly shared his views on the collectivisation programme, and had taken the opportunity to

[3]Her husband, Nikolai Ivanovich Bukharin.

tell him so. Nadezhda Sergeevna was a good, modest person of enchanting appearance and fragile spiritual strength. She suffered terribly from Stalin's coarse, despotic character.

N.I. recalled arriving once at Stalin's dacha at Zubalovo while he was out. As he and Nadezhda Sergeevna walked around the grounds chatting, Stalin returned and, creeping up on them, he said, 'I'll shoot you!' N.I. took it as a joke, but Nadezhda Sergeevna turned pale and shuddered . . .

N.I. had sat next to her at the Kremlin banquet marking the fifteenth anniversary of the October Revolution, and he told me how Stalin got drunk and threw orange peel and cigarette butts in her face. Unable to bear his rudeness, she jumped up from the table and disappeared for the rest of the evening. Next morning they found her dead.

N.I. was one of the mourners standing beside the coffin, and Stalin chose this moment to come up and assure him that he had gone straight from the banquet to his dacha, and that they had telephoned him there to tell him the news. This directly contradicts the account of Nadezhda's daughter Svetlana, and gives the distinct impression that Stalin was trying to divert suspicion from himself.

I don't know if it was murder or suicide, but N.I. certainly didn't exclude murder. According to him, the first person after the nurse to see Nadezhda Sergeevna dead was Enukidze, whom the nurse phoned for fear of telling Stalin first. Perhaps it was because Enukidze knew too much that he was the first of the Politburo members to be arrested.

N.I. said that before the lid of the coffin was closed Stalin asked them to wait, then he lifted up her head and kissed her. 'What are his kisses worth?' N.I. said. 'He's destroyed her!'

Apart from Nadezhda's father, Sergei Yakovlevich, who died of natural causes, all the Alliluyevs suffered terrible ends. Nadezhda's mother, Olga Evgenevna, was afflicted by a serious mental disorder, and her sister Anna was unhinged by years of solitary confinement in Stalin's prisons. But the most haunting of these stories was told to me in the mid-fifties by an elderly Bolshevik woman who had once attended lectures at the Red Professors Institute in the early thirties, and had known a girl who was friendly with Nadezhda Alliluyeva.

Nadezhda was close to a nervous breakdown, said her friend. Weeping and emotional, she would complain bitterly about Stalin's roughness and indifference. They were estranged; he was virtually an alcoholic and would go on drunken binges all night, then sleep until midday. She hated drinking and was unable to do so because of the delicate temperament she had inherited from her mother. Stalin would force her to drink in company, and it would enrage her. When drunk on his own with her, he was intolerable, and when he made obscene remarks about women she often came close to killing him; she was not jealous and did not let his drunken male ravings insult her dignity, but it exasperated her that when everyone shouted 'Great Stalin!' only she knew how 'great' he really was. He even interfered with her relationship with the children. She felt helpless. Her best years were vanishing into the sand. The friend's father, an old Bolshevik, himself visited Stalin at the Kremlin and described how Nadezhda Sergeevna publicly shouted at her drunken husband.

In 1932, about a week before the November holiday, Nadezhda Alliluyeva told her friend that something terrible was about to happen, and that she was cursed from birth. When pressed by her friend to explain, she said that Stalin had told her that she was his daughter. 'You're either mine or you're Kurnatovsky's!' he had yelled to her during a quarrel. He immediately retracted his words, trying to claim that it was just a joke.

Nadezhda was born in September 1901. Her mother had had plenty of lovers in her youth, and when Nadezhda pinned her down she admitted that throughout December 1900 and January 1901 she had indeed been sleeping with both Stalin and her husband, and could not be sure who Nadya's father was, but since she resembled her legal father she had always assumed it must be he. Yet Nadezhda Alliluyeva grew increasingly convinced that she must be Stalin's daughter, and thus the sister of her own children. In the last days of her life she regarded herself as damned, with no place on earth. And so, according to my elderly informant, she killed herself, and afterwards her friend was never seen again.

Nadezhda Sergeevna is now known to have left Stalin a suicide note. The contents of this note were known only to him, but they are easy to guess; any woman with the chance to air all the grievances which have accumulated over fifteen years of marriage will have few difficulties in detailing all her husband's crimes, both to her and in general. After his wife's death Stalin wept openly, and those who saw him were struck by the depth of his grief. He blamed himself for not giving her enough attention or taking her to the cinema, he blamed the bad influence of others, and he blamed her for punishing him by leaving him at such a difficult time. He never remarried. Yet her death untied his hands. Some have speculated that, had she not removed herself, he would have had her liquidated along with all his other enemies. Others find it more probable that Nadezhda would have carried out her own bloody revenge and Stalin's dismembered corpse would have been found in the bath.

The act of suicide contravenes the laws of the Russian Orthodox Church, and suicides are denied a religious burial, yet it may be that God and Church were not one and the same thing for Bolshevik Alliluyeva. The tragedy of her solitary life consisted in the dichotomy between her attempt to turn to God and the impossibility of breaking with the impious world. New generations will bring new insights to bear on this sad event, plays and films will be made about this mysterious couple, the child and the despot, yet history will never finally unravel the tangled story of Stalin and Alliluyeva.

Nadezhda Alliluyeva had to die. Her presence would have hindered Stalin from fulfilling his historic mission. He could tolerate no obstacles on his path, especially female. Prison was the best she could have expected, yet prison was no answer; as long as she was alive she would speak out against him.

Stalin was alone again, and remained so until his death over twenty years later. Marxist delusions of women's social equality were long forgotten, and had come to mean simply women's chance to do the same heavy work as a man and to support him in his cruel politics; there could be no thought of women expressing their emotional and social needs.

In 1941, just before World War II, the Kremlin's Augean stables were thoroughly cleansed by Stalin's secret police, yet with the outbreak of war people's fears of Stalin were now overshadowed by their fear of Hitler. As the Kremlin families were evacuated to Kuibyshev, they gained a welcome distance from Stalin, who remained alone in Moscow with his commanders.

Alone in a cold bed.

V., a ballerina at the Bolshoi Theatre, recalls:

Moscow in 1941 was empty. We had ration cards, but nothing to buy with them. There were queues outside the shops all night. The frosts came early that year. Those of us still left in the capital wrapped ourselves up as best we could. Many apartments stood empty, you could just go in and take what you wanted. Nobody did, though.

Moscow was empty, but in December 1941 the Bolshoi opened a new season. Stalin often attended. In the beginning we were frantic, but we soon got used to it. There was a strange, exalted atmosphere in the theatre. There were always a lot of foreigners – diplomats, pilots, tank-drivers. Everyone was having love affairs, and many of the ballerinas had affairs with foreigners. If one of us came in wearing patent-leather shoes or a foreign frock it was obvious she had caught a foreigner.

Even as a ballet student in the thirties, I knew the Bolshoi was protected by the highest of the high in the Kremlin. The ballet school was under the protection of Abel Enukidze, who used to send sweets and biscuits to the school, and organised magnificent Christmas parties with presents. I was only little then, but I heard the rumours about him and the older girls.

Stalin loved the opera. There were rumours that he had affairs with Natalya Shpiller and Vera Davidovna, both well-known singers from the Bolshoi.

Vera Davidovna spoke recently on television of Stalin's attentions to her, and his offer of marriage. The proposal frightened her, since she was happily married already, and she explained to him that her devotion to her leader was not the same as her everyday love for her husband and family.

Throughout the 1930s and 1940s, the widowed Stalin observed family life in the Kremlin and felt a limitless dissatisfaction: they all had warm hearths, his bed was cold. Brief liaisons could offer such a man no satisfaction: he knew their cost. Attempts at anything more serious would be no better: he knew in advance how they would end.

As Stalin continued his arrests in the Party, he took special pleasure in dealing with his enemies' wives, such as the dangerous Olga Kameneva, sister of Trotsky, who at his orders received a bullet through the head in the yard of Orlov Central Prison, along with the pre-Revolutionary terrorist Maria Spiridonova. Generally, however, Stalin was more lenient, and prison and the camps appeared a more fitting punishment.

Old Bolsheviks returning from the camps told how Nadezhda Krupskaya and Maria Ilinichna, Lenin's wife and sister, visited Stalin at the height of the terror and pleaded with him for the lives of their old comrades. 'Who are you defending? You're defending murderers!' he shouted at them, and the two women were led weeping from the room.

My mother had her own experience of the terror, as the wives of the Kremlin were delivered to the camps and their children into children's homes. Shortly after my birth in 1936 she fell ill, and managed with great difficulty to be sent to recuperate in the Crimea, where she was amazed to see crowds of fabulously elegant women in expensive gowns and bathing-suits on the beach. These were all wives of commissars, marshals and Party secretaries, and they socialised according to their husbands' rank, talking about outfits, their husbands' work and the latest appointments.

When in 1937 my mother fell ill again, she had no trouble in acquiring a ticket to the Crimea. The arrests were at their height in her factory, and she did not want to go, but her mother read the cards and reassured her that she was in no danger, and this time the beach was empty and unrecognisable; all the women who had been there before were now in jail.

Now we can read the memoirs of women who survived Stalin's prisons. My story is also of those Kremlin women who remained free, and of the threat which prison cast over their lives and those of their associates. Women such as Ekaterina Voroshilova and Paulina Zhemchuzhina, who clad themselves in the armour of their blue Party suits, orthodox words and Party devotion. Never knowing what would happen to them, they grew guarded, closed-minded and repressed. Each person close to Stalin lived under the shadow of prison, and this made them morally weak and absolutely submissive. Stalin's personal secretary, Anatoly Poskrebyshev, who had served him with such dog-like devotion, uncomplainingly sacrificed his Jewish wife on the altar of his boss's happiness. Old Bolshevik Yury Pyatakov confessed in speech and writing, in freedom and prison, to crimes he had not committed and eagerly offered to shoot his allies. He even offered to shoot his wife, an impulse evidently familiar to many Kremlin men in those days.

The sufferings Stalin inflicted on his close associates must have helped to ease his own suffering. Yet he became short-sighted, even blind to the future, failing to anticipate that the women who returned from the camps after his death would avenge themselves against him, and that the children to come would denounce his bloody reign.

6

A Soviet Esther

*Kliment Efremovich Voroshilov (1881–1969). Born of poor work-
ing parents in a village near Ekaterinoslav. Started working in a
factory at the age of fifteen and learned to read. Arrested in 1905 as a
strike-organiser and spent the next twelve years working for the
Revolution in exile and the underground. In February 1917 elected
to the Petrograd Soviet, and spent the civil war fighting at Tsaritsyn,
in the Ukraine and the Caucasus. Appointed Marshal in 1935,
Voroshilov was one of Stalin's closest allies and supported all
Stalin's subsequent purges of the army. Between 1953 and 1960 he
was president of the presidium of the Supreme Soviet. Removed by
Khrushchev, he was denounced in 1961 as an accomplice of Stalin,
but was rehabilitated in 1963.*

In the early part of the twentieth century large numbers of Jewish
girls left their villages beyond the Pale of Settlement[1] to follow the
call of the Revolution and settle in the cities. These girls, with their
exotic looks, captured the hearts of many simple Russian boys, and
several of the Party's leaders, including Molotov, Kirov,
Dzerzhinsky, Lunacharsky and Kamenev, were married to Jewish
women. The most striking example of this combination was the
Voroshilovs, Kliment Efremovich and his wife Ekaterina
Davidovna.

One day in December 1944, when I was ten years old, I was picked
up by my 'Uncle Petya', who had worked in the Urals on a secret
tank-building project with my father. Uncle Petya took me with him

---

[1] Before the Bolshevik Revolution, Jews in the Russian Empire were forced to live in strictly
designated areas.

to the Kremlin. We entered a large building, went up to a brightly-lit corridor on the first floor, and were met by a large, unsmiling, dark-haired old woman wearing a beautiful floor-length white satin dressing-gown. The woman silently led me to the kitchen and sat me down at a table, where she poured me some cocoa and spread a slice of white bread with butter and sausage. I can still remember its taste to this day.

After I had eaten, a boy by the name of Klim appeared and took me to another flat, where a large Christmas tree stood in the corner of the sitting room. A stepladder was brought in, and I had just climbed up to decorate the top when a group of men appeared at the door. The man in front was painfully familiar: short, with a black moustache and khaki army tunic, exactly like the photographs, except that his hair was grey, not black, and stuck up like a hedgehog's bristles on top of his head, on which I could see, from my ladder, a small round bald patch. He looked up at the tree, then at me, frozen on my ladder, and said with a slight accent: 'She'll get a bump when she falls!' My heart pounded as Stalin and his friends passed into the next room, and more men quickly led us out.

That night my mother told me that the flat I had been in was Marshal Voroshilov's, that the woman in the dressing-gown was Voroshilov's wife, Ekaterina Davidovna, that Petya was their adopted son and Klim their grandson.

My memory of that dull woman is contradicted by the author Roman Gul, whose book *The Red Marshalls* describes his meeting with Ekaterina Davidovna during the height of the battle for Tsaritsyn in 1918:

> On the second floor of an abandoned mansion which once belonged to a mustard-factory owner live Klim Voroshilov and his wife. Ekaterina Davidovna appears in the darkened bedroom beautifully dressed in a fine caracul cape . . . She dashes around town in a military car, and many Cheka members take a dim view of the concern the commander's wife lavishes on her appearance at such a time.

Gul's Ekaterina Davidovna was bathed in the euphoria of revolutionary victory, the freedom of war, the glory of Voroshilov's military exploits. What happened to transform this elegant, vital woman into the sullen 'Party Aunt' of the 1930s and '40s?

It was in order to discover more about Ekaterina Davidovna's origins and her life in the Kremlin that I visited Nadezhda Ivanovna Voroshilova, widow of my Uncle Petya and mother of Klim.

Nadezhda Ivanovna lives today in a large flat on Granovsky Street, to which the Voroshilovs moved during the Khrushchev period. The spirit of those times is preserved in the huge Kremlin-style dining table, the vast pre-Revolutionary sideboard, the photographs of Voroshilov, Petya, Nadezhda Ivanovna and their sons, and the large ceremonial portraits by the then fashionable touch-up artist Alexander Gerasimov. From Nadezhda Ivanovna's memories of her mother-in-law I discovered a more human side to Ekaterina Davidovna, and things in her past which she felt obliged to hide from the prying eyes of the Kremlin.

She was born Golda Gorbman, one of four children in a poor Jewish family living in the village of Mardarovka, in the Ukraine. After learning to read and write a little in her teens, she left Mardarovka for Odessa, where she trained as a seamstress and enrolled in an adult school. One of her teachers there, a dedicated revolutionary named Serafima Gopner, drew the girl from Mardarovka into the Socialist Revolutionary Party, and in 1906 Golda Gorbman was arrested and exiled to Arkhangelsk, in Northern Russia.

Most of the exiles living there were men, for whom every exiled woman was like a ray of light in the kingdom of darkness. Many revolutionary relationships started in exile, and the dark-eyed little Socialist Revolutionary soon embarked on a love affair with the dashing Georgian Bolshevik Abel Enukidze. Enukidze was something of a star in Arkhangelsk, but for him Golda Gorbman was clearly little more than a passing fancy. The affair did not last, and she was soon to be seen in the company of Kliment Efremovich Voroshilov, a former riveter from Lugansk and a popular Bolshevik organiser, who quickly converted her to Bolshevism. From the outset they made an excellent match. Nadezhda Ivanovna says:

> She possessed an extraordinary sensitivity with Kliment Efremovich. Some years after her death, he told me she had been completely honest with him from the start so there would be no cause for reproaches or recriminations, and that she had told him everything that had happened between her and Enukidze. She put her husband on a pedestal, and he became the sole purpose of her life. She subordinated herself completely to his work and life, and never criticised him or had a moment's doubt about anything he did. This continued for the whole of her life. They seemed to be in total harmony.

Ekaterina Davidovna was released from exile before Kliment

Efremovich, but she soon returned to be with him. As with Krupskaya and Lenin, citizens and exiles were allowed to cohabit only if they were married in church, so she converted to the Orthodox faith and changed her name from Golda to Ekaterina. This deeply distressed her parents, and the rabbi denounced her before a large congregation of worshippers in the Mardarovka synagogue. When Voroshilov's term of exile came to an end, they both left for his home town of Lugansk, and since he had a 'wolf's ticket'[2] she supported them both by doing needlework.

In April 1917 the Voroshilovs were among the crowd of Bolsheviks who gathered in Petrograd to welcome Lenin home, and there she again met her former teacher, Serafima Gopner, who recommended her for membership of the Bolshevik Party.

She spent the entire civil war at Kliment Efremovich's side. In the summer of 1918 she joined him at the Tsaritsyn front, where she worked with the First Cavalry Army and helped to set up a Women's Soviet, taking care of orphaned children and setting up children's homes. One day Marshal Budyonny brought a curly-haired four-year-old boy to her, and the child won her heart. Since she could not have children because of complications arising from her love affair with Enukidze, she and Kliment Efremovich agreed to adopt the child, and they named him Petya. Petya later told his wife that Ekaterina Davidovna had been an excellent mother to him as a child, doing everything for him and using her old dress patterns to make all his clothes.

> Although it was common knowledge that Petya wasn't their son, neither Ekaterina Davidovna nor Kliment Efremovich ever mentioned it. Petya loved them like his own parents, and Kliment Efremovich would shout at him just like a real father. In the 1920s everything was very democratic in the Kremlin, everyone lived as equals, and out at the dachas they all took turns with the cooking. Once Petya was sent off by the cook to fetch bread and refused to go – Kliment Efremovich went wild, chasing him around the bushes and trying to pull his ears.

In 1919 Ekaterina Davidovna and Petya travelled from Tsaritsyn to Moscow, which they left periodically to follow Kliment Efremovich around the country on his various military missions.

In 1922 Ekaterina Davidovna worked for Budyonny's First

---

[2] A 'wolf's ticket', issued to political prisoners or strikers, banned them from finding future employment.

Cavalry Army in Ekaterinoslav, where the Budyonnys and the Voroshilovs shared a house. A. Arbatov, who worked in various Soviet institutions in the town, visited them there on several occasions. Arbatov was no admirer of the new regime, and his memoirs of the period, contained in the Archive of the Russian Revolution, have the ring of truth about them:

> The Department of Social Assistance in Ekaterinoslav had been taken over by a man named Shalyakhin, who immediately declared that money was being paid out to a mass of *petit bourgeois* counter-revolutionary pensioners living at the state's expense, and that this money should be spent on increasing the allowances paid to Red invalids and their widows. Having stopped their payments, Shalyakhin raised the matter at an Executive Committee meeting, and 'jokingly' proposed various ways to quietly eliminate these old people, such as building a large crematorium to which all the pensioners could be sent.
>
> For over three months Shalyakhin battled with the pensioners. This went on until the arrival of Voroshilov's wife. Replacing Shalyakhin as head of the department, she demanded the restitution of all the decrees of Soviet power, and restored the pensioners' benefits, backdated to when they were stopped.
>
> The pensioners stripped the department like locusts; in two days all the cash in the till and three months' savings in the State Bank were gone. Then Shalyakhin declared war on Voroshilova, attacking her before the Executive Committee, the Party and everywhere else. His propaganda had its effect, since her smart appearance, her expensive caracul coat and her elegant silk shawl were more reminiscent of an upper-middle-class lady than the wife of a proletarian leader. Only officers from the General Staff were invited to their home, and her supporters were bourgeois, not proletarian; she herself often said that the Party committee disliked her because of her bourgeois appearance and non-proletarian tastes.
>
> Although a former exile, she was always 'dear Ekaterina Davidovna', not 'comrade', and she flirted with Budyonny's handsome young cavalry commanders, many of whom had belonged previously to the best tsarist cavalry regiments. When one met her on the street with her entourage of officers, provocatively flashing a wide gold watch on her wrist, their elegant talk and manners would remind one of the army of the tsars rather than that of the workers and peasants.
>
> In their apartment, in a splendid old mansion, dressmakers and needlewomen worked day and night for the wives of Voroshilov and

Budyonny. The Voroshilovs and Budyonnys would take car trips out of town together, or steamer-trips down the river Dnepr. At dinner there would be wine and fresh fruit, with cut flowers on the table. I was invited to dinner on the day Ekaterina Davidovna took over at the department. She suffered terribly from Comrade Budyonny's loud and frequent belches, and towards the end of the meal, when he started sticking his fingers in his mouth to rescue some pieces of food lodged in his strong male teeth, she flung down her napkin and left the table . . .

Voroshilov had worked for the Party since 1905, and by 1917 he had a solid record as a proletarian activist. He had educated himself through his love of reading, and he had acquired a selective knowledge of revolutionary history. His development was encouraged by his intellectual wife, and he quickly memorised whole pages from Marx and Engels.

According to Nadezhda Ivanovna, however, things were not quite like that:

> Ekaterina Davidovna was not an educated woman. She could appear so in the company of her officers, but her low-brow tastes were always in evidence. She was intelligent, kind too in her own way, but not an intellectual. I don't recognise her in Arbatov's memoirs. And Kliment Efremovich used to be wildly jealous – he could have killed her!

Returning from her campaigns with Voroshilov to Moscow, she and Petya moved first into the Metropol Hotel, then the Kremlin, where she lived for the next forty years until her death. She continued to study, graduating from the Higher Party School, working on the newspaper *Poverty*, then returning to work for the Higher Party School.

Since Petya did not fully satisfy Ekaterina Davidovna's maternal longings, the Voroshilovs took in her niece, Truda, and Voroshilov's nephew, Kolya. After Petya's marriage she also took in the two children of civil war commander Mikhail Frunze, who had died during an operation. Frunze's death was shrouded in mystery. There were rumours that doctors had 'knifed' him on orders from above, and these fears were enflamed by the publication of Boris Pilnyak's story, 'Murder of a Commander', which was a transparent reference to the murder. Since Voroshilov's friendship with Frunze was well known, it was natural for the Central Committee to appoint the Voroshilovs as guardians of Frunze's orphaned children, and Ekaterina Davidovna's love for them somehow managed to banish the rumours surrounding Frunze's death.

In 1928 Ekaterina Davidovna fell ill, went abroad for a major operation and put on weight. By now she had been appointed political director of the Higher Party School, and was one of the most important women in the Kremlin and an increasingly orthodox member of the Party. Stern and uncompromising, she made allowances for nobody, least of all herself, and those who knew her, including Petya's new wife, found her taciturn and difficult.

Nadezhda Ivanovna and Petya had been schoolfriends; they became close in 1932 at a holiday home and married three years later. She found Ekaterina Davidovna highly repressive on sexual matters:

> Ekaterina Davidovna and I met three years before Petya and I married, yet when our son Klim was born she worked out the dates obsessively to the day, trying to prove that I had been a virgin when we married. I was wary of her coldness. She eyed me for three years before she accepted me as Petya's wife.
>
> By the time I moved in with them, she had closed herself off. Maybe it was because of what was happening around her in the Kremlin that she decided to keep her mouth shut. The Voroshilovs nurtured our marriage, and we filled their life with all the bustle and anxieties of an extended family clan, with our elder son Klim being especially close to Kliment Efremovich, and the younger one, Volodya, to Ekaterina Davidovna. Yet she was unable to express this love. She never embraced, never expressed her emotions, despite the fact that she was a person of enormously strong feelings. She just bottled them up. Her soul was dissatisfied. She wasn't cold, just repressed: always neat, lived by the clock, went to bed early. We young people grew used to it, and Kliment Efremovich would spend the evenings with us . . .
>
> Things were much easier with Kliment Efremovich. It must have been hard for her to be married to a man with such power and such an impulsive, sociable character. Of course his bright expansive nature was popular with other women too, but she didn't notice or didn't want to. She never gave him orders, but he did nothing in the house without her. They never argued.
>
> She had no rings and despised jewellery. When I was married she ordered me not to wear earrings. She always wore a severe, mannish suit, like a uniform. True, her clothes were always well-cut, for she was a fine dressmaker.

Nadezhda Krupskaya, Lenin's wife

Krupskaya with Lenin in the early days of victory

Krupskaya and Lenin in Gorky, shortly before Lenin's death

Inessa Armand

The widowed Krupskaya

Larissa Reisner

Nadezhda Alliluyeva with her son, Vasily

Josif Stalin and his wife, Nadezhda Alliluyeva

The Voroshilovs, Klim (centre, standing) and
Ekaterina Davidovna (right, seated), at Tsarytsin, 1918

The Voroshilovs in old age

Olga Stefanovna Mikhailova-Budyonnaya,
second wife of Marshal Budyonny

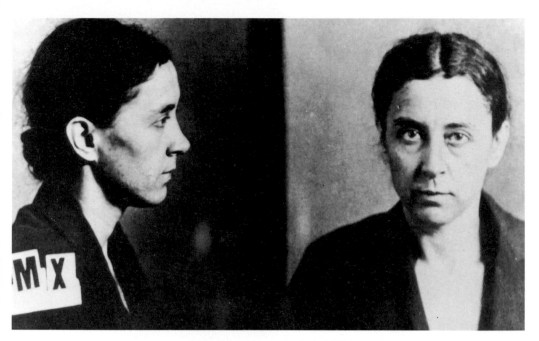

Olga Stefanovna in jail, 1937

Maria Vasilevna, Budyonny's third wife,
with their three children

Ekaterina Kalinina (first right) c. 1936, with Valentina Ostroumova
(first left), Alexandra Gorchakova and Kalinina's brother

Ekaterina Kalinina with her three children

Ekaterina Davidovna had successfully assimilated the manners and habits of the aristocratic ladies whose dresses she had made in her youth. After the Revolution, her contacts with former tsarist cavalry officers helped to form her as a new type of 'Soviet lady' benefactress, adopting orphans and helping poor pensioners in hard times. As age and circumstances turned the 'Lady Bountiful' into the 'Party Aunt', she learned to conceal her spontaneity behind an armour of Stalinist ideological correctness.

When Nadezhda Ivanovna's parents were arrested in 1937 as enemies of the people, Ekaterina Davidovna was outraged and terrified by this threat to her husband's career.

She never said anything, but I could see what she was thinking. Once when we were alone she informed me that my mother was *petit bourgeois*. 'That's not a criminal offence,' I protested. She said nothing. She had obviously been trying to understand why Mother was in prison, and this was the only way she could make sense of it. When my only sister, Vera, moved in with us, I could see Ekaterina Davidovna resented the fact that I had not asked her first. When my husband went to talk to his parents about it she said nothing, but Kliment Efremovich said, 'Don't talk nonsense – I've already informed them all about our "enemies of the people"!' Then Vera fell in love with Frunze's son Timur. This was the last straw for Ekaterina Davidovna. 'One misalliance is enough for this family,' she said, evidently referring to Petya and me, and Vera was ordered to break off her relationship with Timur, although they went on loving each other.

I behaved as though nothing had happened. I never asked Kliment Efremovich about my parents and he never once said anything about 'enemies of the people'. Just before the war he managed to get Mother released on health grounds, and she moved in with us.

Shortly before the birth of our second son, Petya left me in Moscow and went off to work in the Urals. I dropped my studies, visited the theatre and had an affair. Ekaterina Davidovna was outraged.

Unlike most Kremlin wives, she tried not to make use of her husband's privileges. She thought women should work, and it gave her great satisfaction to achieve something without him. It offended her to see me sitting at home doing nothing. She would leave for work early, and to avoid her I would pretend to be asleep in my room and have breakfast with Kliment Efremovich, who worked late into the night. Ekaterina Davidovna nagged him about me, but he would say, 'You've fallen on hard times, Nadya, my girl.' He once read me the fable of the grasshopper and the ant, but that was his only reproach to me.

Stalin didn't like Voroshilov and was always criticising him. Once in 1946 they were boating on the lake together and Stalin said, 'I know you, Klim – you're a British spy!' Kliment Efremovich flushed crimson at this and slapped Stalin in the face, nearly capsizing the boat.

Ekaterina Davidovna told me once in a whisper, looking over her shoulder as she spoke, that she thought Stalin was envious of Voroshilov's popularity. On Kliment Efremovich's sixtieth birthday Stalin made a speech about the model Party worker, and we were all in ecstasies – until we realised he hadn't said a word about Voroshilov.

At dinner Stalin would always check that everyone's glasses were full. He would pour the wine himself and make sure we drank to the bottom, so it was impossible not to get drunk. I remember Molotov being carried out once. Stalin's manners were very coarse, and Kliment Efremovich followed suit, like everyone else in Stalin's entourage. Ekaterina Davidovna lived in a state of perpetual fear. When Frunze's children moved in with us she was afraid that as the daughter of arrested parents I would corrupt them by making critical speeches.

Yet despite Ekaterina Davidovna's growing orthodoxy and her authority in Kremlin circles, she failed to please Stalin. He cannot have been fond of her keen eye, and as a friend of his wife's she must have known more than he would have wished about the party in their flat on that fateful November night in 1932. As her behaviour was impossible to fault, the only punishment available to Stalin was to refuse her any awards or medals. Since every other working Kremlin wife received an award of some kind, the slight must have been deliberate, and according to Nadezhda Ivanovna it hurt her very deeply:

Her fears intensified in 1937, and remained with her for the rest of her life. After 1937 families in the Kremlin kept to themselves. Those who hadn't been arrested barricaded themselves inside with their families, people stopped socialising in the evenings, and everyone grew fat, dull and old. It was as though the Kremlin had been swept by a hurricane.

We all lived in terror. We knew that anything we said or did could land us in prison. In those years Voroshilov wasn't always invited to Politburo meetings. This was a bad sign; we were afraid they might take him at any moment. And when he did attend none of us could sleep. The Politburo met after midnight, and we would stay up all night not knowing if he would return. Ekaterina Davidovna suffered in silence, never betraying her anxieties.

In the last years of her life, Ekaterina Davidovna became deputy director of the Lenin Museum. Stern, severe and undemonstrative as ever, she regarded everything that happened as correct, even the anti-Semitic purges of the 1940s, the arrest of Molotov's wife and the death of Mikhoels, director of Moscow's Jewish Theatre.

Yet after the shooting of the Jews at Baby Yar in 1941 Nadezhda Ivanovna noticed a change in her mother-in-law:

She seemed to become more human. Her sister and her sister's daughter perished in that terrible pit, and it opened her eyes to something. When the state of Israel was declared I heard her say, 'Now we have a homeland too!' This from an orthodox Communist internationalist, anathematised in the synagogue for betraying her faith!

She softened in old age. When she fell ill I took her to the hospital and visited her there, and she thanked me in emotional tones quite unlike herself, as though embarrassed at causing me trouble . . .

She was always convinced that she would outlive Kliment Efremovich, and very early on she started collecting material for his museum. Having broken with her own family, she wanted everything about him to be brilliant and worthy of his name. In fact he outlived her by ten years.

Just before she died she said, 'Nadya, you and Petya don't have a dacha. That's bad, you should have one.' She knew that Molotov's wife, Paulina Zhemchuzhina, had everything and she had nothing, and that it was dangerous for people in our position not to have their own dacha.

I shall never forget her final parting with Kliment Efremovich. She was dying of cancer. She had told us about it, but not him. It was a stormy day in April 1959, and she was being cared for at their dacha by a team of doctors and nurses, while in the next room he was being cared for by another medical team as he lay delirious with flu. She was determined not to die before he recovered.

She grew steadily worse and started to haemorrhage, but still she begged the doctors not to tell him. Finally they decided she must go to hospital. They broke the news to him as gently as they could, and only then did he realise how serious the situation was.

We all knew this would be their last meeting. He sat on the edge of her bed and they sat hand in hand together like Philemon and Baucis. Then we heard her say, 'Do you remember how we used to sing together in Petersburg, Klimushka?'

She sang and he joined in, and the tears streamed down our cheeks as we heard their two quavering voices sing: 'Gazing at the rays of the purple sunset . . .'

She died just a few days before their golden wedding anniversary, thinking as always only of him.

Ten years later, immediately after Kliment Efremovich's death, KGB agents came to the Voroshilovs' apartment, examined all their documents and removed a large quantity of them. These included the memoirs which Ekaterina Davidovna had been writing over several years. It would be interesting to know what has happened to these memoirs. One would love to think they might reveal how Ekaterina Davidovna's youthful passion was so rapidly consumed in the passion of the Revolution. If they do, however, the memoirs will certainly have been destroyed and we shall never see them. Alas, it is more probable that her memoirs, like Nadezhda Krupskaya's, have smoothed out the problems of our history from the perspective of a woman constantly ready for the agents guarding her to switch sides and destroy her. If this supposition is correct, they may be lying somewhere in the Party archives, waiting for somebody to embark upon the fascinating task of reading between the lines.

7

The Three Wives
of Marshall Budyonny

Semyon Mikhailovich Budyonny (1883–1973). Born in a poor peasant family on the Don. After the civil war he was appointed assistant Commander-in-Chief of the Red Army, in 1937, commander of troops in the Moscow military district, and from 1939 to 1940 deputy Defence Commissar. During the war he was a member of the general headquarters of the Supreme Command, and promoted to a succession of military posts.

Posterity has dealt roughly with those of Stalin's government who died in their beds, and this is especially evident in the case of Semyon Mikhailovich Budyonny.

For almost the entire twentieth century Budyonny was worshipped in Russia as a hero. Every Soviet schoolboy longed to be like Semyon Mikhailovich, with his horse and his sabre. A new breed of horse was named after him, and endless songs testified to his cavalry skills and his courage in battle. He spoke the language of the ordinary people, and if he changed under the pressures of age and adulation, nobody seemed to notice.

In his youth Semyon Mikhailovich had dreamed of being a stud-farmer. Instead he became a professional horseman, the finest in the tsarist cavalry and a graduate of the Petersburg Equestrian Academy. Enlisting in 1903 at the age of twenty, he was promoted to cavalry sergeant-major, did battle with the Khunguz in the war against Japan, fought on the Austrian, German and Cossack fronts during the First World War, participated in the illustrious Baratov campaign in Persia and was decorated with four St George Crosses.

In 1917, just as he was about to be promoted to officer, he suddenly went over to the Bolsheviks, joking later that he preferred to be a marshal in the Red Army than an officer in the White. During the civil war Budyonny's First Red Cavalry seized numerous towns from the Whites, including Rostov and the Cossack capital of Novocherkassk, and it was during these battles that he acquired his legendary status.

For women who loved physical strength in a man, Budyonny was powerfully attractive: stocky and well built, with large peasant features, quick brown eyes and luxuriant whiskers. Yet the woman chosen by this hero in 1903 as his life's companion was neither a beauty nor an intellectual but an illiterate Cossack peasant girl named Nadezhda Ivanovna, who came from the next village. After marrying her in church he set off with the army and did not see her again for seven years. Seven years after that, in October 1917, his cavalry regiment disbanded and he returned to his village to raise a Red detachment there.

By now in her thirties and having learned to read and write a little, Nadezhda Ivanovna went with her husband to fight at his side and organise food and medical supplies for the regiment's hospital unit. It seemed as though Budyonny had found the ideal wife, but Nadezhda Ivanovna apparently found it hard to accept her husband's new position in life, and later, when they shared a house with the Voroshilovs in Ekaterinoslav, she would often shout at him for not allowing her to invite her Cossack friends home.

In 1923, after the civil war was over, the Budyonnys moved to Moscow. The following year Nadezhda Ivanovna shot herself.

Her death spawned a thousand rumours. Some said that Budyonny shot his wife because he was tired of her. Others that she committed suicide because he had found another woman. Or that when he was away fighting for the Tsar she had given birth to a dead baby and buried it in the kitchen garden. Or that he had discovered from the women on his landing in Moscow that she was having an affair with a student, and when Semyon Mikhailovich discovered his faithless wife with her lover she pleaded that she wanted a baby and since he could not give her one she decided to have one with the student – even though she knew she could never conceive again after what she had done . . .

Years later Semyon Mikhailovich told his grown-up daughter by his third wife that he and Nadezhda Ivanovna had grown apart and no longer had any family life together. One evening while Nadezhda Ivanovna was with friends at the theatre, he said, he came home from work to find a crowd of men gathered in the courtyard outside his flat on Granovsky Street, blocking his way. It was dark, and since the secret police did not protect its VIPs as diligently as they do now, he removed the safety-catch from his pistol as he walked through the crowd. Entering his flat, he sat down on the bed and started to take off his boots. At this moment his wife walked in with her friends, saw the pistol lying on the table and laughingly brandished it at her head. Through the open door, he called out to her that the pistol was loaded. 'It's all right, I'm not scared!' she laughed. A shot rang out, she fell to the ground, and all the witnesses in the room turned to stone.

By the end of that year Budyonny was living with a beautiful singer he had met while on holiday in the Caucasus.

Olga Stefanovna Mikhailova, with her gypsy good looks and dark, lilac-tinged eyes, had a lovely contralto voice and dreamed of being a singer. Semyon Mikhailovich, himself an accomplished accordionist, loved and encouraged her musical aspirations, and after they married she entered the Moscow Conservatory, joining the Bolshoi Theatre in 1930, and singing the parts of Vanya in *Ivan Susanin* and Lelya in *The Snow Maiden*.

Olga Mikhailova and Budyonny were together for thirteen years, each leading their own separate lives and never really managing to make one together. Budyonny wanted children, but Olga Mikhailova did not want to spoil her figure or to take time from her precious work. The role of brood mare did not appeal to her any more than it had to Inessa Armand. But while Armand never quite knew what she wanted from her grand revolutionary dreams, this woman of the twenties, born in poverty of a railway worker from Kursk, knew clearly that she wanted to dazzle audiences as a famous singer.

Budyonny, himself the possessor of a God-given gift as a horseman, honoured his wife's talents, yet her aspirations failed to coincide with his old-fashioned, middle-aged dreams of family warmth and children's voices; her nephew and niece came to stay with them occasionally, but their presence could not fill the childless house.

In the summer of 1937, as the madness, spy mania and suspicion reached their height, Olga Mikhailova was arrested. There are many differing accounts of her arrest. According to a woman who lived in the Budyonnys' building as a child, local gossip had it that the beautiful singer was a Polish spy, and her husband had abandoned her. The story I heard as a child was that she was having an affair with a foreigner, and that Budyonny took her to prison in person in order to save the KGB the trouble. (I imagined him, like Kazbich in Lermontov's *Hero of Our Time*, throwing his poor wife across the saddle of his bay stallion and galloping her over to the Lubyanka.) In fact she was arrested either on the street or at the apartment of the singer Alexeev, with whom she was having an affair, and she spent the next nineteen years in a succession of jails and camps.

Shortly after Olga Stefanovna's imprisonment, Semyon Mikhailovich's marriage to her was annulled and he married for the third time. It was said that Budyonny's third wife was the young servant girl in his house, that he had chosen her in order to save time looking for anyone else, and that when he went to her mother the old woman fell at his feet, crying, 'Make us happy, Sir!' This wife was also said to have fifty fur coats, and that when she hung them out to air at their dacha it was quite a sight. Everyone agrees, however, that Maria Vasilevna was a sweet, modest girl who ran the large Budyonny household splendidly. Thirty-three years younger than Budyonny, she lived happily with him for the rest of his life and bore him three children.

Ekaterina Sergeevna Katukova remembers her thus:

> She was a good-natured woman with a lovely laugh. She was always rushing around after her three children.
>
> In the late 1940s it was an unbreakable tradition for the men to see in the New Year with Stalin, while the wives and children spent the evening at the Budyonnys' dacha. At 2 a.m. Stalin would release the men and they would arrive at the Budyonnys to be met with delicious home cooking, cakes, presents and a Father Frost for the children. It was wonderful![1]

Maria Vasilevna lives today in a large Moscow apartment situated in a rambling, nineteenth-century building adorned with plaques bearing the names of Marshals Budyonny, Zhukov, Voroshilov and others. A small youthful woman of seventy-five, with a kind face and calm bright eyes, she sits in her small kitchen at a huge oilcloth-covered table. Covering the wall behind her back, as though standing guard above her, hangs a huge family portrait executed in the familiar traditions of socialist realism – harsh, aggressive and formal. Semyon Mikhailovich is solemn and brave with his famous whiskers. Maria Vasilevna, glamorous in a dark

---

[1] Father Frost is the Russian Santa Claus.

dress with the fashionable stand-up collar and décolletage known in the early 1950s as the 'Mary Stuart style', appears virtually the same age as her husband, not because the artist has aged her, but because several years have been taken off Semyon Mikhailovich. The couple sit surrounded by characterless children, clearly of no interest to the artist as he focuses on the bold Cossack warrior and the little girl from Kursk destined to be his life's companion.

Budyonny's widow is understandably distressed by the contemptuous reactions to him today. Insisting that most of what is written about Budyonny is lies, Maria Vasilevna talks candidly about her life.

In 1936 I left Kursk to study at the Stomatology Institute in Moscow. An aunt of mine lived in Moscow, and her daughter, my cousin Olga, was married to the famous Marshal Budyonny. I hardly ever saw Olga, she was always busy working, and Semyon Mikhailovich almost never saw her either, but I always felt nervous of meeting him when I went to visit.

Once I rang the bell and he opened the door. He asked me who I wanted to see, and I barely managed to whisper my aunt's name.

I used to help my aunt with the cooking and housework sometimes, and after Budyonny's wife went to prison in 1937 I would often cook him dinner, and he would always thank me and smile.

One day Auntie asked me if there was anyone special in my life. There wasn't. She must have told Budyonny, for the next day at dinner he asked me, 'How do you feel about me?'

Not suspecting anything, I said, 'You're my favourite hero!'

'How would you like to marry me then?'

I was flabbergasted. Finally I whispered, 'I'm afraid!'

He laughed. 'Go to your parents and ask their advice. Then give me your answer.'

He left the room and I ran to my aunt, who said, 'Marry him! He's a good man, I can vouch for that. He's got to marry someone, so it might as well be you. Even if Olga gets out of prison they'll never be together again. How could Budyonny be married to an ex-prisoner? Go on, marry him!'

I went to Kursk to talk to my parents. When Mother opened the door she assumed I'd been expelled from the Institute. When I told her I was getting married she sat down on a chair and asked me who it was.

'Semyon Mikhailovich Budyonny!' I said. (People in Kursk didn't know yet that his wife was in jail.)

'Have you got yourself into trouble?' Mother demanded.

I said nothing, just handed her a letter from Auntie explaining that Olga was in prison and Semyon Mikhailovich had asked me to marry him.

I talked with my parents for a long time. When I started back to Moscow, Mother embraced me and wept, 'They'll lock you away behind the Kremlin walls and we'll never see you again!'

When I got back I went straight to Budyonny's place and cooked him his dinner. He greeted me but didn't mention his proposal. I felt awful. After he finished his soup he asked, 'So what's it to be?'

'It's yes!' I said, my ears burning.

'I was afraid to ask,' he said, blushing too. 'I thought you'd say no!' Then he went off to work.

My aunt had fixed me up in the corner of a room belonging to the cleaning woman, but when he came home that evening he said, 'Don't go, stay with me. You're mistress of the house now!'

He was so confused he didn't know what to call me, and I kept calling him 'Semyon Mikhailovich'. That made him angry. 'Don't be so formal! I'm your husband now – Semyon Mikhailovich sits on a horse!'

We were happy together right from the start. We never quarrelled. Our son Seryozha was born on 13 August 1938, and our daughter Ninochka on 6 September 1939. Misha, our second son, was born in 1944. Semyon Mikhailovich was terribly happy. He hadn't had children with his other wives, and he'd always assumed it was his fault.

After the first two children arrived I left the Institute. It made me very sad. Semyon Mikhailovich was sad too, but we didn't want to hand our babies over to nannies. 'You look after the children, and I'll pay your wages,' he said. I never worked outside the house again, though I learned English, bee-keeping, vegetable-growing, how to use a sewing machine and the usual domestic skills.

My aunt stayed with us for a while, then moved to be with her sister in Leningrad, where Semyon Mikhailovich helped her to find a flat. It was painful for her to see us so happy together when her own daughter was in prison and she herself had given me to him.

Semyon Mikhailovich and I were very close. He thought the world of his children. Their favourite game was to climb into bed with him for a cuddle, and he would tell them a story, then stop and tell them to finish it.

He was always afraid something would happen to me. 'I bring bad luck,' he said. 'One wife shot herself, another was arrested – you must be terrified!' We even moved out to another flat so he wouldn't be surrounded by memories.

He always tried to keep me away from Kremlin society, but the first time he took me out was to a government reception marking the anniversary of the Revolution. He introduced me to all the other guests. I was shy because of being so much younger than anyone else. When he went up to the podium I sat with Askhen Mikoyan, who took me under her wing; she was a good wife and mother. I didn't have much to do with the other politicians' wives, though; they were all strong women and much older than me. I was just a child, and I couldn't stop thinking that I'd built my happiness on someone else's suffering, and that if Olga hadn't been arrested we wouldn't have had our three children. I found that terribly hard to bear.

The first time my parents visited us they travelled to Moscow in a special government train. My father later told me he'd found it very difficult and felt intimidated by Budyonny, but he walked in with his hand outstretched and they started talking, and he soon felt he'd known Semyon Mikhailovich all his life. Semyon Mikhailovich's sister Tanya and his mother, Malanya Nikitinichna, lived with us too, and after Seryozha was born I brought my parents to Moscow and we all lived together.

In 1938, when they started arresting the cavalry commanders, most of them highly respected men and revolutionary fighters, Semyon Mikhailovich protested to Voroshilov. Voroshilov sent him to see Stalin, and Semyon Mikhailovich said to Stalin's face, 'If they're jailing the people who made the Revolution they'd better jail us too!' To which Stalin replied, 'You must be crazy, Semyon!'

When Beria redeployed our troops in the Northern Caucasus during the war without telling him, he was furious and went to Stalin, who said, 'Beria's from the Caucasus, he knows best what to do with our troops down there.'

'But Beria's a *Chekist*, not a soldier[2]. There's a difference!' Semyon Mikhailovich retorted.

Once after the war Budyonny took me to a banquet in the Georgievsky Hall of the Kremlin. At the end of the meal he went off somewhere. The guests sat at tables laid out in the hall, and Stalin was passing between them with his glass in his hand. My heart was in my stomach as he moved towards me. He stopped behind my chair, and said, 'Who's this, then?' When I told him he exclaimed, 'So what's our Semyon Mikhailovich doing abandoning his wife to chat with the working class? We're all so envious of his happy family life!'

[2]*Chekist:* member of the Secret Police, the *Cheka.*

Shortly afterwards the Kremlin wives and children saw in the New Year as usual at our dacha and I did all the cooking. When the men arrived after midnight my Semyon Mikhailovich was holding a huge bunch of flowers. 'Give these to your wife,' Stalin had said to him. 'You've been with me and the women are alone – they'll be angry with me.'

My life with Semyon Mikhailovich was so happy. He didn't talk much about love, but once he said, 'Thank you, Maria, for prolonging my life and giving me a family. I long to come home to you after work. All my life I've dreamed of having children.'

Semyon Mikhailovich had bought us a dacha of our own at Bakovka, so we didn't use government dachas. 'I'm older than you,' he said. 'If something happened to me, you and the children could be chucked out of a government dacha within twenty-four hours.'

My husband was a good man. He loved his people and tried to help everyone who came to him. When we were on holiday in the Caucasus we used to walk to the hills every day, and crowds would gather around us with flowers, jostling to get close to him. I tried to keep out of the way. When our doctor saw what was happening he advised us to take our walks earlier, but people still kept crowding around us.

During the war the children and I were evacuated from Moscow with Semyon Mikhailovich's mother and sister. His mother longed for the war to end. She would say, 'I hope I live to see the day. If I die now I won't know how it ended!'

Maria Vasilevna showed me a letter Budyonny wrote to her on 19 September 1941, from the bloody battles of the first days of war. The letter was written in pencil in a large, clear hand on a sheet of paper torn from a notebook, with not a single grammatical error:

Darling little Mother,
I have received your letter and remember that day in September 1937 when we joined our lives. I feel as though we have known each other since we were children. I love you infinitely and my heart will love you until it stops beating. You are the most beloved and precious creature to me, for you have given me our own darling little babies. I am sure that all will end well, and that we will be together again. Give my greetings to Mother and the rest of our family. Kiss Seryozha and Ninochka for me. I wish you health and happiness. I kiss you, my darling.
Your Semyon.

When asked about the fate of Budyonny's previous wife, Olga

Mikhailova, Maria Vasilevna explained that she had always been afraid to ask her husband about the circumstances of her cousin's arrest. Olga Mikhailova had returned to Moscow in 1956, sick and terribly aged. Convinced that everyone hated her and suspected her of trying to poison Budyonny, she described how she had been repeatedly raped in the camps by gangs of men. Semyon Mikhailovich thought all this was the product of her sick mind, and arranged for her to go to hospital, then helped her to find a flat and urged her to visit. But she almost never did, thinking Maria Vasilevna would not like her company, and nothing Maria Vasilevna could say would dissuade her.

Insisting that Budyonny had had nothing to do with his second wife's arrest, Maria Vasilevna produced, from a large file of documents, a letter which he wrote to the Chief Military Prosecutor on 23 July 1955, eighteen years after she went to prison:

In the first months of 1937 (I forget the exact date), J. V. Stalin informed me that Ezhov[3] had told him that my wife, Olga Stefanovna Mikhailova-Budyonnaya, was behaving in an improper manner and compromising me. He warned me that this was not to our advantage and could not be tolerated. According to Ezhov's information, Comrade Stalin said, foreigners were drawing her into their net, or could well do so. He therefore recommended that I discuss the matter further with Ezhov.

Shortly after this I had a meeting with Ezhov, who informed me that my wife, along with the wives of Bubnov and Egorov, was visiting the Italian, Japanese and Polish embassies, and had once stayed at the dacha of the Japanese embassy until three o'clock in the morning. Ezhov also informed me that she had an intimate relationship with a singer at the Bolshoi Theatre named Alexeev.

She herself had told me before my conversation with Ezhov that she had gone with her women friends to the Italian embassy to sing for the ambassador's wife. When I asked Ezhov what specifically could be described as politically compromising in her behaviour, he replied that there was nothing so far, but they would continue to keep watch on her and I should mention nothing to her.

In June 1937 I paid a second visit to Ezhov at his request. This time he said that my wife had taken to the Italian embassy a programme of the racing and show-jumping events at the Hippodrome. 'So what?' I said, 'These programmes are sold everywhere – they don't mean a thing!'

[3]Nikolai Ezhov, chief of the NKVD, the Commissariat of Internal Affairs.

'I think we should arrest her and interrogate her and make her tell us about her relations with Bubnova and Egorova. Then if she's innocent we can release her.'

I told Ezhov I saw absolutely no grounds for arresting my wife, since I had been given no evidence of her committing any political crime. As for her intimate relations with Alexeev (about which I had been informed by Ezhov and the Ministry of Internal Affairs), this was an entirely personal domestic matter, which might well end in divorce.

In August 1937, when I was out of Moscow on a ten-day visit to the Gorokhovetsk camps, Olga Stefanovna was arrested. I had played no part in her arrest, on the contrary I had opposed it, since nothing Ezhov told me led me to believe there were any grounds for it. I knew the Ministry of Internal Affairs official, Dagin, personally after working with him in Rostov, but I did not invite him to my house and never talked to him about my wife.

Later, after my wife's arrest and that of a number of cavalry commanders including Alexandrov, Tarasenko and Davydovich, I came to the conclusion that Ezhov had organised the whole thing with the purpose of provoking intrigues and rumours which could be presented to our Party and government with a view to arresting me.

I feel obliged here to include a brief character reference of Olga Stefanovna. She comes from a poor family. Her father was a railway worker, then a transport official. I married her in 1925. After our marriage she entered the Moscow Conservatory, from which she graduated in 1930. She studied diligently and was socially active. She never expressed the slightest hint of criticism of Soviet power. Her needs were modest, and she showed no signs of greedy materialism.

In conclusion, I must say that I do not believe she could commit any crimes against the Soviet government.

Semyon Mikhailovich Budyonny

Budyonny's letter is a startling insight into the hidden workings of the infernal machine. Visiting foreign embassies, now a cause of little more than envious curiosity, was for years regarded as highly suspect, if not criminal, as was carrying the racing programme of the Hippodrome. No matter that this was a blatantly nonsensical fabrication – anything could be fabricated in those days.

Whether or not Budyonny heeded Ezhov's advice to say nothing to his wife about the suspicions against her, the shadowy presence of Alexeev indicates that his second marriage, like his first, was not happy, and his own negative male emotions must have compounded the practical impossibility of rescuing her.

Many of the leaders' families were destroyed by Stalin in 1937, and the Budyonnys were no exception. Had Maria Vasilevna been taken during Stalin's second round of arrests of Kremlin wives in the late 1940s, Budyonny would have fought for her like a lion, rather than allow her to be devoured by the machine of state. Mother of his children, his faithful wife, flesh of his ageing body, this strong little woman was one of the few Kremlin wives to bring some domestic warmth to the hell of the thirties and the austerity of the war years. Fluttering like a butterfly into the Kremlin during the bloody days of 1937, she survives to defend the memory of this Hero of the Soviet Union.

8

In the Inquisitor's Chair

When Stalin persecuted his brave marshals and generals they dragged down with them their wives, who behaved with varying degrees of courage. Must we blame a woman for behaving like a woman, for fearing prison, interrogation, torture and the firing squad and losing her head?

The KGB file on Budyonny's second wife states:

> Born 1905. Native of Ekaterinoslav. Daughter of a railway official. Before her arrest a soloist at the Bolshoi Theatre of the USSR. Wife of Marshal of the Soviet Union Semyon Mikhailovich Budyonny.

Olga Stefanovna's handwritten evidence of 14 March 1938 states:

> I was born in 1905. My father, an orphaned peasant, left his village and worked for thirty-six years on the railways. I started my education in Kursk in 1915. I have painful memories of the tsarist regime, since my father sent me to a high school, where my common speech, shabby clothes and peasant status provoked the other pupils' derision. The class teachers forbade the children of wealthy parents and government officials to play with me, telling them in my presence that they must have nothing to do with me. 'Your papa's a peasant!' they would taunt me, and to avoid the sneers my father joined up with the local bourgeoisie.
>
> I left school at the age of fifteen and married a man named Runov, who was station manager at Vyazma. I lived uncomplainingly but unenthusiastically through the years of havoc and civil war. The inevitable happened: the Germans and White generals switched sides, the Tsar was finished and no one could be called a peasant any more. That satisfied me, even though I was hungry.

Runov was an alcoholic, who drank away our wages and pawned my meagre wardrobe. In 1924 I left him and travelled to Georgia for two weeks' holiday at the health resort of Essentuki, where my friends Kulik, Tyutkin and Georgadze introduced me to Semyon Mikhailovich Budyonny. Since he was a widower he proposed that we have an affair. I agreed, and moved in with him.

As for my personal relations with Semyon Mikhailovich, I loved him at first for his kindness. He loved me very much, but he also made me feel that I was a trivial creature of few merits – which is perfectly true – and that I took advantage of the material benefits of his position. He received cars and dachas from the Central Executive Committee because he had earned them, he said; my job was to take care of him and look after his health and well-being, and if I wanted fame I must earn it for myself.

The file on Olga Mikhailova says nothing of what happened to her between this handwritten testimony and a letter she wrote shortly afterwards to Ezhov, in which she bitterly attacks her husband:

During the twelve years I lived with Budyonny I discovered him to be a harsh man, who would let no one stand in the way of his ambitions. In these twelve years Semyon Mikhailovich beat me, intimidated me, tyrannised me, threatened to report me to the KGB as a spy and even to murder me. The investigation requires me to reveal all crimes or criminal intentions against the Soviet state. I have said nothing before, since this would have meant speaking of Budyonny and I lived in fear of his revenge.

During the twelve years of our marriage I collected numerous facts indicating that he was involved in criminal activities against the leaders of our country, notably Stalin and Voroshilov. I shall talk about these facts in my statement.

Years later, after Olga Stefanovna had been released from the camps, she told Maria Vasilevna Budyonnaya that her interrogators had beaten and tortured her, forcing her to testify against Budyonny and telling her that he was already in jail and had incriminated her.

Evidently destroyed by her experiences of prison and interrogation, the poor woman proceeds to weave an elaborate fantasy, in which reality and fiction are mixed together to create such half-truths as:

During the bitter battles with Trotsky in 1927 I asked Semyon Mikhailovich whom we should support, Trotsky or Stalin. Semyon Mikhailovich said this was a difficult question and it was no good rushing to extremes; we should wait a bit and see how things developed, then decide.

Or:

Semyon Mikhailovich had some shady connections on the Don. Once on our way back from holiday he was greeted in Vladikavkaz by a railway worker who later came to our carriage and talked at length over a bottle of wine about how he and his detachment had encircled some Reds, and a partisan detachment had caught him in a deadly grip by the throat, and they barely managed to drag him away from the commander's corpse.

Olga Mikhailova's KGB files at the Lubyanka Prison also contain evidence from a fellow prisoner named 'K', who was clearly a plant:

I shared a cell with Olga Mikhailova, a singer at the Bolshoi Theatre and former wife of Marshal Budyonny. According to Mikhailova, Budyonny not only knew about an anti-Stalin, anti-Soviet conspiracy within the army, but was a leading member of it. Mikhailova said she had considered reporting him, but she did not know whom to approach, fearing that Voroshilov would not believe her and it would get back to Budyonny. She said that when the conspiratorial cells in the army were smashed and the ringleaders rounded up, Budyonny was convinced that he too would be arrested, and that during the Central Committee plenum of 1937 he had been acting very strangely . . . She said she now realises that on his trips to Siberia between 1923 and 1930, ostensibly to meet his old partisan comrades, he was in fact organising insurrectionary detachments . . . Mikhailova was convinced that Budyonny wanted to get rid of her before she compromised him. Only she knew the full extent of his anti-Soviet views, and he feared that if she left him for Alexeev he would lose his influence over her and she might damage him.

As far as I know, Mikhailova revealed none of the above facts to the investigation, since, according to her, she was not in her right mind at the time. Secondly, she was asked almost nothing about Budyonny. Thirdly, she was afraid to talk about him. Fourthly, she has only just begun to make sense of things. And finally, she expected a just rebuke for not reporting these matters earlier. Mikhailova is now in a state of deep depression, and it is hard to talk to her or get her to reveal anything. *14.7.1938*

There follow a number of questions concerning Olga Mikhailova's connections with foreign embassies. She admitted occasionally visiting embassies without her husband, such as when the Italian ambassador, Attolico, invited her to sing. She also reported the questions she was asked:

> At the Japanese embassy they asked me where Budyonny was, and I told them that he was said to be in the Far East preparing for war against Japan . . .
>
> When foreigners asked if they could see our dacha I replied that it was being decorated. When they asked me for our telephone number I told them the telephone was broken. When they asked me if I liked Karlsbad, I replied that the waters were good but the cures were expensive.

Evidently driven almost to the point of madness, Olga Mikhailova told the interrogation about her lover Alexeev, and about Semyon Mikhailovich's jealous threats to have her thrown into jail. Alarmed by these threats, she said, Alexeev had suggested that he go to the People's Commissariat of Internal Affairs and report her for some minor misdemeanour, whereupon she would spend a couple of years in a camp, he would save up a lot of money and when she got out they would live happily ever after.

Alexander Ivanovich Alexeev, leading tenor at the Bolshoi Theatre, elegant, intelligent and aristocratic, was clearly in love with Olga Stefanovna. His evidence in her case is exemplary and contains no hint of criticism of her: 'Yes, we occasionally discussed the current political situation. She always behaved impeccably and I never heard her express any negative opinions.' When asked about her relations with Budyonny, Alexeev replied that things between them were strained because of Budyonny's jealousy. When asked if he had proposed reporting Olga Stefanovna to the NKVD for some minor misdemeanour he categorically denied suggesting any such thing.

The investigation dragged on until 3 August 1939, when Sergeant of State Security Kurkova finally stated, 'There is no criminal evidence against the accused Mikhailova to present to the court,' and urged that the case be annulled and Olga Stefanovna released from custody. On the same day Kurkova writes to her superior, 'Mikhailova is seriously ill and in need of urgent medical attention.'

Lavrenty Beria, who had succeeded Ezhov as head of the NKVD, was informed, but despite this and the lack of any evidence against Olga Mikhailova, in November 1939 the charges were spelled out before a Special Session of the Soviet Court:

1) That while married to Budyonny she conducted an intimate liaison with Bolshoi Theatre artist Alexeev (decd.), who is suspected of espionage activities.[1]
2) That while taking the waters in Czechoslovakia she associated with enemies of the people, known spies and conspirators.

The case continues:

The wives of former deputy Defence Commissar Egorov and former Education Commissar Bubnov, also both arrested on espionage charges, describe Mikhailova in their evidence as a member of their circle. Egorova and Bubnova were not questioned about Mikhailova's connection with their espionage activities. Mikhailova admits that she is guilty of making dubious contacts during her unofficial visits to foreign embassies, but she denies charges of espionage. On the basis of the above prosecution evidence, the case is to be forwarded to Special Session for consideration of same.

Junior investigator Kurkova, November 1939

So Kurkova finally gave in, crushed by the mighty machinery of Soviet power, and on 18 November 1939 poor Olga Stefanovna, by now seriously deranged, was sentenced to eight years in a corrective labour camp.

Over the next six years she was incarcerated in a number of different camps and prisons. Among the KGB files on her is a letter dated 15 August 1945 from the Ministry of Internal Affairs (the NKVD) in the province of Vladimir:

When in Vladimir jail Mikhailova told her fellow inmates of her hostility to the Soviet state, spreading slanderous lies about the leader of the Soviet government and the country's political structure, and announcing that after her sentence expired she would continue her active struggle against Soviet power. Since Olga Stefanovna Mikhailova is a socially dangerous element she must not be released . . . It has therefore been decided to keep her in jail for a further three years.

In April 1948 Olga Stefanovna was living in a camp in the

---

[1]Alexeev died in 1939 of throat cancer. The monument on his grave is one of the finest at the Novodeviche Monastery.

Eniseisk region of Krasnoyarsk, where the following unsigned letter was written:

> I was arrested in 1938, and after my sentence expired in 1953 I was deported to the province of Krasnoyarsk. It was during the building of the Eniseisk invalid home in July 1953 that I first heard of Olga Stefanovna Mikhailova, who was working as a cleaner in Middle School No. 45. I knew her only as the wife of Budyonny, and had met her at several Kremlin receptions. I tried to speak to her but found her pathologically solitary and terrified of social contact. Her memories, logic and speech were painfully muddled, and she limited herself to brief remarks about her arrest. She said she had only been arrested because she was the Marshal's wife, and they had broken her spirit. She also informed me that she herself had interrogated the Ministry of Internal Affairs, that Semyon Mikhailovich was ninety-four years old and seriously ill and refused to meet anyone, and so on. Mikhailova was so ill she could certainly not have left Eniseisk alone even if she were released.

This letter in Mikhailova's file lies next to the original of Budyonny's letter of 1955, which Maria Vasilevna had shown me. Budyonny's letter was written eighteen years too late, yet it had the desired effect, and the following year she was finally released. Were it not for the infernal machine, Olga Mikhailova could have married her singer and Budyonny his Maria. As it was, she emerged alone and broken into a world which no longer had any place for her.

Arrested at the same time as Olga Stefanovna was her friend Galina Antonovna Egorova, wife of Marshal Egorov, and the woman at whom Stalin had thrown bread pellets on the night of his wife's death. The two slim KGB files comprising Egorova's case contain the following information about her:

> Born 1898, province of Bryansk. Film actress. Graduate of Social Studies Faculty at Moscow University. Non-Party. Russian.
>
> Evidence that as an agent of Polish espionage she passed information about the Worker Peasant Red Army to the Polish government, and that knowing of the existence of an anti-Soviet fascist plot within the army and of her husband's leading part in it, she failed to report this to the authorities.
>
> Orders to arrest and search.

Egorova's signed evidence of 17 January 1938 was written in a frightened, childish hand:

... Between 1916 and 1917 I studied at the Petrograd Conservatory, and was there during the February revolution. Mentally confused and unclear as to what was happening, I went home to Bryansk. After October 1917 I worked in the Commissariat of War. There I met Egorov, and in August 1919, after we married, I moved with him to Moscow ...

In 1927 I met some film-makers and acted in a couple of films. My downfall started when I was drawn into the diplomatic world. My head was turned by the dazzling company, the stylish clothes, refined manners, foreign languages, flirtatiousness, dancing and fun. It was a new and seductive life, which flattered me and appealed to values established in childhood by my bourgeois education.

At first I only attended official receptions with my husband, but bit by bit I was drawn into a series of unofficial engagements with foreigners, informal breakfast and dinner parties, skiing holidays, trips to the theatre, tickets to the diplomatic box, and so on. My presence in the diplomatic world soon made me an object of attention, but I was of particular interest to officials at the Polish mission.

'Are you a Pole?' ambassador Lukasevich asked me, then demanded my maiden name and *wrote it down in his notebook.*

My friendship with ambassador Lukasevich deepened, and soon all formality was dropped and we became friends. Flowers and Polish sweets were delivered via the Department of Foreign Affairs or to my home, and this was followed by personal phone calls, an invitation to attend the opening party for a Polish exhibition, and so on. My feelings for Lukasevich grew, and I fell in love with him. It thrilled me to see him, dance with him and talk to him. I couldn't resist answering his questions, and I blurted out more and more state secrets to him.

Lukasevich was mainly interested in the activities of our government officials and army commanders. On several occasions I talked to him about hostile groups within the ranks of the Soviet army, and about the anti-Soviet views of certain individuals. I told him that Tukhachevsky, Uborevich and Yakir all bore a grudge against Voroshilov and wanted to replace him, and that each of these men considered he had the skill and experience to do so.[2] I also told Lukasevich about a second group around Egorov and Budyonny, which was in opposition to

[2] Each surname mentioned is invariably underlined by the interrogator in red or black pencil.

Tukhachevsky. I provided biographical facts and information about the places where Budyonny and Egorov had studied, served and fought, and Lukasevich asked me about Voroshilov's relations with them.

At the beginning of 1934 Lukasevich finally told me that the moment had come when our friendship required some unequivocal proof, and he asked me to supply him with information about our military command, specifically our air force and armed forces and the command structure of the Red Army in the event of war.

I understood that I was committing a serious crime against my country, but because of my infatuation with Lukasevich, the fact that he was unmarried, led a glamorous social life and had capital abroad, I felt unable to refuse.

I knew about the proposed command structure in the event of war, since I had heard commanders of the Worker Peasant Red Army discussing in our flat how Voroshilov would be made Commander-in-Chief and Tukhachevsky or Egorov Chief-of-Staff. As for information about our air force, I tried to find out about this from General Alksnis, but when I next met Lukasevich at a banquet I had to confess that I had been unable to meet Alksnis. Lukasevich then asked me if it was true that Egorov had travelled to the Far East.

'Yes,' I said.

'What for?' he asked.

I replied that he had gone to inspect the fortified regions in the Far East, and that I would be joining him there. Lukasevich asked me to find out about these fortifications and the construction of a new metalled road. I promised to do so. In Khabarovsk I learned about our shore fortifications, the building of a new highway along the edge of the ocean from Tikhaya Bay, and the delivery of aeroplane and submarine parts.

I informed Lukasevich of all this at our next meeting, during a dance on the tennis court of the Italian embassy. I had still been unable to discover any information about our armed forces and air force.

All our subsequent meetings were deliberately distant and of a strictly official nature. This was because Soviet society could no longer turn a blind eye to Bubnova, Budyonnaya and me, and regarded our association with foreign diplomats as highly improper. In April 1934 I was summoned to see Voroshilov who warned me about this, and word spread through the diplomatic community that 'Soviet ladies had received a reprimand'. I talked to Lukasevich about it during a reception at the Italian embassy, and he said we must behave formally to avoid unpleasant consequences for both of us. From then on,

Lukasevich transferred all his favours – the first dance, sitting next to him during dinner and so on – to Tukhachevsky's wife, and shortly afterwards he left Moscow for Poland for good. The Polish military attaché, Colonel Kovalevsky, kept contact with me, and I did not see Lukasevich again . . .

1937 passed uneventfully, since I was unable for various reasons to attend any receptions. Between 1932 and 1935 salons had sprung up in Moscow, reminiscent of the glittering receptions held by wealthy Russians in aristocratic Russia, or of subversive aristocratic circles such as the Decembrists. Such salons were held by Bubnova and us to read a new play or film-script, or to hear a quartet perform a little concert.

But there was a more sinister side to these gatherings. For some reason they were invariably attended by people who had been passed over for the top jobs, people with warped minds and personal grudges against the existing state of affairs in Russia, who would slander the positive aspects of life in our country.

As we women busied ourselves in the kitchen, we would echo the views of our husbands as we discussed the latest appointments and cursed the government. Bubnova complained that Andrei Sergeevich was being held back, despite having been one of the top five with Lenin. Tukhachevsky, a blue-blooded aristocrat, always affable and surrounded by ladies, had formed a group within the army and was campaigning openly, making no attempt to disguise his hostility to the government. This crowd of unacknowledged geniuses aspired to the leadership, caring nothing about how their aims were accomplished. Flattery, lies and brazen sycophancy – they stopped at nothing. It was plain for all to see. When someone finally discovered their plans and stopped them in their tracks they became angry, and their anger pervaded our gatherings. Their admiration for foreigners and their scepticism about the possibility of progress in our country meant they needed people to blame, and they found these in the leadership . . .

Budyonnaya's crowd was a little different, consisting of civil war veterans and cavalry soldiers. Semyon Mikhailovich mirrored these men's qualities and defects, and saved them from committing any kind of impropriety. I have known Semyon Mikhailovich since 1920: a cheerful, sharp-witted man, but ambitious, vain and something of an actor, whose political and cultural development meant that he could no longer be content with a simple Cossack girl.

His meeting with Olga Stefanovna Mikhailova took place near Kislovodsk, where I was on holiday with my husband at a sanatorium. One day Egorov, Budyonny and I went for a drive to Lermontov rock, where we were soon joined by Kulik and Georgadze, accompanied by two women, one of whom was Olga Stefanovna. I left soon afterwards with Egorov, while Budyonny stayed behind with his new friends. That was how his affair with Olga Stefanovna started. The following morning there was a jealous scene between Olga Stefanovna and Kulik, who had brought her to the Caucasus.

The Cossack girl shot herself, and literally two days later Olga Stefanovna moved in with Semyon Mikhailovich. Beautiful, young, a soloist at the Bolshoi Theatre, an accomplished French speaker, all this thrilled and delighted him. She brought so much to his life. Yet after twelve years of happy married life, Olga Stefanovna was suddenly arrested. I had never seen Semyon Mikhailovich so crushed as he was at our dacha then. I had never imagined Budyonny could cry, but the tears were pouring down his cheeks. Her arrest wasn't just a blow to his pride, he suffered terribly from the loss of this woman he loved, as well as the loss of his comfortable, familiar family life.

He saw in the New Year with us at our dacha. After dinner he sat down beside me and asked me if I knew about his wife's arrest. I said I did and asked him what had happened. He told me that she and Bubnova had turned out to be spies, Bubnova for three foreign governments and Olga Stefanovna for the Poles, and that Olga Stefanovna had carried out these espionage activities for seven years, had had an affair with a Pole at the embassy and had been paid twenty thousand roubles for her pains. He also told me that she and Bubnova had said under interrogation that I was the leader of their spy-ring and that I had given them their assignments. He warned me to prepare myself for any eventuality.

Galina Antonovna continued her handwritten evidence on 26 April 1938:

In the evidence which I presented to the investigation in January of this year I omitted a number of circumstances which have a direct bearing on the character of my husband, A. I. Egorov, as well as on my own person ... I refer to the double life led by Egorov and his close associates. Although successfully presenting themselves as defenders of the Revolution and commanders of the Red Army, they were in fact out- and-out White Guards. It suited their purposes to go along with the Red Army for the time being, but their hearts were in the enemy camp on the other side of the barricades.[3]

---

[3]Note the aggressive style here, and the preponderance of clichés evidently prompted by the investigators, as Egorova attempted to formulate her evidence in the style required of her.

As dawn was breaking these men would gather after their night's work and have dinner together. When Stalin was at the table they would congratulate each other on their spoils [sic] and raise their glasses to Soviet power and victory over the Whites. When Stalin wasn't there, all of them, including Egorov, would express their hostility to Soviet power and to Stalin personally, and drink to the imminent defeat of the Red Army. . .

Early in 1920 I remember Alexander Ilich Egorov returning home in a state of high anxiety, and when I asked him the matter he told me Stalin's train had been accidentally switched to the wrong track and there had nearly been a catastrophic accident. Then his comrade Mantsev came in and the two of them had a long and heated discussion, from which I gathered that Stalin's train had almost been derailed. *Mantsev said: 'Bugger it, what a mess!'*[4]

When I asked Alexander Ilich why, despite his apparent friendship with Stalin and membership of the Communist Party, he behaved in such an anti-Soviet manner, he replied that he and his friends remained officers, that is *men unable to reconcile themselves to Soviet power* [underlined by the investigator]. Alexander Ilich thought constantly about escaping abroad. In 1921, at the end of the civil war, he wrote to me urging me to learn more foreign languages since new times were coming, links with foreign countries were being made and we should not rule out the possibility of moving there. He also encouraged me to frequent banquets attended by foreign ambassadors, and he knew of my relations with Lukasevich. In answer to Lukasevich's questions about Egorov's anti-Soviet views, I replied that these views were shared by Bubnov and Budyonny, and that I understood from my conversations with Budyonny, Bubnov and Egorov that they were all supporters of Rykov.[5]

Egorov used me to persuade Lukasevich to set up a meeting for him in Warsaw with Stakhevich, the Polish Chief of Staff. When we visited Rome in 1934, we were invited to dinner by the Italian ambassador to the USSR, Attolico, and since the conversation was in English, I interpreted for Egorov as he expressed his admiration of the Italian government – which amounted effectively to a direct condonement of Italy's fascist regime.

Apart from this handwritten evidence, Egorova's files contain absolutely no evidence of any crime. Yet the Supreme Court's

---

[4] Underlined in the investigator's red pencil.

[5] Alexei Rykov, a contender for power after Lenin's death, was arrested by Stalin in 1929.

minutes of her committal proceedings in Moscow, on 27 August 1938, state: 'The case to be heard *in camera* without witnesses or counsel for the prosecution and defence, and the accused to be held in custody until the trial.'[6] The minutes of the Supreme Court session the following day continue:

> The presiding judge asked if the accused was acquainted with the charges against her. The accused replied in the affirmative. The accused was informed as to her legal rights. The accused made no plea or challenge to the court. The judge asked the secretary to read out the charges, explained to the accused the nature of the accusations against her and asked her if she pleaded guilty or not guilty. The accused replied that SHE WAS NOT GUILTY, and that she REJECTED THE SIGNED EVIDENCE SUBMITTED DURING THE FIRST INTERROGATION.
>
> Nobody had forced her to give incorrect evidence, she said, she had simply been stunned by her husband's sudden arrest and her own, and had lost her head and slandered herself. She had no explanation as to why her husband had produced incriminating evidence against her . . .
>
> When asked if she had anything to say, the accused replied that since she had no way to prove her innocence she could only beg for mercy. The court retired to deliver its verdict, and at 21.55 the sentence was read out.
>
> SENTENCE. In the name of the Union of Soviet Socialist Republics . . . G. A. Egorova is found guilty of all charges against her, and the military collegium of the Supreme Court of the USSR therefore sentences Galina Antonovna Egorova to the SUPREME MEASURE OF DEATH BY FIRING SQUAD, with the confiscation of all personal property.
>
> The sentence is final, and according to the USSR Central Executive Committee's ruling of 1.12.1934, is to be carried out FORTHWITH.

One might ask why all these mighty men were in such a hurry, and what possible danger was presented to them by this 'spy', who gave away secrets which everyone knew.

The final documents in Egorova's meagre KGB file date from 1956. A letter marked 'Top Secret' and issued by the head of the operations section of the Committee of State Security of the USSR declares: 'In our judgement there is no case against Galina Antonovna Egorova. We possess no information as to any links between her and Lukasevich or Kovalevsky.'

Another document, dated 13 March 1956, states:

[6]The decision to hear cases without defence or prosecution lawyers was taken after the death of Kirov in 1934, and remained in operation until Stalin's death.

The case against A. I. Egorov, former Marshal of the Soviet Union and deputy Defence Minister of the USSR, has been annulled through lack of *corpus delicti* . . . Having examined the files relating to the case of his wife, it has been established that since the only proof of Egorova's guilt was a note containing excerpts from her husband's evidence against her, this evidence is now invalid and the case against her is annulled through lack of *corpus delicti*.[7] The KGB and the Soviet of Ministers of the USSR have no information as to G. A. Egorova's membership of any international intelligence agencies.

[7]This note, the only 'evidence' against Galina Egorova, is missing.

9

The President's Wife

Mikhail Ivanovich Kalinin (1875–1946), born of a poor peasant family in the village of Verkhnyaya Troitsa, in the Kashin district of Tversk. On leaving school at thirteen, he became a footman in St Petersburg, attended a factory school in the evenings at sixteen, and two years later was working as a lathe operator at St Petersburg's Putilov works. In 1898 he joined the Social Democratic Party. He rose steadily through the Party ranks, and from 1919 until his death he was President of the Soviet Republic.

It appears from all the evidence that while Stalin tended to spare self-effacing family women such as Ekaterina Voroshilova, Maria Kaganovich, Maria Budyonnaya and Nina Khrushcheva, he bore a special grudge against the more emancipated women of the Kremlin – possibly because they reminded him of his Nadezhda.

Strong, competent and independent, Ekaterina Kalinina was one of those who incurred his displeasure. One thin file at the Lubyanka yields her prison record:

> Ekaterina Ivanovna Kalinina, *née* Lorberg. Nationality: Estonian. Date of birth: 1882. Father: day-labourer. Mother: laundress. Party membership: All-Russian Communist Party (Bolshevik). Profession: government official. Previous employment: weaver. Education: primary. Employment before arrest: Commissarist of Justice, member of the Supreme Court of the Russian Soviet Federated Socialist Republic. Place of residence before arrest: the Kremlin, Moscow.

Since these extraordinary notes inexplicably omit any mention of the prisoner's family status, it should be added that Ekaterina Ivanovna (Ioganovna in Estonian), mother of five children, three of her own, two of them adopted, was the wife of Mikhail Ivanovich Kalinin, President of the Supreme Soviet of the USSR.

The girls in Mikhail Ivanovich's village had all turned their classmate down when he asked them to marry him. They could not make him out. He didn't plough his parents' land or tend their vegetables, he had gone off to St Petersburg to become a lathe operator, and people said he had got caught up in the Revolution and had been on the run from the police since the upheavals of 1905. When he brought his seventeen-year-old Estonian bride back to Verkhnyaya Troitsa the following year, nobody knew much about her either.

Ekaterina Ivanovna came from a large Estonian peasant family and was sent out to work in a spinning mill at the age of eleven. Moving to St Petersburg, she joined the strike movement of 1905 and was hidden from the police by a Bolshevik woman named Tatyana Slovatinskaya, who found her a job in a textile mill and took her in as a servant when her continued revolutionary activities lost her her job. It was at Slovatinskaya's house that she met the revolutionary Mikhail Kalinin and went back to Verkhnyaya Troitsa with him.

Seven years younger than Kalinin, Ekaterina Ivanovna was a tall, strong, graceful woman, with a snub nose and plump red cheeks. Neat and hard-working, she cleaned and scrubbed his cottage until it shone, reorganised everything her own way, was out in the kitchen garden at dawn and could scythe as well as any man. The weaver and the lathe operator were well matched, and she proved a good wife, mother and comrade to him.

Shortly after the birth of their first baby, the nobly named Valerian, they left Verkhnyaya Troitsa for St Petersburg, returning for brief visits until in 1910 Ekaterina Ivanovna moved back to the village with her children, of whom there were now three. As the villagers gossiped about Mikhail Ivanovich's revolutionary activities she kept her peace and made plans to have a new house built in the village, a clear sign that the family intended to settle there.

War upset all her plans. She no longer made any secret now of the fact that her husband was in jail in St Petersburg awaiting deportation to Eastern Siberia as a revolutionary. Throughout 1914 she regularly left the children with his mother, Maria Vasilevna, to visit him in the capital, and at the end of 1916 she petitioned the government to allow him to travel to Siberia independently rather than under armed guard, and for her and her children to accompany him there.

The girls from Verkhnyaya Troitsa who had rejected Kalinin must have been kicking themselves a few months later when the rough, self-educated Kalinin found himself not in some remote Siberian hut but at the pinnacle of Soviet power. And after the death of Yakov Sverdlov in 1919 there appeared no better candidate to head the new Soviet state than this genuine worker of peasant origin, one of the people and a true Russian. He had clean hands too, and this was a significant factor at a time when rumour had it that Sverdlov had been murdered for his part in the Romanovs' death.

In the Kremlin the Kalinins shared a flat with the Trotskys, who also had three children, and Ekaterina Ivanovna made friends with Nadezhda Krupskaya. The object of fierce scrutiny, Kalinina disarmed all critics with her simplicity, her native tact, her passionate desire to be useful and her diligence in every task she undertook. Thrown from the confines of her female world into the wide open spaces of political life, she enrolled in nursing courses and helped organise schools and kindergartens. As she set about tackling her own residual illiteracy she developed a taste for this new life of cultural interests, stimulating company and discussions of sexual equality and personal liberation.

In the summer of 1919, as the tide of civil war finally seemed to be turning in the Bolsheviks' favour and Kalinin had been appointed president of the new Soviet state, Ekaterina Ivanovna left the children first with her mother, then with his mother in Verkhnyaya Troitsa, and set off with her husband to tour the country on the 'October Revolution' agit-train.

The 'October Revolution' was a mobile means of mass education, the equivalent of our radio, press and television, designed to introduce people throughout large areas of Russia to the principles of the new life, to tell them who their friends and enemies were, and show them the path to literacy. The new president's presence was considered essential. Also on board were Commissars Kamenev and Lunacharsky, plus numerous journalists, workers, foreign Communists and writers, all working in shifts to distribute pamphlets, give talks, show films, make local inspections and force open the rich peasants' grain-stores in areas hit by famine.

Her hair cropped short after an attack of typhus, Ekaterina Ivanovna was the 'October Revolution's' chief administrator. Quick-witted and efficient, she helped to set up kindergartens and gave talks in hospitals about the care of the wounded. Her energy was prodigious, and all who saw her then remarked on her incorruptibility and her outstanding organisational ability.

In the summer of 1921 she returned with her children to Verkhnyaya Troitsa, where she was promptly elected to the district executive committee. In these lean times even people in the Kremlin went hungry, and she stayed on in the village with her large family until the end of that year, helping her mother-in-law by working in the kitchen garden. Gradually the threat of starvation receded, and in 1922 she returned to Moscow, where she completed her nursing courses, studied homoeopathy, adopted two civil war orphans and was appointed deputy director of the Liberated Labour weaving mill.

Her granddaughter, Ekaterina Valerianovna, told me: 'Everything revolved around Granny – she was the centre of the family. She was a stickler for neatness, I suppose it's an Estonian trait. It was an obsession with her . . .'

However, as Kremlin life became established and special privileges became the norm, Ekaterina Ivanovna's appetite for public service and her dramatic rise from weaver to factory manager took a toll on her time and energy. People increasingly criticised her for giving too little time to her children. There was no stopping her now: after tasting life outside the home nothing could induce her to return to it. The solution was to hire a housekeeper. When the beautiful, educated, aristocratic Alexandra Vasilevna Gorchakova moved in to take charge of the house and children, freeing Ekaterina Ivanovna to work undistracted by female worries, it seemed as though this former peasant, now one of the most powerful women in the Kremlin, could want for nothing more.

Yet in 1924, Ekaterina Ivanovna left her husband and children in Alexandra Gorchakova's capable hands and went off with a woman friend named Valentina Ostroumova, a stenographer in Kalinin's secretariat, to the remote Altai region. As industrialisation gathered pace in the Urals, the two women flung themselves into trade union work and organised a series of 'Down with Illiteracy!' groups. Valentina Ostroumova wrote to Kalinin in Moscow:

The regional committee has decided to promote Katya, and the president praises her work to the skies. She'll soon be catching you up! People's attitude to us is positive, and most of them (the masses anyway) don't know about her connection with you, so there's none of that unnaturalness she experienced in the factory.

Ekaterina Ivanovna Kalinina

Five days later, after her arrest

Above Young Paulina Zhemchuzhina, 1926. Nadezhda Alliluyeva, whose hand is on her knee, has been cut out; every family album was filled with such excisions

Opposite above Vyacheslav and Paulina Zhemchuzhina-Molotova with their daughter, Svetlana

Right Zhemchuzhina after her release from prison, with her grandchild

Nina Teimurazovna Beria

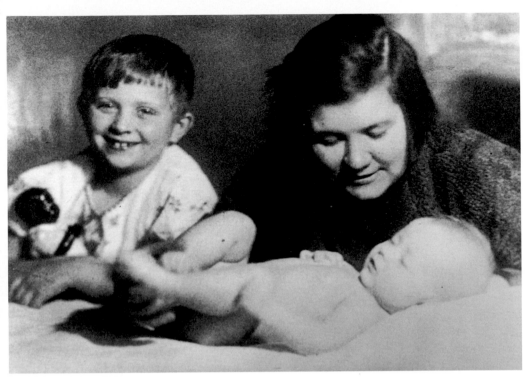

Nina Petrovna Khrushcheva with her two children

Khrushchev with his family

Victoria Brezhneva

The Brezhnevs

Anna and Konstantin Chernenko

Before Perestroika: Raissa Gorbacheva with Galina Brezhneva (right)

Raissa and Mikhail Gorbachev

Raissa Gorbacheva

This remark may be the key to the conflicts which drove Ekaterina Ivanovna to leave her family and rush off to the ends of the earth. She explained her predicament later in a letter to her husband from Altai:

> I wasn't a real person in Moscow, I was a false figure in that society which I belonged to only through you. It was a dishonest situation. A couple of people were sincere with me, but with the rest it was all lies and pretence and it disgusted me. Because I belonged to the top rank I couldn't speak and think as I wanted, like ordinary officials. I was told this to my face by fellow Communists in the top and middle ranks. What happens to the ideals we worked for if we divide up the Party into ranks, and even classes? You can't make wheat bread from rye – if they want to sort people into groups they can leave me out. I don't need cars and privileges, I don't need your false respect – all that stops people seeing me as I really am, just a plain ordinary weaver.

Ekaterina Ivanovna was forty-two, a normal woman crying out against the destruction of her ideals. All around her, inside and outside the Kremlin, the stereotypes of the new power were taking shape, festooned with the slogans of the new vocabulary but based as ever upon the timeless truth that the man with the stick is boss.

As her children grew up, Ekaterina Ivanovna's socially active nature and the revolutionary dreams of her youth were being stifled by the growing anomalies of Kremlin life. A step away from her lived poor, unhappy Nadezhda Alliluyeva, almost twenty years her junior but equally conscientious and sincere, complex yet simple. The two women had much in common, but the difference in their ages and the impossibility of helping each other meant that they could never be close.

Unable to be a politically active woman in this changing world, Ekaterina Ivanovna fled to the Urals hoping to find herself and to affirm her value as an individual. But the invisible chains of the power structure dragged her back. In the summer of 1924 Alexandra Gorchakova silenced Kremlin gossip by bringing the children to see their mother in Altai, and they spent the summer together, enjoying the natural beauties of the Urals, bathing in its clear streams and picking mushrooms and berries. Then, possibly against her better judgement, Ekaterina Ivanovna returned to Moscow and to her hated position as quasi-First Lady of State. There she fell ill, went to the Pasteur Institute in Paris for treatment (occupants of the Kremlin all made use of capitalist hospitals in those days), and after recovering helped to set up several large state farms.

Ekaterina Ivanovna's escapes to Verkhnyaya Troitsa in 1921 and three years later to the Urals seem to have been prompted by different reasons, but both were clear evidence of the ambiguous position in which she felt herself to be. It is possible that personal motives were at work here. It may have been that her relations with Mikhail Ivanovich lacked emotional commitment, that they had agreed to lead separate lives and that all that kept them together was the children. It may have been the familiar pattern of couples unable to live together, but missing each other when apart. The problem may have lain with Kalinin's attraction for the beautiful Alexandra Gorchakova, who moved into their home and showed him how things should be, while his semi-literate upstart Estonian took over a factory and vied for power. It is also possible of course that, encouraged by the recent emergence of the 'woman question' and ideas of free love, Ekaterina Ivanovna was confronting her husband and demanding the right to live by the same standards. Cracks started to appear in more than one Kremlin family at this time, and several leaders acquired new lovers on the other side of the wall.

Whatever the causes of Ekaterina Ivanovna's restlessness, the Altai region seems to have drawn her like a magnet, and in 1931 she set off there again. By now she was forty-nine, the same age as Krupskaya when she entered the Kremlin as its new queen. This was the high point of Ekaterina Ivanovna's life too. She worked on the construction of the Chemalsk hydro-electric power station and a new rest home for the Executive Committee, she kept pigs, she grew vegetables, and she rejoiced again in the opportunity to make use of her organisational skills. In her enthusiasm for her new life she had no qualms about using Kalinin's and others' names to promote the development of the Altai, and she wrote numerous letters begging for help. During these early years of collectivisation the president's wife believed or tried to believe what the Party said, and she worked tirelessly to help this new world come into being and prosper. Her letters to her husband are filled with a youthful love of life, and give the impression that the Urals had everything that could possibly make a woman happy.

When a new holiday home opened in the Altai the leaders started arriving there from Moscow. Kalinin himself visited in 1934, shortly after he had celebrated – predictably, without her – the fifteenth anniversary of his presidency. Her presence in Moscow would have been easy enough to arrange, but the event evidently meant little to her, and he arrived home a few days later to find a letter from her apologising for forgetting to congratulate him.

At the end of 1934 Ekaterina Ivanovna returned exhausted to Moscow. In her absence the Kremlin had witnessed a number of crucially important events, including the death of Nadezhda Alliluyeva, the murder of Kirov and Stalin's reprisals against various leading Party members. But she could not fail to see the cruel realities of Kremlin life, for by now these were plain for all to see.

In was in 1937, at the height of the arrests and shootings of the 'enemies of the people' and their wives, that Ekaterina Ivanovna started working at the Soviet Supreme Court. March 1938 saw the trial of Trotsky, Bukharin and the 'Right-Trotskyite bloc', and in August Beria replaced Ezhov as head of the Ministry of Internal Affairs, the NKVD. In September the Kalinins were on holiday separately, she in the Caucasus and he in Sochi, writing a pamphlet entitled 'The Glorious Path of the Komsomol'. On her way back to Moscow she visited him in Sochi. She left for Moscow on 4 or 5 October, and shortly after her departure he wrote to his daughters, 'Mother has just visited and put some dynamite into our stagnant life.'

A few days after Ekaterina Ivanovna's return home to Moscow her old friend Valentina Ostroumova came to visit and the two women had a heart-to-heart talk about politics. On 17 October Ostroumova was arrested.

Bukharin's wife, Anna Larina, who shared a cell with Ostroumova in 1938, recalls in her memoirs the dramatic developments in the investigation of her case:

Valentina Petrovna's hatred for Stalin was such that she was prepared to repeat everything she had said to Kalinina about him: 'A tyrant and a sadist, destroying the Leninist leadership and millions of innocent people . . .' Concerned about the position of Kalinin's wife, she initially denied that the conversation had taken place. It later transpired that both Beria and the investigator had precise and detailed knowledge of the content of their conversation, so that Beria was able to tell Ostroumova that Kalinin's wife had confessed everything. Believing Beria, Ostroumova confirmed what had been said between them. The investigator then arranged a face-to-face meeting between the two women, at which Ekaterina Ivanovna denied everything and Valentina

Petrovna realised that she had been tricked. At least that was how Ostroumova described the incident . . . Soon afterwards she was led from the cell and we never saw her again.

When Ekaterina Ivanovna was arrested they found her letters to her husband hidden behind a picture. Did somebody know where these were hidden? Was her conversation with Ostroumova bugged? Was there an informer in the Kalinins' flat? Or were the two women simply tricked into making their confession?

The minutes of Kalinina's first interrogation, on 9 December 1938, begin with the interrogator demanding information on the two women's 'Right-Trotskyite counter-revolutionary activities':

KALININA: I did not carry out any Right-Trotskyite counter-revolutionary activities. The only thing I could be accused of is having associated with people convicted as Right-Trotskyites. I know Ostroumova as a Party member, and have never heard her make any anti-Soviet remarks.

QUESTION: Ostroumova states that she involved you in her counter-revolutionary activities. Is that true?

KALININA: She's lying. I have never been involved with her in any counter-revolutionary activities. I know nothing of her counter-revolutionary activities.

Kalinina is told she is to have a meeting with Ostroumova. Ostroumova is led in.

QUESTION TO OSTROUMOVA: What do you know about the counter-revolutionary activities of Ekaterina Ivanovna Kalinina?

OSTROUMOVA: As I already indicated in my previous interrogation, I have conducted subversive espionage work against the Soviet state for several years. Apart from information of a purely intelligence nature I collected defamatory rumours about the leaders of the Party and the Soviet government. One of the sources of these rumours was Ekaterina Ivanovna Kalinina and her associates.

Kalinina's apartment was a kind of salon where people hostile to the Party line would meet to criticise the Party's collectivisation policies. Amongst those who used to attend was Abel Enukidze. Kalinina cannot fail to remember our bitter attacks on the Party and our bitter hatred of Stalin, whom we regarded as the chief culprit of its new course . . .

QUESTION TO KALININA: Do you confirm Ostroumova's evidence?

KALININA: It's lies, all lies!

OSTROUMOVA: Kalinina was very friendly with a Trotskyite named D. This woman was a friend of the Trotsky family and had had an intimate relationship with Trotsky before he was deported from the USSR.

QUESTION TO KALININA: Do you confirm your links with the Trotskyites?

KALININA: I confirm only that D. was a personal friend of mine. I deny that this friendship was of an anti-Soviet nature.

The typed minutes of this meeting were signed by both Kalinina and Ostroumova and form the main part of the KGB's one thin file on Kalinina's wholly unsubstantiated case. The file also contains minutes of the interrogation of D., who confessed to 'allowing her flat to be used twice in 1927 for the purpose of illegal counter-revolutionary meetings at which Trotsky spoke.' D. was further forced to confess that she had attended one of these meetings, although she had not actually said anything.

Even a ten-year-old affair was cause for vicious retribution in those days:

I started visiting the Trotskys' flat in the Kremlin as a friend of the family, and between 1922 and 1923, when Trotsky's wife was abroad for medical treatment, I formed an intimate liaison with Trotsky.

What this has to do with anything, let alone Kalinina's case, is a mystery. It merely indicates how little there was against her in the first place.

One can only guess what happened to Ekaterina Ivanovna between her first and second interrogations, for the tone of her replies changes abruptly after her encounter with Ostroumova. We now come to the hardest part of her story, in which she reveals her part in the arrest of her brother:

INTERROGATOR: You are accused of conducting counter-revolutionary propaganda against the USSR. Do you admit your guilt?

KALININA: No, I do not. I have never conducted counter-revolutionary propaganda, I have always struggled against enemies of the Party and the Soviet Union and exposed them.

INTERROGATOR: Whom have you exposed?

KALININA: I exposed my own brother, Vladimir Ivanovich Lorberg. In 1924 I learned that he had been an *agent provocateur* of the tsarist secret police, and I demanded that he go to the OGPU and give himself up. He did so, and was arrested and shot.

INTERROGATOR: How did you learn that your brother had been a tsarist agent?

KALININA: I was told by my brother Konstantin Ivanovich Lorberg.

INTERROGATOR: What exactly did he tell you?

KALININA: He told me that the Narva Social Democrat organisation in the town of Kalinin [*sic*] had exposed Vladimir Lorberg as a secret agent who had betrayed a number of comrades to the tsarist police.

INTERROGATOR: What did you do when you received this information?

KALININA: I immediately summoned Vladimir Lorberg and asked him if it was true. He admitted that he had had connections with the tsarist secret police and had betrayed members of the Estonian social democratic organisation to them. I then demanded that Lorberg go to the OGPU and confess.

INTERROGATOR: Why did you not inform the Party yourself?

KALININA: I wanted my brother to tell them in person, and I warned him that if he did not I would do so myself. I myself helped him to make contact with the OGPU, and telephoned OGPU agent Bokio asking him to meet my brother.

If Alliluyeva was almost expelled from the Party for unpunctuality and Stalin threatened to set the Control Commission on to Krupskaya for disobedience, one can imagine how threatened Kalinina must have felt by the shadow of her erring brother. Since what was considered heroism in those days would now be considered a contemptible crime, it is hard for us to know whether she was slandering herself to save her life, or whether in 1924, the critical year of her life, her blunt, straightforward nature was outraged by her brother's past, and determined that he atone for his crime even at the cost of his life. It may well also be that she ran off to Altai in that year in order to escape the affair and lie low for a while.

After the interrogators had finished with her brother, they accused her of meeting a White émigrée woman named Levinson when she was in Paris for medical treatment, and of answering Levinson's questions about life in the Soviet Union. She then starts to slander herself in earnest:

I confess to being a member of a right-wing counter-revolutionary organisation. I was drawn to this in 1928 by my hostility to the Party's collectivisation policies. Between 1928 and 1930 I regarded the peasant as an extreme individualist, and with this mentality I thought it would be impossible to change him into a state farmer . . .

In the statement I made after my meeting with Ostroumova I

admitted being a member of a counter-revolutionary organisation. I deny charges of espionage.

The interrogator interrupts her: 'Espionage charges will not be dropped. You are a spy!'

Finally comes the sentence: fifteen years' imprisonment in corrective labour camps, with a further five years' political disenfranchisement. Ostroumova was shot shortly afterwards in jail.

The only recorded memories of Ekaterina Ivanovna in the camp were those of a writer named Razgon, who recalled her working in the camp bath-house and shaking the lice from the prisoners' clothes while they were washing. Her fond granddaughter, Ekaterina Valerianovna, says: 'She didn't have to do it – I'm sure she didn't think how disgusting the lice were but how nice it would be for people to wear clean clothes, even for a little while.'

It is typical of Stalinist justice that Kalinina's files should contain no evidence from her husband. By arresting her, Stalin clearly intended to keep his president under his thumb, while showing the world that the great man was being magnanimously defended from his counter-revolutionary wife, and that in purging the Kremlin of the enemy within, the innocent were not touched.

In a letter Kalinin wrote to a friend in the 1930s, he describes privileges more appropriate to an operatic tenor than to a head of state:

> People say power hasn't changed me, but in my heart of hearts I'm thrilled by the meetings, the motorcars and the popular attention, especially that of women . . .

Anna Larina, the widow of Bukharin, spoke of the powerlessness of the man who occupied the Soviet throne:

> In the Tomsk camp, which contained mostly the wives of so-called 'traitors to their country' (most of whom were shot), there was also a Moscow professor's wife who had evidently landed up with us by accident. This professor once received an award from Kalinin, and used the occasion to present his case. Kalinin replied, 'My dear chap, I'm in the same position! I can't even help my own wife – there's no way I can help yours!'

Years passed, war broke out, and in 1944, as victory approached, the leaders talked of an amnesty. The ailing Soviet president was a particularly passionate advocate of the amnesty. This made Stalin smile: Kalinin must be missing his wife.

Kalinin's helplessness casts new light on Budyonny's inability to help his second wife, yet Kalinin did have the advantage over everyone else in Russia of being the first to know of Stalin's latest decrees. On learning of the amnesty which he was to sanction, he immediately summoned his children and dictated a letter to Stalin requesting that their mother be pardoned. On Victory Day Ekaterina Ivanovna's sister travelled to the camp where she was incarcerated and gave her the petition to sign. Ekaterina Ivanovna refused, protesting that she was guilty of nothing, but her sister shouted at her, the petition was sent, and finally the Presidium of the Supreme Soviet of the USSR, headed by Ekaterina Ivanovna's husband, decreed: 'Ekaterina Ivanovna Kalinina to be released forthwith . . . and all rights restored. *Secretary of the Presidium of the Supreme Soviet of the USSR, A. Gorkin.*' This must have been the only Presidium decree not to bear Kalinin's signature. It was dated 14 December 1946; if family memories are correct and the decree was not backdated, this means that it took eighteen months for the proud Estonian's letter to travel from the camp to Stalin's desk, and from Stalin's desk to the Presidium.

Over the following years Ekaterina Ivanovna battled tirelessly to clear her name. On 24 August 1954 she delivered a handwritten letter to USSR Public Prosecutor Rudenko:

On 22 April 1939 I was found guilty of belonging to a Trotskyite organisation, of having links with Trotskyites and advocating terror . . . The methods used in the interrogation forced me to give false evidence. My first interrogators, Ivanov and Khoroshkevich, whom I regard as direct agents of Fascism, broke all Soviet laws with regard to investigation procedures, failing to show me any specific prosecution material, merely shouting at me that I was a terrorist *provocateur*, a spy and a member of a counter-revolutionary organisation, and that they could prove it so I had better admit it. I suggested that if the prosecution had slanderous material against me they should check it with me, and they replied that there was nothing to check, everything had been checked before my arrest and it only remained for me to admit it.

When I was transferred to Lefortovo jail fifteen days later I sat without clothes in winter in a freezing basement and was beaten, which made me break down and state falsely that I had expressed anti-Soviet views about collective farms. The minutes were drawn up by the interrogator, I just signed them . . .

On the night of 9–10 December I had a face-to-face meeting with Ostroumova. No minutes of this meeting were taken and we signed nothing, but three months later we were made to sign some minutes supposedly of this meeting. I don't know when and where these minutes were concocted, but they bore no relation to the evidence Ostroumova gave in my presence, even though they were signed by her.

. . . I asked the interrogators to let me have a defence lawyer, since my reading and writing is poor; I'm not Russian and can't always express my thoughts.

. . . In view of the above, I ask you, citizen Public Prosecutor, to protest against this unjust sentence and to release me from a non-existent crime dreamed up to the advantage of our enemies.

The difference in the language of Kalinina's letter and that of her interrogation minutes makes it clear that the minutes must have been fabricated after the interrogation to bolster the case against her. They also indicate that Ostroumova may not in fact have slandered herself and her friend after all.

The final document in Kalinina's file states:

It is clear that at the moment of Kalinina's arrest there was no evidence against her of any anti-Soviet activities, apart from the unspecified evidence of Ostroumova. Arrested on 25 October 1938, Kalinina was illegally held in custody until 13 February 1939 and the Public Prosecutor's permission was received only after she had made her confession . . . It is therefore established that Kalinina's arrest was an act of retribution by Beria and Kobulov, who were directly involved in the investigation of her case and are now exposed as enemies of the people.

The fact that this document is dated on the same day as Kalinina's letter shows that the new Khrushchev era was in a hurry to expiate old sins, and that the process was starting at the very top.

Ekaterina Ivanovna's granddaughter has collected numerous books, photographs and papers relating to her grandparents. Recently, when the Kalinin Museum, established in their memory, was dismantled, she gathered all the archive material she could. Yet her grandmother apparently never talked of her prison experiences, and it had not occurred to Ekaterina Valerianovna to investigate her files at the Lubyanka.

She describes Ostroumova as a strong woman working hard in difficult circumstances to support two children on her own. She was puzzled that Ekaterina Ivanovna never mentioned her or visited her two children when she was freed, yet when told about Ostroumova's evidence against Ekaterina Ivanovna she exclaimed, 'Poor Valya, people said she was dreadfully tortured in jail – they had to carry her in at the end!'

This generous and sensitive woman realises that one cannot judge those who have endured torture. Nor will she betray her extraordinary, contradictory grandmother, who fought so valiantly to remain true to the people and escape her hated role as First Lady of the Kremlin.

10

A Pearl set in Iron

Vyacheslav Mikhailovich Skryabin (revolutionary name Molotov –
1890–1986), born into an educated family in Vyatka province.
Drawn to revolutionary politics in 1905 at the age of fifteen, he
spent two years in prison and exile and became friends with Stalin.
He then studied economics in St Petersburg and joined the Pravda
editorial board. In October 1917 he became a member of
Petrograd's Military Revolutionary Committee, then chair of its
Economic Council. During the civil war he occupied leading posts
in various towns, and in 1921 Lenin appointed him Secretary of the
Party's Central Committee. Appointed president of the Council of
People's Commissars, he became Stalin's Number Two and in 1937
conducted a massive purge of the Ukrainian CP. After Stalin's
rapprochement *with Hitler in 1939 he replaced Litvinov as head of*
the Commissariat for Foreign Affairs, where he remained until
1949. After Stalin's death he was forced to issue a public self-
criticism, and was banished to a diplomatic post in Mongolia after
his unsuccessful campaign against Khrushchev. In 1961 he was
expelled from the Party, along with Kaganovich and Malenkov,
and spent the years until his death tending his garden and writing.

In Russian, Zhemchuzhina means pearl. A lovely name – rather too
lovely for the hungry Soviet people, but not for a Kremlin wife.

Paulina Semyonovna Zhemchuzhina, a poor Jewish girl from a
Cossack village in Zaporozhe, was nineteen when elected to attend
the International Women's Conference held in Moscow in 1921.
She had been a Bolshevik for three years and her red kerchief
merged with thousands of others gathered in the Kremlin that
summer. Vyacheslav Molotov, however, who was helping to

organise the conference, spotted her immediately and she did not return to Zaporozhe. Sharp and clear-headed, Paulina Zhemchuzhina quickly grasped what was what in the Kremlin, and became one of its most important women.

To begin with, the Molotovs shared a flat with the Stalins in what is now the modern Palace of Congresses building, and since the two wives were nearly the same age they became friends. No one knew Nadezhda Alliluyeva better than Paulina Zhemchuzhina. It was she who led the distraught Nadezhda from the room in November 1932 after Stalin publicly humiliated his wife at dinner. During their long walk around the Kremlin together afterwards it was Zhemchuzhina again who comforted Alliluyeva in her distress. And when Nadezhda's nurse discovered her body the next morning, the first people she called were Abel Enukidze and Zhemchuzhina.

Many historians assume that Stalin nurtured a secret hatred for Paulina Zhemchuzhina, and wonder why he waited until 1949 to arrest her. Stalin would have had no problem in disposing of her in the thirties had he wished to do so; the NKVD did its work perfectly, prying into people's most intimate secrets, especially those living in the Kremlin. Moreover, Paulina Zhemchuzhina had made one glaringly obvious mistake: her elder brother was an American capitalist who had left Russia at the turn of the century, and she sometimes wrote to him. That was certainly a crime!

Yet Zhemchuzhina went from strength to strength, first as deputy commissar of the food industry, then as commissar of the fish industry, then as director of the state perfume industry, *Glavparfumeria*. Like everyone else, she had occasional problems at work. According to Molotov, the Germans preferred Soviet perfumes to French brands, and in 1939 she was reprimanded and temporarily expelled from the Party when *Glavparfumeria* was infiltrated by German spies trying to steal the secrets of its success. But she was quickly reinstated and made director of the knitwear and fancy goods industry.

For the whole of her life Zhemchuzhina remained dedicated to the Party and its leader, and each of her appointments was personally authorised by Stalin.

In Molotov's memoirs he describes his relationship with Stalin before the Revolution:

We wrote to each other from exile, and after we became friends we shared a flat. Then he stole my girlfriend Marusya. Stalin was a good-looking man whom women found attractive, and he had a lot of success with them.

Even though Molotov acknowledged Stalin's supremacy in everything and became his shadow, such treachery can rankle all one's life. Although it is generally assumed that his wife was best friends with Stalin's wife, contemporary accounts agree that Paulina Zhemchuzhina was bitterly critical of Nadezhda Alliluyeva for killing herself, and that, far from mourning the loss of her friend, she condemned her for selfishly leaving Stalin and the children at such a difficult time.

Paulina Zhemchuzhina's love for her husband and family fused with her devotion to Stalin and the Party. It also appears possible that she loved the leader as a woman too, and that this devotion tied his hands.

Zhemchuzhina's photographs show a strong, biblical face, a slim figure, haughty gaze, curly hair and elegant hands. She can hardly have pleased Stalin as a woman; she was too active and political for his taste. Yet it was Molotov himself who said that women fell in love with Stalin, and it can have been no secret that Stalin had once stolen his Marusya. He did not need to steal Paulina; they were liberated Marxists and close neighbours. The other Kremlin wives, fearing that Stalin would not stay unmarried for long, were determined not to release him into the hands of some outsider eager to take her place in the Kremlin. But who could object if he sometimes drank from the cup of love with his former wife's best friend and his best friend's wife? There was nothing crude or vulgar here, and there was nothing crude or vulgar about the complex and contradictory Zhemchuzhina.

Paulina always had the best. The Molotovs had the best flat in the Kremlin, and under her watchful eye Molotov had built the best dacha, in which state and international receptions were held. When the Molotovs eventually moved to another flat next door, the Stalins' home was constantly filled with tension. Stalin preferred to spend time at the Molotovs. Clever Zhemchuzhina knew how to create calm and surround people with warmth and comfort; Stalin liked that. Molotov describes in his memoirs how the two families would spend intimate evenings around the table together, and how Zhemchuzhina, unlike Nadezhda, would unhesitatingly take Stalin's side.

When the place of First Lady of the Kremlin fell vacant after

Nadezhda Alliluyeva's death, Paulina Semyonovna quietly filled it. Unofficially at first, just for a couple of months, not because she wanted to, but because there was no one else to do it. Throughout the thirties and almost the entire period of Stalin's life without Alliluyeva, Paulina Semyonovna was there at his command. And since she herself had at her command an army of guards and servants, she was able to shoulder many of his problems, including the education of his daughter, Svetlana. The Molotovs' daughter had been born shortly after the Stalins', and they had named her Svetlana too. Who better than Paulina to supervise the upbringing of the best Kremlin girls?

She took this task extremely seriously, and if Svetlana Stalina did not always agree with her, Paulina did not insist, but ensured that her own daughter followed it. There were gymnastics and music lessons. ('It enhances a girl's image to sit down at the piano while the party is in full swing and play a polonaise,' she said.) There were classes in German and French, and English lessons with Doris Hart-Maxin, known to millions for her English-language broadcasts from the Soviet Union.

Doris Hart was a well-heeled English girl who had fallen in love with Communism in the early thirties and was seconded by the British Communist Party to work under Ivan Maisky at the Soviet embassy in London. There she met Alexei Maxin, the ambassador's chauffeur, who took her for drives in the ambassadorial Rolls Royce, and finally invited her to live with him in Moscow, where she ended up working for Moscow Radio. Although she generally refused to give lessons she made an exception for the two Svetlanas, and English lessons with Doris Maxin became a status symbol for the Kremlin aristocracy.

Doris recalls:

> The two girls came together and studied together. They were sweet, modest girls. They wore wretched, thin fur coats. When Svetlana Molotova caught me looking at hers, she said, 'Mama doesn't want people in town to know who I am – we have to be modest, the whole country's looking at us.'

A man who studied with Svetlana Molotova at the Institute of Foreign Relations ten years later remembers her differently:

> She was chauffeur-driven to the Institute wearing a new outfit every day. Going up the stairs one would be assailed by the smell of French perfume, and know that Svetlana Molotova had just passed.

*

The boundlessly energetic wife of a Kremlin leader, the mature and powerful Soviet commissar, mistress of a large household – as the months turned to years, Paulina Semyonovna Zhemchuzhina unobtrusively stepped into the place of First Lady and made it her own. As the years turned into decades, she would anticipate Stalin's mood and step aside, then slip back to her place like a cat. Beria must have had his eye on her the moment he arrived at the Ministry of Internal Affairs, and her subsequent problems make it clear that he had been collecting material against her from the start, yet Stalin opposed him, and so perhaps did Molotov.

She was unbowed by her problems, for she was not a fearful or cautious woman. The daughter of the Molotovs' chauffeur was with her in the Crimea on 22 June 1941, the day the Nazis invaded Russia:

> Early in the morning of 22 June Vyacheslav Mikhailovich telephoned her from Moscow urging us to return at once. Paulina Semyonovna calmly packed her bags and summoned the hairdresser, and at midday, as she listened to Molotov's declaration of war over the radio, she had a manicure.

For several years after the war Paulina Zhemchuzhina and her considerable entourage would visit socialist Czechoslovakia to take the miracle-working waters of Karlovy Vary. On their way there they would stay with Marshal Katukov, commander of Soviet troops in the German Democratic Republic, whose Dresden home became a place of pilgrimage for the Soviet élite enticed by Germany's fur and fabrics, and the Sèvres and Meissen porcelain miraculously preserved from the Nazi defeat. Ekaterina Sergeevna Katukova, a sharp, intelligent woman, had in the thirties married a Kremlin official who was arrested and shot, and she herself had spent two years in Butyrki prison before marching from Moscow to Berlin with the Marshal and marrying him. She recalls the arrival of Paulina Semyonovna and her daughter at her Dresden villa:

> There were both lavishly dressed and covered in furs – Svetlana was wearing a mink stole. Paulina Zhemchuzhina was a clever, powerful woman. There were about fifty people travelling with them on the same aeroplane, but they all lived separately. It was a problem finding room for them all. I travelled on with Zhemchuzhina and her entourage to Karlovy Vary, and although they had stayed for several days at our villa, she no longer acknowledged me once we arrived.

It was three years after the war ended that Zhemchuzhina's troubles began. While Ekaterina Voroshilova, Maria Kaganovich and other Jewish wives held their Jewishness deep within them, Paulina Zhemchuzhina embraced with open arms the newly-formed Soviet Jewish Anti-Fascist Committee and the new state of Israel. The Soviet government was the first to open diplomatic relations with Israel, and she threw a reception in honour of Israel's new ambassador to Moscow, Golda Meir. When prominent Jews urged the Party Central Committee to establish a Jewish autonomous region in the Crimea, she supported the idea and her regular meetings with Golda Meir spawned rumours that the two women had been at school together and were drawing up a blueprint for the scheme.

By the end of 1948 relations between the USSR and the new state of Israel had deteriorated disastrously, all talk of a Jewish homeland in the USSR was rejected, and leading members of the Jewish community were being arrested as 'rootless cosmopolitans'. This did not deter Paulina Zhemchuzhina from meeting Meir and members of the Anti-Fascist Committee. What was she thinking of? Had this loyal Stalinist forgotten her place?

The women of the Kremlin had changed a lot over the past two decades. In the 1920s they had been mistresses of their fate. In the 1930s they became 'Party Aunts', imbued with Party spirit. In the 1940s they relaxed a little, and the more they relaxed the more they were punished.

Beria had already assembled his evidence; now it was time to round up his witnesses and move into action. With the Jewish witch-hunt at its height and Stalin more distant from Zhemchuzhina and the domestic warmth she provided, Beria showed the leader his evidence. She was apprehended at work and interrogated, but released soon afterwards. Realising that her arrest was imminent, she left Molotov to live with her brother and sister, telling her husband, 'If the Party demands it, we'll separate.'[1]

For the next eight months Paulina Semyonovna did not communicate with her family for fear of incriminating them. Occasionally Svetlana's husband would visit his disgraced mother-in-law in the evening after work to give her news of the family and drive her to the gates of their government dacha on the outskirts of Moscow.

---

[1]Molotov told this to the poet Felix Chuev, who met him frequently in the last years of his life and published a book of interviews with him.

It is hard to imagine this once proud and fearless woman crushed by the Party machine and uncomplainingly awaiting prison, while behind the gates her loving husband rested from his Party labours and endured a mass of inconveniences as a result of her absence. He did not go to Stalin and demand that his wife be left alone, he did not challenge Beria to a duel, he suffered in silence in the name of Communism and the bright future, which he believed in as he believed in her guilt.

The following February, Paulina Zhemchuzhina was arrested along with her brother and sister at their home. Molotov described to Felix Chuev how she was summoned before the Central Committee and accused of 'sustaining criminal relations with Jewish nationalists for several years, and conducting enemy work with them against the Soviet Union'.

Molotov told Chuev:

> My knees trembled when Stalin read out to the Politburo the evidence against Paulina Semyonovna which he had received from his Cheka agents. He and I quarrelled about it, but there was nothing to be done. The Cheka had pounced, she couldn't escape. She was charged with associating with Zionist organisations and with the Israeli ambassador Golda Meir, and with wanting to turn the Crimea into an autonomous Jewish republic. She was too friendly with Mikhoels – she should have been more careful with her friends.[2]
>
> When I told her the charges against her she screamed, 'And you believe them!'
>
> She spent two years in jail and over three years in the camps. When Beria saw me at Politburo meetings he would whisper in my ear, 'Paulina's alive!'

In this weird comedy only two men, Stalin and Beria, had the power to take decisions, while their henchmen sat in the Politburo, each with his own vivid fears and weaknesses, not daring to raise questions about his own wife.

In leaving her own home to save her husband, Zhemchuzhina destroyed her sister, who later died in prison. She herself was held at the Lubyanka and interrogated. The film star Tatyana Okunevskaya, who was imprisoned there at the same time, recalls hearing a shrill female voice shouting through the open door of her cell, 'Phone my husband! Tell him to send my diabetes pills! I'm an

---

[2]Mikhoels was manager of Moscow's Jewish Theatre.

invalid! You've no right to feed me this rubbish!' Okunevskaya says, 'I learned that this was Zhemchuzhina, Molotov's wife, and that he had abandoned her and might even be imprisoned himself.'

Molotov could indeed be said to be imprisoned in the Kremlin, sustained at Politburo meetings only by Beria's words, 'Paulina's alive!'

The case of Paulina Semyonovna Zhemchuzhina consists of four pale-blue files, the first three containing the minutes of the interrogation of the accused and the witnesses, the fourth containing various documents relating to the case, including the accused's personal correspondence with various people, birthday greetings, petitions and appeals.

The writer Galina Serebryakova writes to her from the camps. A man named Belinkov writes pleading for the release of his son Arkardy, arrested for writing an 'anti-Soviet novel'. Workers write from various prisons. There is a note from Academician Lina Solomonovna Stern asking her to pass on a letter to Molotov, and there is a copy of this letter, in which Stern begs Molotov to use his position to speed up the travel documents for a party of learned physiologists visiting Australia.

All these letters have been answered. Zhemchuzhina conducted a correspondence with Serebryakova, asking about her latest novel and offering to have it typed for her. She tried to ease the fate of Arkardy Belinkov, who was seriously ill. She wrote to public prosecutors and judges asking them to carry out further investigations; they replied and the cases were investigated.

The compromising material in the fourth file includes a photocopy (unsigned) of a letter written on 10 May 1946 to her brother Karp, the American capitalist:

> My dears,
> Since someone is visiting your part of the world I am using this opportunity to drop you a line. We are all well. Throughout the country rebuilding work continues apace as we struggle to heal the wounds inflicted on us by the fascist aggressor, and the people are toiling selflessly to fulfil the new Five-Year Plan. Little Svetlanochka has left school with a gold medal, and is now studying at the Institute of Foreign Relations. Her English is excellent, so if your daughters visit us she will have no problems in talking to them. I am working in the textile industry but unfortunately I haven't been well lately. Greetings and kisses to Sonya and the children.

Another letter dated 18 April 1945, is from Mikhoels:

Dear, respected Paulina Semyonovna,
I hope you will forgive me for daring to trouble you. I am led to do so by a matter of public importance concerning our critic Abram Solomonovich Gurvich, who at a comparatively early age has suffered a paralysis of the limbs. According to the doctors, his illness is curable. Knowing your generosity, I am asking for your kind help in arranging for him to be admitted to the Kremlin hospital. I repeat, I am loath to trouble you, and hope that you will forgive me.
    With deep respect and gratitude, Mikhoels.

Mikhoels was no longer alive by the time of Zhemchuzhina's first interrogation on 8 June 1948, which included a meeting with Fefer, a member of the Jewish Anti-Fascist Committee. Since it is questionable whether Zhemchuzhina played any significant role in schemes concerning a Jewish Crimea, it seems likely that the Jews found to testify against her discovered her to be an easy target as a woman. Her real crime before the Soviet government was her Jewishness, and the first part of her lengthy interrogation was intended to establish whether she had attended synagogue on one occasion three years earlier. To visit a place of worship was considered incompatible with Party membership and thus virtually a crime. Hence Zhemchuzhina's steadfast denial of the undeniable evidence that she had been there.

FEFER: When Mikhoels was a member of the Jewish Anti-Fascist Committee, he told me Zhemchuzhina used to attend plays at the Jewish Theatre, and that he chatted with her once in the artistic director's room during a performance. She said she was deeply interested in our affairs, the life of Jews in the Soviet Union and the work of the Jewish Anti-Fascist Committee. Mikhoels said: 'She is a good Jewish daughter.' He told me he once complained to her that there was so much hostility to Jews and she replied: 'It's bad at the top.'
    INTERROGATOR'S QUESTION TO FEFER: What did that mean?
    FEFER: I looked at Mikhoels and asked him how I should take these words, and he said he understood her to mean it wasn't just a local problem, but that many of the leaders supported this policy of oppressing and discriminating against the Jews.
    QUESTION TO ZHEMCHUZHINA: What do you say to that?
    ZHEMCHUZHINA: It's pure lies, invented either by Mikhoels or Fefer.
    QUESTION TO ZHEMCHUZHINA: Were you at the theatre, and did you talk to Mikhoels?

ZHEMCHUZHINA: I was at the theatre, but I deny Fefer's account of my conversation with Mikhoels.

QUESTION TO FEFER: Were you present at the synagogue on 14 March 1945?

FEFER: I rarely attend synagogue, but on that day I was there. On 14 March prayers were said for Jews killed in the Second World War. Many people attended, including the actors Peisen, Khromchenko and Utesov, as well as several academicians, professors and even generals. I also saw Zhemchuzhina there with her brother. I went in and sat down in the fifth or sixth row, facing the altar. According to synagogue tradition, the women sit upstairs, but exceptions are made for particularly important women and an exception was made for Zhemchuzhina.

QUESTION TO FEFER: Was Zhemchuzhina seen by everybody present?

FEFER: All the Jewish high-ups there recognised her – everybody knows her.

QUESTION TO ZHEMCHUZHINA: Were you at the synagogue?

ZHEMCHUZHINA: No, I was not, it was my sister.

QUESTION TO FEFER: Are you quite sure that it was Zhemchuzhina you saw at the synagogue?

FEFER: Quite sure. All the Jews in town were talking about it.

QUESTION TO ZHEMCHUZHINA: Do you still deny you were there?

ZHEMCHUZHINA: I was not at the synagogue.

Later that day Zhemchuzhina had a meeting with Zusskind, administrator of the Jewish Theatre, and member of the Jewish Anti-Fascist Committee.

INTERROGATOR'S QUESTION TO ZUSSKIND: Did Zhemchuzhina attend the funeral of Mikhoels?

ZUSSKIND: Yes she did. On the evening of 15 January 1948 I stood beside the grave taking the wreaths from all the various organisations and there I saw Paulina Semyonovna. We exchanged greetings. I expressed my grief at Mikhoels' death, and Paulina Semyonovna asked me if I thought it was an accident or murder. I said that on the basis of the information I had received it appeared that Mikhoels had died in a car crash, and was found at seven in the morning near his hotel. Paulina Semyonovna rejected this – she said she thought it was murder, and things weren't as simple as people would have us believe.

QUESTION TO ZHEMCHUZHINA: Did you say that?

ZHEMCHUZHINA: No.

QUESTION TO ZUSSKIND: Were you at the synagogue on 14 March 1945?

ZUSSKIND: Yes, I was. I saw Paulina Semyonovna there – she was sitting right opposite me.

QUESTION TO ZUSSKIND: Are you sure it was Zhemchuzhina?

ZUSSKIND: Absolutely sure, I am inventing nothing. We exchanged greetings.

QUESTION TO ZHEMCHUZHINA: Your presence at the synagogue is confirmed by both Fefer and Zusskind, who know you well and greeted you there. What have you to say?

ZHEMCHUZHINA: I was not at the synagogue.

The same line of questioning was pursued on 26 December 1948 in a confrontation between Zhemchuzhina and an elder of the Moscow synagogue, who confirmed that he had seen her in the synagogue three years before and had arranged for her to sit downstairs. Yet again, Zhemchuzhina denied that she had been there.

Paulina Semyonovna's interrogation started in earnest on 4 February 1948, after her arrest:

QUESTION: Is Zhemchuzhina your real name?

ZHEMCHUZHINA: No, my real name is Pearl Semyonovna Karpovsksaya – Zhemchuzhina is my underground name.

QUESTION: You worked in the underground?

ZHEMCHUZHINA: Yes.

QUESTION: Where?

ZHEMCHUZHINA: In the Ukraine, when it was occupied by Denikin's troops.

QUESTION: Who assigned you to do underground work in the rear of the Whites?

ZHEMCHUZHINA: I assigned myself to work there because the situation was desperate. In 1918 I was accepted into the Russian Communist Party (Bolshevik) by the Zaporozhe city Party organisation, and shortly afterwards I became leader of the Zaporozhe Party committee. In the autumn of 1919 Denikin advanced on Zaporozhe, and the whole regional Party apparatus was evacuated to Kiev. I was evacuated there too, along with a group of local committee workers. In Kiev we presented ourselves to the central committee of the Ukrainian Communist Party (Bolshevik) and were sent off in groups to work with various fighting units of the Red Army. I was appointed political worker with a regiment of the Ninth Army, which was stationed near Darnits, where I stayed for about two months. After that our regiment was forced to disperse under attack from the White troops, and I escaped back to Kiev.

QUESTION: It appears from your evidence that you were sent to the front to do political work with the troops, but that instead you escaped to Kiev. How would you regard this?

ZHEMCHUZHINA: I would now regard it as desertion from the battlefield, but I was young then and did not understand what was required of me. We had been told by the commissar of our regiment that the situation was hopeless and we should destroy all personal documents and get out to Kiev. That is what I did.

QUESTION: What did you do on arriving in Kiev?

ZHEMCHUZHINA: By then the town was in the hands of White General Bredov. I hid out for three days in the Mikhailov Monastery, unable to contact any of my comrades or receive instructions, until finally I escaped to Zaporozhe, which was still under White occupation. In Zaporozhe I made contact with the Party organisation and was sent to Kharkov to do underground Party work.

QUESTION: Why did you not stay in Zaporozhe?

ZHEMCHUZHINA: People in Zaporozhe knew I had been working for the Party committee, and I would have been identified. Only twenty-four hours after my return Denikin's counter-intelligence troops started hunting for me, and they came to my home while I was out and searched it.

QUESTION: How did they treat your family?

ZHEMCHUZHINA: They didn't touch them.

QUESTION: How do you account for that? It's well known that people of Jewish nationality are generally punished by the Whites for no reason.

ZHEMCHUZHINA: I cannot explain it.

QUESTION: You cannot, because nothing of the sort happened?

ZHEMCHUZHINA: We were searched, the Whites ransacked my things, but I cannot explain why they dealt leniently with my family . . . In October or November 1919 I was in Kharkov. There I made contact with Dashevsky, who ran the passport section of Kharkov's underground Party organisation. Dashevsky gave me a new passport in the name of Paulina Semyonovna Zhemchuzhina, and since then I have used this name . . .

QUESTION: How long did you work for the central committee of the Communist Party of the Ukraine?

ZHEMCHUZHINA: Not long. In 1921 the Ukrainian Party organisation sent me as a delegate to the International Women's Conference in Moscow, and I stayed in the capital to work as Party organiser in the Rogozhsko-Simonov district . . . While attending the International

Women's Conference I met Molotov, who was then secretary of the Central Committee of the Communist Party, and at the end of 1921 I became his wife.

Zhemchuzhina's next interrogation was six days later:

QUESTION: Are you prepared to talk truthfully about your crimes against the Soviet state?

ZHEMCHUZHINA: I have committed no crimes against the Soviet state. I deny the charges of having criminal contacts with Jewish nationalists.

QUESTION: You deny them because you want to hide the anti-government nature of your contact with Mikhoels and other nationalists? Tell us how often you met Mikhoels.

ZHEMCHUZHINA: Not often. Our first meeting was in 1938 or 1939 at Moscow's Jewish Theatre, where I attended a performance of *Tevie the Milkman*. Mikhoels came to my box in the interval and introduced himself as the theatre's manager. After this I had no further contact with him until the beginning of 1944, when a fellow director in the textile and fancy goods industry asked me to invite him to talk to us about his trip to America. He accepted my invitation, and he gave his talk a few days later ... In 1948 he visited our directors twice to invite me to a performance of *Freilechs*. He also requested me to arrange for an actor at the Jewish Theatre to enter the Kremlin Hospital for treatment, but I refused his request.

QUESTION: Tell us about the errands you performed for Mikhoels.

ZHEMCHUZHINA: In 1948 or 1947 Mikhoels asked me to pass on a letter to Molotov, who was then on a working trip abroad. I gave this letter to a secretary at the Soviet of Ministers to be forwarded to Molotov by the next post.

QUESTION: Did you know the contents of this letter?

ZHEMCHUZHINA: No, I did not read it and he did not inform me of what it said.

QUESTION: You're lying again! It is known that you not only agreed to pass on the letter but promised Mikhoels to raise the questions contained in it!

ZHEMCHUZHINA: I deny that. I saw nothing wrong in taking the letter from Mikhoels, and as for its contents, I repeat that I knew nothing about them.

INVESTIGATOR: Since you brazenly deny the known facts, the investigation is forced to expose you.

They lead in prisoner Lozovsky, formerly head of the Informburo and member of the Soviet Jewish Anti-Fascist Committee.

QUESTION TO LOZOVSKY: Did Jewish nationalists send slanderous letters to the Soviet government?

LOZOVSKY: Yes. In 1944 Mikhoels and Epstein, formerly chief secretary of the Soviet Jewish Anti-Fascist Committee, received several letters from Jews in the Ukraine complaining of harassment from the local authorities. They came to me asking me to protest about this to the Soviet government. By then our nationalist work was well advanced, and after discussing the matter amongst ourselves we decided to write to Molotov presenting the facts cited in these letters, with the aim of forcing the Soviet government to grant concessions to the Jews. Since we received no answer, Mikhoels, Epstein and I agreed to write a further letter to Molotov on the matter, but fearing that this too would be ignored we decided to ensure a positive response from him by using our contacts.

QUESTION: You mean Zhemchuzhina?

LOZOVSKY: Yes, her.

Zhemchuzhina was then interrogated about her part in promoting a Jewish republic in the Crimea. For this they brought in Lozovsky's deputy, Yusefovich, another member of the Soviet Jewish Anti-Fascist Committee.

YUSEFOVICH: Mikhoels and Fefer were the first to discuss the idea. We all agreed that the climate in the Crimea made it the most favourable place for the foundation of a Jewish republic.

QUESTION: It's not a question of the climate, but of whether these plans to establish a Jewish state was at the behest of your American bosses. Why conceal this?

YUSEFOVICH: That is true, but I only realised it afterwards, when US Congressman Goldberg visited the USSR . . . During Goldberg's first meeting with us in Moscow he expressed his satisfaction with our nationalist work and said the Crimea should be a Jewish glory, a Jewish California. He spoke of the Crimea's proximity to Palestine, and of the need to establish closer links between Soviet and Palestinian Jews. He clearly represented the interests of American Jewish organisations in establishing a Jewish state on Crimean territory, which could be used as a political base against the Soviet Union.

QUESTION: What was your connection with Zhemchuzhina's criminal ambitions?

YUSEFOVICH: With Goldberg's encouragement, Mikhoels and Fefer decided to use Zhemchuzhina to raise the issue with the Soviet government. Mikhoels said that he could rely on her support. We Jewish nationalists regarded Zhemchuzhina as our benefactor, who lent a favourable ear to our requests and to Jewish problems in general. Mikhoels met her and explained our plans regarding the Crimea, and she promised to help us. Soon after this, in early 1944, he and Fefer drafted a letter about the hand-over of the Crimea to the Jews.

The same evidence was heard by all members of the Soviet Jewish Anti-Fascist Committee interrogated during Zhemchuzhina's case, except for Academician Lina Stern. Lina Stern was questioned interminably about the letter she sent Zhemchuzhina to pass on to Molotov, but she refused to say anything but 'my relations with Paulina Semyonovna were of a warm and friendly nature.'

During the next stage of Paulina Semyonovna's interrogation her faith in her colleagues' sincerity was further shattered when those who had ingratiated themselves with her when she was in power met her face-to-face, and said:

You were a despot. When anyone tried to argue with you, you would shut them up. People were afraid of you because you were as cruel as Mother Morozova.[3] I'm not sticking up for you – it's all your fault I'm in prison now! You dragged us all down with you, why should we defend you?

Zhemchuzhina abused her position as Molotov's wife to trick the government into thinking everything was perfect at work. All the staff of the Central Directorate knew the illegal, anti-government methods she was using to procure extra funds ... She often boasted that our Central Directorate was far better supplied than the ministry as a whole.

On Saturdays she would gather a group of her friends together and invite us out to her dacha, where we would have a fine time eating and drinking. Knowing what we were up to, the collective at the factory didn't bother to do any work.

She took all her colleagues' bonuses, and even their awards and medals ...

Nor was Paulina Semyonovna spared by her close relatives;

[3]Mother Morozova was a Moscow merchant of legendary cruelty.

scared to death by the Lubyanka and demoralised by the investigation, they obviously hoped that a frank confession would save her:

Polya, you weren't telling the truth. Remember when you returned from America in the spring of 1936, and you gave me a letter and twenty dollars from Karp?

ZHEMCHUZHINA: I never gave you anything.

Polya, I've told the investigation everything about your friendship with Mikhoels, about your meetings with him and all your conversations on so-called Jewish matters. I advise you to confess your crimes honestly.

ZHEMCHUZHINA: I have nothing to confess, I'm guilty of nothing.

Remember, Polya, how you told me Mikhoels had described life abroad, and he said they had real freedom over there, and that we're not free here in the Soviet Union? And he complained that the Soviet government had even closed our schools? You told me yourself how he asked you to speak up for the Jews!

ZHEMCHUZHINA: I had no such conversation with Mikhoels.

And you said that when Mikhoels visited you he felt as though he was visiting the Rabbi?

ZHEMCHUZHINA: I said no such thing.

Polya, you said the Jews were persecuted under the Tsar and they're still persecuted today, and that the government closed their eyes when they heard about cases of anti-Semitism!

ZHEMCHUZHINA: I deny it.

A large part of Paulina Semyonovna's interrogation was devoted to prurient questions and statements about her sexual life, with frequent accusations of promiscuity and debauchery. She had a particularly painful confrontation with one of her colleagues, Ivan Alexeevich X. The slanders quoted above are little better, but at least these deal ostensibly with 'political' matters, about which a fair amount had already been written in the press, whereas this man's words would simply disgrace his surviving relatives.

QUESTION TO X: In your previous interrogation you revealed that the Central Committee of the All-Russian Communist Party (Bolshevik) received a letter in 1939 which contained certain allegations against you. Who informed you of this letter?

X: Zhemchuzhina. She called me into her office and told me I had been accused of making anti-Soviet remarks.

QUESTION: What measures were taken about this letter?

x: None. Zhemchuzhina just warned me to watch my step in future and not to indulge in any more anti-Soviet remarks.

QUESTION: So Zhemchuzhina took you under her wing?

x: I shall always be grateful to her for that.

QUESTION TO ZHEMCHUZHINA: When did you learn about the letter alleging X.'s anti-Soviet views?

ZHEMCHUZHINA: I know of no letter regarding X., and had no discussions with him on the subject.

x: Paulina Semyonovna, you called me into your office – it will be engraved in my memory for the rest of my life! Such things are never forgotten!

ZHEMCHUZHINA: I repeat, I received no letter regarding X.

QUESTION TO X: How did your relationship with Zhemchuzhina develop?

x: She proposed intimacy.

ZHEMCHUZHINA'S REPLY: Ivan Alexeevich!

x: Paulina Semyonovna, don't deny it! You can't push me away!

QUESTION TO ZHEMCHUZHINA: Whom did you inform of your relationship with X.?

ZHEMCHUZHINA: I informed no one, since I had no relationship with X. I always regarded Ivan Alexeevich as unreliable, and I told him so frankly several times, but I never thought he was a scoundrel.

x: Paulina Semyonovna, how can you call me a scoundrel? Think of my wife and children! If you'd thought about my family then you wouldn't have insulted me!

ZHEMCHUZHINA: Ivan Alexeevich, are you inventing fantasies about me here in the hope of being pardoned and returned to your family? Is this how I should take your plea to think of your family?

x: You won't provoke me, Paulina Semyonovna. I remind you of my children and my broken family to make you admit your guilt towards me and them. Despite the fact that I had a wife and children, you forced me into an intimate relationship . . .

ZHEMCHUZHINA: I repeat, I had no intimate relationship with X. Indeed I often criticised him because people used to say that his naivety and good nature often affected his judgement at work.

At the end of her lengthy interrogation, Paulina Semyonovna denied her connection with the 'Case of the Jewish Nationalists', but admitted herself guilty of:

. . . defending arrested enemies of the people Serebryakova and Belinkov, and Party-workers Dokuchaeva, Gubanova, Fedosova and

Grakhova.[4] The list of enemies of the state defended by me is not limited to those cited in the minutes; there are incomparably more of them, but the passage of time makes it hard for me to remember them all.

The sentence was five years – hardly an exceptional one for the period – in the Kustanai camp in Siberia.

Paulina Semyonovna's files contain several reports on 'Prisoner No. 12' from female secret agents at the camp:

She said she used to live very well, and had a lot of lovely dresses. There was one she specially liked – a bottle-green worsted . . .

We made ravioli together, and she said she had a husband called Vladislav and a little girl called Svetlana. Every year on International Women's Day she celebrates the daughter's birthday . . .

In the first year she drank a lot of vodka and wine . . .

She said she once met Vladimir Ilich Lenin at some congress, I don't remember which . . .

In January 1953 an operations group from the Ministry of State Security arrived at the camp with urgent instructions to transfer Paulina Semyonovna to Moscow, ostensibly since 'Prisoner No. 12 suffers from attacks of tachycardia as a result of experiencing extremes of joy or distress.' In fact Paulina Semyonovna was being returned to the Lubyanka to be charged for her involvement in the 'doctors' plot'.[5] The agents were forbidden to tell 'Prisoner No. 12' the reason for her transfer, but she greeted the news with characteristic stoicism, saying, 'I'm an adult woman, I don't need reasons, it's as the government decides.' When she was searched before the journey to Moscow, she said, 'You can turn everything upside down, but I swear on my daughter's life that you won't find anything criminal. For me the interests of the state come first.' Nothing incriminating was found, of course, though agents removed several notebooks filled with material from the Nineteenth Party congress and résumés of the Marxist-Leninist classics.

Paulina Zhemchuzhina's second term at the Lubyanka opened up yet another circle of hell. Contained in her files are excerpts from the

[4]Most of these women were probably not Jewish.

[5]In January 1953 nine doctors were accused of having assassinated a number of Soviet leaders, the crime apparently being part of a 'Zionist conspiracy'.

interrogations of doctors Vinogradov, Kogan and Vovsi, who all confirmed that she was a Jewish nationalist. The writer Lev Sheinin was the exception in refusing to slander her: 'Zhemchuzhina and her daughter attended a performance of my play *The Duel* at the Lenin Komsomol Theatre. She praised the play and regretted that her husband could not see it since the theatre had no government box.'

Although Paulina Zhemchuzhina's 'criminal' letters were addressed to Molotov and were handed personally to him, her files predictably contain no testimony from the man with whom she had shared twenty-seven years of her life. Where was he all this time? It may be that he was interrogated, but that the interrogations of such important men were not recorded in criminal files. Yet Zhemchuzhina had left him shortly before her arrest, and the question on 'Family Status' in her prison form is marked 'Single'.

Throughout February 1953 Zhemchuzhina was interrogated interminably at the Lubyanka. Then suddenly, on 2 March, it stopped. The day of Stalin's funeral, 9 March 1953, was Molotov's birthday. After stepping down briskly from the tribune of the Mausoleum, Khrushchev and Malenkov went to him and asked him what he wanted for his birthday. 'I want my Polya back!' he said tersely, and left the room with bowed head.

Rumours of Stalin's illness had percolated into the prison, and she must have been the only prisoner in the Gulag who evidently desired his recovery. On 10 March she was summoned to see Beria, who greeted her with the words: 'You're a heroine!' She pushed him away, demanding, 'How is Stalin?' On hearing the news, she fell senseless to the floor. Also present in Beria's office was her husband, Vyacheslav Mikhailovich Molotov.

According to most accounts she was released on 10 March, but her files make it 23 March, in which case Beria must have postdated his signature on the release document. But on this document one phrase is witness to the age: 'It is now established that the statements of Kogan and Vovsi in Zhemchuzhina's case were falsified and extorted through brutality and beatings.'

How simply this is said. Zhemchuzhina's is the only case I have read which contains a confession of torture. Which of us would not confess if beaten or starved? How did they torture Zhemchuzhina, who confessed nothing?

When Zhemchuzhina was arrested everyone assumed that she

would not survive the camps, and her daughter heard nothing from her. Yet despite suffering three heart attacks and undergoing major heart surgery in the seventeen years before her death, people described her as looking better than ever, and all the ailments to which she had been prone seemed suddenly to vanish.

Svetlana Molotova's eldest daughter, Larissa Alexeevna, a translator of English art books and specialist on the art of the Pre-Raphaelites, was six when Zhemchuzhina returned from the camps:

They called me 'Granny's tail'. When she returned I went to live with them, and the Molotovs brought me up. She was devoted to me and took me everywhere, even to Party meetings. She and Grandfather were actively involved in my education. Everything that is good in me is their doing, everything bad is my own. She taught me everything. They developed my memory and comprehension. From an early age they would sit me down in the evenings and make me tell them everything I'd see during the day – the waving trees, the smells. Then I had to repeat it again in German.

Mother was just a big child. She was terribly over-protected when she was young, and never grew up. She took our problems under Khrushchev terribly hard – she read all the lies and it probably hastened her death. She died suddenly of a heart attack . . .

Granny was determined not to repeat the same mistakes with me. 'Life is hard,' she would say. 'Things can change any moment, you must be ready.'

She was like a giant bird, sheltering her nest with her wings. She helped everyone and people would crowd to see her, even when Grandfather was in disgrace under Khrushchev. People saw her as a real lady, kind and considerate.

After 1943 the Molotovs donated their medal coupons to a children's home.[6] (They both had a large number of medals, but didn't advertise the fact.) In 1957, after Grandfather was banished in disgrace to Mongolia, the Foreign Ministry received a telegram from the children's home asking why the money had stopped coming. It was then that they realised that the funds weren't from the Ministry at all but from the Molotovs' own pockets. A few years ago I was at the cemetery and saw an old woman at my grandparents' grave, who turned out to have been a nanny from the children's home. She was bowing from the waist and saying, 'Thank you, Paulina Semyonovna! Thank you,

[6]People received coupons for medals then, and these could be exchanged for cash.

Vyacheslav Mikhailovich! You were holy people. While you were alive the orphans did not die!'

Granny could endure anything. She went off to jail in a squirrel fur coat, and she came back in the same coat, now in tatters. All she would say of her experiences was, 'You need three things there: soap to keep you clean, bread to keep you fed, and onions to keep you well.'

The moment she returned she collapsed onto the sofa in the dining room where she lay for six months, and from the sofa she directed the house. Her hands had started shaking, but she tried to control it by doing needlework. She often said she had always believed that Grandfather would save her, and we would all be happy again. Their love was an exceptional thing. They never shared their pain, and their actions always matched their words. She created a splendid domestic routine for him − neither of them ever raised their voice or swore, he would just say, 'I'm sorry we quarrelled, Polenka, I was wrong.'

When asked why Molotov did not defend her, Paulina Semyonovna's younger granddaughter, Lyubov Alexeevna, says,

He thought that by speaking up for her he would destroy her. Those government men were all hostages!

She was the dynamo of the family, the spirit of the house. She taught us grandchildren everything: cooking, sewing, knitting. She taught her own servant, a simple country girl, to be an excellent cook, and she waged an incessant war in the house for cleanness and order. If she decided something, that was how it was done. She was an incomparably stronger character than Grandfather, of course − he lived by her rules. Meals were served at exactly the same time every day, with certain foods on certain days. On Wednesdays there were always milk noodles − come hell or high water there were always milk noodles. It was a family tradition for meals to be quickly served and cleared away. When Stalin ate with them he used to say, 'I never have enough time for my food. Eat with me and we'll take our time.'

In some ways her routine was a bit hard on Grandfather, but he put up with it because he needed her to organise his life for him.

Paulina Semyonovna and Vyacheslav Mikhailovich loved each other very deeply. They didn't coo over each other, but they were real lovers. I've never seen two people so much in love. Grandfather always came first for her, then us . . .

She never spoke of prison and the camps, I only found out about it after she died. She dedicated her life to the Party. In her last years she would summon up her last strength to attend meetings. Her faith in its ideals was totally genuine, without hypocrisy.

Excluded from power by Khrushchev, and suffering for her husband, Zhemchuzhina despised the post-Stalin government for its treachery and fired off a series of letters demanding a range of privileges including an increased pension and access to a dacha outside the town. 'You don't respect him, but at least I was a people's commissar and member of the Central Committee,' she said. As a result the Molotovs were allowed a ministerial dacha in Zhukovka, and in 1967 their pension was increased to 250 roubles.

All who knew Paulina Zhemchuzhina confirm that she remained passionately devoted to Stalin's memory. After he was unmasked in the late-fifties, she told his daughter, Svetlana, 'Your father was a genius. He destroyed the fifth column in our country, so when war came the Party and people were united.' Puzzled by this loyalty, Svetlana recalled how Paulina Semyonovna always added finely chopped onion to her borshch, saying, 'That's how Stalin liked it!'

She died on 1 May 1970. Her elder granddaughter, Larissa, recalled:

> Just before her death she had a manicure. As she lay dying she called out to Vyacheslav Mikhailovich. Years later, when I sat by his deathbed, he mistook me for her, calling, 'Polya, Polya!'

All who met the widowed Molotov in the last years of his long life confirm his undying devotion to his wife's memory. Many years after her death, Felix Chuev recalled:

> On the November 7th holiday Vyacheslav Mikhailovich would produce cognac and pour it out, crying, 'Lenin – One! Stalin – Two! Paulina Semyonovna – Three!' And smash the bottle.

He told Chuev:

> It was my great joy to have Paulina Semyonovna as my wife. Not only was she beautiful and clever, she was a true Bolshevik, a true Soviet person. Life treated her badly because she was my wife, yet despite her sufferings she never blamed Stalin, and refused to listen to those who did, for history will discard those who blacken his name.

Paulina Zhemchuzhina's life, so characteristic of the interwoven faith and lies of the Stalin era, has passed almost unnoticed into history. Who was she, Party machine or woman? Among all the reports and interrogations contained in her files there is a small piece of paper covered in her handwriting:

> With these four years of separation four eternities have flowed over my strange and terrible life. Only the thought of you forces me to live, and the knowledge that you may still need the remnants of my tormented heart and the whole of my huge love for you . . .

To whom were these words addressed? To her daughter? To her husband, who could not defend her? Or to Stalin? 'Only the thought of you', 'My huge love' – such phrases conjure up a worthy but evil hero, a dark passion.

Zhemchuzhina's granddaughters say that after Molotov's death, and even during *perestroika*, they were visited by secret service agents who took away numerous papers with them. One wonders what these papers contain and where they are today. They might help to cast light on this powerful and contradictory figure. Even discounting the possibility that Paulina Semyonovna loved Stalin, the Stalin–Zhemchuzhina–Molotov triangle conceals explosive passions of Shakespearean dimensions. All her life she thought and acted in unison with Stalin, she even appeared to 'understand' his persecution of the Jews. Perhaps she felt no cause to forgive him for her arrest, since she considered herself guilty. Perhaps it was easier for her to accept her own guilt than his, since to acknowledge his injustice would mean to destroy her ideals. Perhaps she knew everything, understood everything, hated everything and suffered. We may never know.

II

Bluebeard's Women – The Girl in the Apricot Cloud

Lavrenty Pavlovich Beria (1899–1953). Son of a Georgian peasant. In 1915 he attended Baku technical school, and in 1917 he joined the Bolsheviks. In 1921 he became head of the Georgian, then the Transcaucasus security police. In 1931 he was appointed first secretary of the Transcaucasus Party, and in 1935 he went to Moscow, where three years later he replaced Ezhov as head of the Ministry of Internal Affairs (the NKVD). He started by purging the police, and went on to establish a regime based on torture, terrorism and forced labour. In 1945 he was appointed Marshal, and put in charge of Soviet Russia's atomic research programme. After Stalin's death, he was arrested and shot in mysterious circumstances.

The prisoner is being interrogated by the Prosecutor:

QUESTION: Do you confess to the charges of criminal depravity against you?

REPLY: Some of them, yes.

QUESTION: And that your criminal depravity led you to associate with women attached to foreign intelligence agencies?

REPLY: Maybe, I don't know.

QUESTION: And that you instructed Sarkisov and Nadaria to keep lists of your mistresses? We have here nine lists containing the names of sixty-two women. Were these the lists of your mistresses?

REPLY: Most of the women were my mistresses, yes.

QUESTION: Were you infected with syphilis?

REPLY: I caught syphilis during the war, in 1943 I think, and had treatment.

The prisoner is then charged with raping a fourteen-year-old schoolgirl, who has his baby; the prisoner states that it happened by mutual consent.

Who is this prisoner? A medieval monster? A modern sex maniac? Leader of a gang of rapists? No, this was Hero of Soviet Labour Lavrenty Beria, Marshal of the Soviet Union, Minister of Internal Affairs of the USSR, Politburo member of the Central Committee of the Russian Communist Party (Bolshevik), deputy President of the Soviet of Ministers.

Beria's lengthy trial parades before us the mass murders committed over the course of several decades, the horrifying acts of lawlessness, betrayal and brutality. Coming right at the end, as is usual in such cases, are the little details which complete this picture of depravity: women.

Amid the flowers and crêpe-de-Chine brightness of post-World War II Moscow the air was thick with anxiety, and mothers would warn their daughters not to talk to anyone on the streets for fear of Beria's Cheka bandits, who were known to prowl the capital snatching girls to bring back to his mansion; one was said to have been abducted near the Theatre of the Red Army, where we lived.

Khrushchev's son-in-law, Alexei Adzhubei, writes:

Beria's house was on the corner of Sadovo-Triumfalnaya and Kachalov streets, not far from Uprising Square. The building stood back from the street, concealed by a high stone wall. The sentries standing guard outside would watch everyone passing, and Muscovites would quicken their step and keep quiet.

Adzhubei describes attending a party in 1947 to celebrate the engagement of Beria's son Sergo to the beautiful Marfa Peshkov, granddaughter of the writer Alexei Maximovich Gorky.

Marfa and the groom sat stiffly at the table, the guests seemed not to be enjoying themselves much, and only Marfa's younger sister Darya, a theatre student, let herself go . . .

Shortly after this Beria moved his mistress into the house. When I see L. now it strikes me that beauty and wickedness are quite compatible . . : She was seventeen years old then, and had a child by him. People said the girl's mother made a fuss and slapped Beria in the face. The girl settled in comfortably and the mother evidently grew used to it too. His wife, Nina Teimurazovna, tolerated her presence – she obviously had no choice.

There are many mysteries surrounding the evil name of Beria, and much has been embellished by past generations, but the greatest mystery of all is that of his wife, Nina Teimurazovna.

One evening during the interval at the Bolshoi Theatre I saw a woman of unearthly beauty slipping with a shy, distracted smile through a ring of soldiers. Her hair was golden, her features were sweet and gentle, and her dress was an airy, apricot cloud, flowing, rippling and floating about her body. This was Nina Teimurazovna Beria. As I watched this lovely creature all the rumours about Beria floated from my unconscious. With such a wife? Impossible! Why would a proud and beautiful woman endure such humiliation for the sake of the material privileges it brought her.

Thaddeus Wittlin's biography of Beria, *Commissar*, published during the seventies in the United States and recently translated into Russian, contains a lurid account of Nina Teimurazovna's first meeting with Beria:

During his stay in Abkhazia, Beria lived on his luxurious special train, in which he had travelled to Sukhumi. It was switched onto a siding some distance from the station building. The train consisted of three Pullman cars: a sleeper, a saloon car equipped with bar, and a restaurant car. The evening before Beria planned to depart for Tbilisi, he was approached near the station by a young girl of about sixteen years of age, of medium height, with black eyes and a creamy white complexion. The girl had come from her Mingrelian village neighbouring Beria's to plead for her arrested brother . . .

Beria noticed the beauty of the girl. Asking for more details about her brother he invited her into his train – but not to the saloon or the restaurant. In his sleeping car he told the girl to undress. When, frightened, she started to leave the car, Beria locked the door. Then he slapped her face, twisted her arms behind her back, pushed her onto the bed and pressed her down heavily with his body. The fragile girl was overpowered and raped. A few minutes after everything was over, Beria let her go. He could now order a guard to take the little waif to jail, or he could just kick her out onto the railroad track. But looking at her beautiful, tear-streaked face, Beria knew that in less than half an hour he would desire her again. He locked her up in the compartment and went to the restaurant car for supper and some vodka.

Beria kept the girl all night. The next morning he told his orderly to bring breakfast for two. Later, before leaving for his duties, Lavrenty locked up his victim again. Beria was not only spellbound by the freshness and charm of the girl, he realised that she was the type who appealed completely to his senses. She was young and innocent, but looked mature. She was delicate but by no means thin. She had small breasts, big eyes that cast demure glances and a full, ripe mouth. Lavrenty realised that it would be stupid of him to throw such a creature away right now.

Beria spent a few more days in Sukhumi to supervise the progress of the Five-Year Plan for the improvement of the country roads and highways, and the construction of new dwellings, hospitals and schools. Throughout this time he kept his prisoner locked in the train . . . Thus little Nina became his wife.

Wittlin has merely lifted this episode from Svetlana Stalin's book *Only One Year*, and embellished it. And although Svetlana Stalin's accounts of her own experiences are an invaluable source of information, her version of the Kremlin legends which others have told her often appear closer to disinformation.

Ekaterina Sergeevna Katukova's description of Nina Teimurazovna, whom she met several times in Karlovy Vary during the 1930s, appears closer to the truth:

She had golden hair with a coppery tinge, huge brown eyes, thick eyelashes curling upwards like a doll's, a delicate complexion and a good figure marred by slightly crooked legs. She dressed beautifully. One dress of hers was incredibly lovely, it was made from twenty-five metres of chiffon. She never wore diamonds – no one wore diamonds in those days. She and I would play tennis together. She was an excellent tennis-player. Sometimes she would play with her guards. Her husband didn't allow her to play with strange men. In Karlovy Vary I would run off to drink the waters, but she always had to be driven there. He didn't let her mix with other people. Her luxury villa was surrounded on all sides by guards. She wasn't allowed to do anything. She was very close to her son . . .

She took great care of herself. I was once given some face cream which I shared with her, then forgot about. In Dresden I often helped visiting ministers' wives to buy tea sets, hats and furs, and if they hadn't finished their shopping they would leave me the money and I would post the things off to them with the receipts. I never heard a word of thanks from Zhemchuzhina or Khrushcheva, but Nina Teimurazovna telephoned me the minute she got back to Moscow, thanking me for the face cream and inviting me to their dacha in Barvikh. When I arrived she was bicycling in the yard, with a soldier behind and a soldier in front. It was like a cage . . .

In Dresden she once said to me, 'I keep looking at you and admiring the way your husband loves you.'

'What, doesn't your husband love you?'

'I'm terribly unhappy. Lavrenty's never at home. I'm always alone . . .'

Everyone who knew Beria's wife in those years agrees that she was a good, kind and desperately unhappy person. People at the Timiryazev Agricultural Academy, where she worked, remember her for her kindness. Since Kremlin wives were not allowed to intervene in politics she was obviously unable to do much, but various attacks against agriculture were softened thanks to her influence, and her teacher, Academician Pryanishnikov, was spared.

In 1990 Nina Teimurazovna Beria was eighty-six years old and living in a small flat in Kiev which she rarely left. Bilingual in Russian and Georgian, she chose to speak in Georgian when interviewed by journalist Teimuraza Koridze in *Sovershenno Sekretno* (*Top Secret*) newspaper.

I was born into a poor family. After Father died it was terribly hard for Mother. You could count the rich families in Georgia on the fingers of one hand then. They were anxious times – revolutions, riots, political parties. I grew up with my uncle, Sasha Gegechkori, who took me in to help Mother. We lived in Kutaisi, and I went to the first women's school there. Sasha often went to prison for his revolutionary activities, and his wife Vera used to take me to visit him. I was young and it fascinated me. My future husband was in the same cell as Sasha. I didn't notice him, but he apparently remembered me.

After Soviet power was set up in Georgia, Sasha was transferred to Tbilisi and elected president of the Tbilisi revolutionary committee. I went with them.

I was already grown up by then, and Vera and I didn't get on. I remember I had one pair of good shoes, and she told me not to wear them every day so they'd last longer. I always walked to school by the back streets so people wouldn't notice my clothes.

In the first days of Soviet power I joined a student demonstration against the Bolsheviks. They turned the water cannon on us and I ran home soaked. When Sasha's wife found out what had happened she grabbed a strap and thrashed me, shouting, 'You live with Sasha Gegechkori – you don't join demonstrations against him!'

Once, on the way to school, I met Beria. After Soviet power came to

Georgia he was always visiting Sasha. He insisted that I talk to him, saying, 'We'll have to talk sooner or later, like it or not!'

I agreed, and we met in Tbilisi's Nadzaladevi Park. My sister and brother-in-law lived in that part of town, so I knew the park well. We sat on a bench. He wore a long black overcoat and student cap. He told me he'd been watching me for a long time, and that he liked me very much. Then he said he loved me, and he wanted me to marry him.

I was sixteen-and-a-half then, and he was twenty-two.[1] He told me the new government was sending him to Belgium to learn about petroleum extraction, but only on condition that he was married. I thought about it and agreed. It seemed better to be married and have my own family than to live in someone else's home, even if they were relatives. So without telling anyone, I married Lavrenty. The rumours immediately started that he'd abducted me. Nothing of the sort happened. I married him of my own free will.

Her indifference to her future husband appears truthful: she married him to have a home of her own. So either the three Pullman carriages and the rape scene at Sukhumi were dreamed up, or Nina Teimurazovna is lying to protect her husband. This seems hardly likely: Beria was a family friend of the Gegechkoris and several people who knew them then are still alive. Besides, why should she lie about her youth, at such an advanced age? In order to soften his posthumous reputation?

In 1926 I graduated from the Agronomy Faculty at Tbilisi University and worked as a scientist at Tbilisi's agricultural institute. We never did go abroad. First Lavrenty postponed our trip, then problems cropped up and he was up to his eyes in government work. We lived poorly, like everyone else then. It was considered wrong to live well, because the Revolution had been made against the rich.

In 1931 Lavrenty was made First Secretary of the Central Committee of the Georgian Communist Party. He was out at work day and night and had almost no time for his family. It's easy to criticise him now, but there were fierce battles going on. Soviet power had to win. You remember what Stalin wrote about the enemies of socialism? Those enemies really existed.

The inventory of Beria's office, taken after his arrest, reveal the following items:

[1] Nina Teimurazovna, like Nadezhda Alliluyeva, was under the legal age of consent.

Ladies' stockings of foreign make – 11 pairs.
Ladies' silk combinations – 11 pairs.
Ladies' silk vests – 7 pairs.
Ladies' sports outfits.
Ladies' blouses.
Material samples for ladies' dresses.
Ladies' silk scarves and handkerchiefs of foreign make.
Countless intimate letters from women.
A large quantity of items of male debauchery.

One can only guess what these last might be; the lexicon of Party and Cheka *apparatchiks*, serving always to veil the real meaning of words in euphemisms, evidently collapsed in this search for words.

Before being executed the prisoner admitted his 'criminal moral depravity', and his dark deeds with women were well authenticated at the time. He was said to rape young women prisoners in his office and shoot them to stop them from talking, or select the younger ones for special attention. In the 1940s the KGB organised stenography courses for which young, pretty women were picked; many later described these courses as Beria's secret harem, and those still alive today say that the things that went on there would scar you for life.

Even the daughter-in-law of the virtually all-powerful Voroshilov was afraid of this man so recently arrived in power. In the summer of 1941, Nadezhda Voroshilova was walking down the street towards the Kremlin with the Voroshilovs' niece, Valya, when a black car slowed down and crawled along the kerb behind them, and a KGB agent jumped out towards them, shouting, 'Hey, haven't I seen you before?'

> Valya turned off towards the TASS building, and I walked on in silence, with the colonel pursuing me, still shouting. I had heard of Beria's debauchery, and how his colonels would snatch women off the street, and I quickened my step. The man kept up with me, the car crawled on behind, I ran, desperate to reach the Kremlin, where he would surely turn back. He ran, the car speeded up, people turned to look. When finally I reached the gates of the Kremlin I looked around, and sure enough he was gone.
>
> At home after I'd caught my breath I told Ekaterina Davidovna. I expected her to laugh, but instead she looked at me with terror in her eyes, saying, 'It's Beria! Say nothing! Don't tell a soul!'

Nadezhda Voroshilova explains:

Everyone was afraid of everything then, every one of us had some family tragedy. Stalin and the NKVD made everyone feel guilty of something, regardless of their position in society. All of us had someone in prison. With the Voroshilovs it was my parents, with Kaganovich it was his brother, with Budyonny his wife. Everyone bore the stigma of jail – it was policy.

Thaddeus Wittlin's book *Commissar*, written for Western consumption, paints a lurid picture of Beria's adventures:

His car usually stopped near the Soviet Army Theatre, where a girls' high school was located. Soon after two o'clock the girls would leave the building for their homes. From behind a curtain half covering his car's greenish windows, Beria would observe the girls like a prowling panther watching a herd of young does . . . When he spotted a plump girl of fourteen or fifteen years old, with rosy pink cheeks and lips moist as the morning dew, Beria would jerk his chin in her direction and Colonel Sarkisov would leave the car and start towards the chosen girl . . . From his car, often using field-glasses, Beria could see terror flash into the eyes of his horrified victim . . .

Actresses and dancers were especially defenceless against the KGB machine. The singer Zoya Fyodorova was picked up one night by one of Beria's officers, who told her they were going to a large party. She later told her friend Ekaterina Katukova how she was driven to a dacha and led into the dining room, where a table was laid for two.

'Where are the others?' she demanded.

'Don't worry, they'll come,' he said, and disappeared.

Zoya had just given birth to a baby daughter, and her milk was leaking, her head ached and her nerves were at breaking-point. Finally Beria came in. Zoya said, 'If there are no more guests, let me go.'

'Aren't we going to have a little chat?' he said.

'The milk's burning in my breasts, I have to feed my baby and you talk rubbish to me!' she shouted.

Beria was furious and called an officer to take Zoya away. Another officer, evidently misunderstanding what had happened, handed her a bunch of flowers at the door. When Beria saw, he shouted, 'May they rot on your grave!' She was arrested shortly afterwards.

Zoya Fyodorova's murder in Moscow at the age of seventy-six was the subject of much talk at the time. Less well-known is the fate of the film star Tatyana Okunevskaya.

Women of our mothers' generation still remember the lively, temperamental beauty of Tatyana Okunevskaya, whose severe brow and dazzling smile ruled men's dreams and stared down from giant hoardings in every Russian town. Her first serious film part, as the heroine of Maupassant's *Boule de Suif*, was followed by various classical and revolutionary stage roles. But it was the film *Hot Days* which turned her into a star. At the end of the war she starred in the popular Yugoslav partisan film *Night over Belgrade*, and she would end her concerts at the front with the film's hymn-like battle-song: 'The flame of anger burns in our breast . . .'

By the end of the war Tatyana Okunevskaya and her husband, Stalin Prize-winning novelist Boris Gorbatov, were regarded as one of the most brilliant couples in Moscow. They began to be invited to foreign receptions at embassies, including the Yugoslav embassy, where the handsome young ambassador invited her to Yugoslavia to attend the opening night of *Night over Belgrade*. The highlight of her visit was a concert for Marshal Tito and his staff. The concert was a dazzling success, and next day she met Tito alone. In her unpublished memoirs she writes:

> I was driven to the court of the king who had abandoned Communism. Through an ordinary gate walked Marshal Tito. At the concert he had been in uniform, now he was dressed in civilian clothes. In one hand he carried a pair of secateurs, in the other a large bunch of black roses.
> At the Marshal's feet lay a splendid sheepdog, gazing into my eyes. Tito said, 'Now we'll see how you feel about me – if it's bad, Rex will rip you to shreds! I can read his mind.'

A strange, unpleasant joke. Since the Marshal was meeting the actress who had sung the praises of their countries' friendship, the intimidating tone is puzzling. But Okunevskaya accepted everything with undaunted enthusiasm:

> Tito then led me into dinner. Two dozen members of his General Staff rose from a huge square table to welcome us, shoulder to shoulder, tall, young and handsome in their magnificent braided uniforms. I was seated in the centre on an antique high-backed chair, like a princess.

Later, during Tito's visit to Moscow, a lavish reception was organised in his honour, at which the Yugoslav leader crossed the floor to ask Tatyana Okunevskaya to dance. As they danced he told her that his people would never forgive him if he married a foreign woman, but he begged her to come to Belgrade, promising that he would build her her own studio there and let her live and work as she liked. The romance went no further, and was followed by a brief and stormy affair with the Yugoslav ambassador.

But by 1945 Tatyana Okunevskaya's other life was catching up with her. When I visited her in her small apartment on Petrovo-Razumovsky Street she told me about the very different existence concealed behind her glamorous life as a star: about her father, an officer before the Revolution, who was jailed in the 1930s and shot, and about her brother and grandmother, who perished in the camps. Pursued by the shadow of her criminal relatives, she had allowed herself too many liberties, turning the head of Marshal Tito, who turned out himself to be an 'enemy of the people', then sleeping with his ambassador. The spiral of her misfortunes started with an invitation to a private concert at the Kremlin, where People's Artists and the friends and mistresses of the leaders were to perform.

> I was told these concerts were held late at night to relax the leaders after their meetings. I was to be collected by Beria himself. Boris wasn't in Moscow then – all journalists were in Germany attending the Nuremberg Trials. I felt a strange sensation of dread . . .
>
> A colonel escorted me to a car, and I got into the back beside Beria. I recognised him at once. He was ugly, flabby and unhealthy-looking, with a greyish-yellow complexion. He told me the meeting at the Kremlin hadn't yet ended, and we would have to wait at his house.
>
> Once inside, the colonel vanished. There was a table laden with food. I said I never ate before a concert and I certainly never drank, but he insisted, Georgian fashion, virtually pouring the wine into my lap. He ate greedily, tearing at the food with his hands, chattering away and begging me to take a sip.
>
> After a while he stood up and slipped silently through one of the doors. All sounds were muffled, even the traffic from the Sadovo ring-road . . . By now it was three in the morning – our dinner had lasted two hours. He came back, drank more wine and paid me banal compliments, telling me that a certain Koba, who had never seen me in person, wanted very much to do so. I wondered who Koba was . . .[2]

[2] Koba was Stalin's Georgian nickname.

He slipped out again. I had heard they worked until dawn, but I was exhausted. Coming back he announced that the meeting had ended, but that Koba was so tired the concert had to be postponed. I stood up and asked to leave. He said that now I must drink, and that if I didn't he would not let me go. I drank. Grabbing me, he pushed me through yet another door. Dribbling repulsively in my ear, he whispered that we would have a little rest, then I would be taken home. I remembered nothing more.

When I came to, all was quiet. Nobody was there. The door opened silently and a woman appeared and led me back to the room where I had spent the previous evening. A table laid for breakfast floated into my consciousness, and a clock said ten o'clock. I went out, climbed into a waiting car and returned home. I had been raped. Something terrible, irrevocable, had happened. I felt numb.

Shortly after this, Tatyana Okunevskaya was arrested.

I was ill in bed with a high fever. Boris was rushing around preparing to leave on a journey somewhere. Finally he left, and my chauffeur came in and told me the yard was full of soldiers. Two of them came in, and said, 'You're under arrest!' I realised then that Boris knew everything and had been making his escape.

Tatyana Okunevskaya wrote later to the Procurator General:

When I was arrested the minister said, 'You can see she needs a bit of punishment!' And, 'Just think, what beauty, what intelligence and talent – everyone admires you, and I've arrested you!'

They shouted that I was a whore, that I held orgies, that I danced naked on the table and men played cards on my stomach. They wouldn't let me say anything – they just kept asking about Tito and his dog, and whether I believed in God.

The questions and evidence contained in Okunevskaya's two weighty files at the Lubyanka insult the dignity of every woman with their prurient interrogation into the intimate details of her sexual life. These files, like those of Olga Budyonnaya, Ekaterina Kalinina and Paulina Zhemchuzhina, contain no evidence from her husband. Boris Gorbatov lived in the same town, just a ten-minute bus ride away. He could have been summoned and interrogated, and might well have eased her fate.

Her letter to the Procurator continues:

One night during the interrogation I was called out and driven off to another prison, where I was thrown into a freezing, pitch-dark cellar.

'Take your clothes off!' they said.

I thought I had misheard, but I hadn't. I stripped naked and stood barefoot on the icy floor. I held my stockings so I could put them on later, but they took them away and gave me back just my dress and shoes.

I lost track of the hours – the only thing left was the bread they brought me once a day. At four on the first day they threw down a board for me to lie on, and its iron clamps froze my legs. After my third piece of bread they took me out into the freezing yard and led me to interrogator Sokolov. I was not allowed to wash, and my face was black with dirt. I was also menstruating, and as they had taken away my handkerchief and cotton-wool I was soaked in blood. Sokolov looked at me and asked me how I felt. Understanding everything, I said, 'Wonderful!'

The charges finally brought against Tatyana Okunevskaya were as follows:

> . . . conducting virulent anti-Soviet discussions with her acquaintances, criticising the policies of the Party and the Soviet government, praising the bourgeois order, worshipping the conditions of life in the capitalist countries and systematically meeting with foreigners.

Thirteen months of solitary confinement were followed by the camps at Dzhezkazgan, where Tatyana Okunevskaya felled timber in the frozen forests. The women in her cell were mainly local leaders' wives, who assumed that she must be in for some crime, but she was loved by the people with whom she worked at the camp's forests and building sites. 'It was the ordinary people who saved me,' she writes in her memoirs:

> There, where everything is designed to turn a person into an animal, where a mother snatches bread from her daughter, and the daughter pushes the mother into the ditch, a woman with the eyes of an icon approached me in my darkest hour and said, 'The women want you to have this kerchief – cover your face with it or you'll freeze.'

Some time after Beria's downfall Tatyana Okunevskaya was finally released. She roamed Russia with nowhere to live, trying to adjust to her freedom. All her films had been withdrawn, and Gorbatov, who had divorced her and remarried, was now dead.

In old age Okunevskaya is a slim, elegant woman who keeps fit with daily gymnastics. The insignificant men who insulted her beautiful body are now in the ground, and only the memory of Beria survives.

Kremlin wives too were vulnerable to Beria's tactics. He arrested Komsomol leader Alexander Kosarev in person. Kosarev's wife, Maria Viktorovna, threw herself at his feet, crying, 'Sasha, come back!' Beria then arrested her too, and she spent seventeen years in a camp.

Fifteen-year-old Anna Mikhailovna Larina first met Beria during a visit to Georgia with her parents when he was head of the Georgian secret police.

> Sitting at his desk, Beria said to my father, 'I never knew you had such a lovely little girl!' I blushed with shame, and my father said, 'I don't see anything lovely about her!'
> Beria turned to his aide, saying, 'Mikha, let's drink to the health of this lovely little girl! A long and healthy life to her!'

When Anna Mikhailovna met Beria again four years later in Batumi, he again praised her beauty; her third meeting took place in 1938 in his office at NKVD headquarters, where the newly appointed People's Commissar had summoned her after the arrest of her husband, Nikolai Bukharin.

> 'I must say you've become extraordinarily beautiful since I last saw you.'
> 'What a paradox, Lavrenty Pavlovich – after ten years in jail you'll be able to send me to Paris for a beauty contest!'
> After a short pause, he suddenly said, 'Tell me, why do you love Nikolai Ivanovich?'
> I avoided the question, saying love was a purely personal matter and didn't have to be justified to anyone.

Beria sentenced Larina to fifteen years in a camp. When he summoned twenty-three-year-old Glafira Blukher, wife of the jailed Marshal Blukher, he did not threaten her or question her about her husband, he just looked at her.

> Beria conducted the interrogation himself, clearly out of simple sadistic curiosity. His appearance was repulsive and his demeanour was haughty. He conveyed an utter indifference to his victim's humanity – as though he was peering through a magnifying glass at a tiny insect.

After five months in solitary confinement, Glafira Blukher was transferred to the Butyrki prison, then to the Karaganda camps.

The stories of those victims who managed to outwit Beria make more cheerful reading. One woman wrote to me describing how in 1938 she worked at a secret factory outside Moscow, and when replacing a sick typist she addressed an envelope not to Stalingrad but to Stalin*gad*.[3]

> I never meant to call Stalin a swine, but they arrested me anyway and harassed me with endless questions about the envelope, demanding that I tell them which organisation I belonged to and who I was spying for. The interrogator later said, 'For heaven's sake, why didn't you leave out the "g"? That would have made it Stalin*rad*,[4] and everything would be OK.'
>
> I was a good-looking girl, although my looks were a bit too perfect – cold as a statue and thin, the Venus de Milo come to life. After six months in jail I was suddenly taken off in the middle of the night, driven to the railway station, bundled into a carriage and locked in. We travelled for what seemed like an eternity, then the carriage was shunted off to a siding and some Cheka agents came and pushed me blindfolded into a car. I managed to peer through the blindfold and saw that we were driving out of a large building, which I recognised as Moscow station.
>
> The car stopped and they untied the blindfold. We were in a forest, at the edge of a snow-covered clearing bordered by a straight line of fir trees and a giant oak. Before us stood a large dacha. Two soldiers led me in and untied my hands. I sat down in a big armchair and looked around. The sofas and chairs were draped in white canvas covers, a reproduction of Perov's 'Huntsmen at the Stopping-Place' hung on the wall. I became calmer. A door led into another room. I tried it but it was locked. It opened, and out jumped a monkey in a short dressing-gown. He had dark hairy legs, crooked knees and *pince-nez*, just like in the photographs. The monkey smiled and said in a hoarse, high-pitched voice, 'I've decided to interview you myself. You make mistakes in important letters. You say it's an accident? Rumours of your beauty have reached Moscow, but you're even better in the flesh!'
>
> Sitting down beside me on the sofa, the monkey began to scrutinise me, but I was no longer afraid. I knew why I had been brought here, but

---

[3] In Russian this comes out as 'Stalin swine'.
[4] 'Stalin happy'.

it was plain that my looks did not appeal to him. Men liked women to be plump then, and I never had any luck with them.

'Shall I take my dress off, or will I do as I am?' I asked him. 'I haven't washed for a week.'

The monkey flashed his gold teeth and frowned. He didn't like this. I threw off my rags and stood before him. The room was hot, but without the warmth of those rags my skin was covered in goose-pimples. As I stood there, shivering, I saw myself from a distance. My collarbone stuck out, my stomach caved in, my breasts sagged. The monkey stepped back, evidently revolted. I saw that he wanted to leave, and heard myself say, 'Sit down.'

We had a long talk. I am good at drawing people out, and I seemed to awaken the human being in him. He told me how tired he was, and that nobody understood him at home – thankfully he didn't tell me about his wife's gynaecological problems.

'Your crime's nothing,' he said with his slightly Georgian accent. 'I just wanted to see you for myself. Let's keep our meeting a secret. Be a clever girl and don't say a word about this to anyone.'

He left the room. Pulling on my rags, I stretched out on the sofa and fell into a deep sleep, oblivious to whether I was dirtying the government chair-covers with my prison filth. I was woken next morning by a soldier who led me to the next room. There I was given something hot, good and simple to eat, as well as an old but respectable overcoat. I was then driven to the centre of Moscow and left there with a train ticket and a note, in which the monkey wished me success in the building of Communism. It was unsigned.

For years afterwards I would scan the newspapers for this freak's progress up the crooked ladder of success.

When I returned to work a few people looked askance at me – few came back from prison in those days. But I had betrayed no one, and they all knew why I had been arrested. Beria left me alone not so much because I wasn't his type, but because in 1939 he was at the start of his career and not entirely sure of himself yet. Also, I was twenty-six then, and it must have been obvious to him that I wasn't a virgin. He preferred innocent girls, who would be afraid and cry at his sadism. He didn't do anything to me, yet I felt the danger from him – the danger of a man with limitless power, who can do whatever he likes.

Beria's shadow hovered wherever bright young women were found. Here is the story of an ordinary Moscow woman, now in her sixties, who fell into Beria's clutches in the summer of 1952 when she was an innocent twenty-one-year-old student. She and her two girlfriends had just received their graduation diplomas from the Institute of Foreign Languages, and were walking cheerfully down Kachalov Street.

I was wearing a coral-coloured dress with little white flowers, and a string of pearls around my neck. I don't know if I was pretty, but I had gleaming white teeth and a nice smile which everyone noticed. Outside the large building where Beria lived stood a group of men – Beria was with them too, but our thoughts were elsewhere.

I left my friends at the corner of Kachalov and Sadovo-Triumfalnaya streets, and as I stopped at the ring-road crossing to catch the trolleybus home, I was approached by a soldier. I later learned that this was Colonel Sarkisov, Beria's chief procurer of women.

'I want a word with you,' he said. 'You've been invited to see someone.' I recalled seeing Beria a minute ago on the pavement.

'That man wants to see you. He's inviting you to dinner.'

'But Comrade Stalin warns us to be vigilant!' I babbled.

'You saw who I was with,' the colonel repeated, shaking with laughter at my words. 'There's nothing to be afraid of. He's quite safe. He's been watching you. He wants to help you.'

I had my diploma and the offer of a teaching job – what more could I want? I was afraid, mortally afraid. The colonel and I stood for a long time talking at the crossroads, then we crossed the Sadovoe and argued for another fifteen minutes on the other side. He kept repeating that 'that man' (he never once mentioned his name) wanted to help me.

I kept repeating, 'But Comrade Stalin warns us to be vigilant!' This did not stop him. 'It won't harm you to come – it'll harm you more not to. Who do you live with?'

'My mother.'

'Right, we know where you live.'

My head thumped, and I felt even more afraid.

'We know all about you. We'll come around in the car at nine and wait outside the main entrance. There's nothing to be afraid of. You're in no danger.'

He left, and I caught the trolleybus home. A '*seksot*' maniac[5] jumped up behind me on the bus, accompanied me to my stop and escorted me home in broad daylight. After checking the number of my apartment, he ran downstairs. From the sitting-room window, I saw him climbing into a black motorcar, which drove off at speed.

[5]Special services agent.

Mama was at work. I sat in the room, my head aching. Three girls had been walking down the street, and I had been picked. Why? Somehow the most primitive, honest reason never occurred to me, for I had been brought up to believe that all people were good, and that bad ones existed only in books.

As nine o'clock approached, I took out my new blue silk suit, the pride of my wardrobe, and ironed it. I assumed we would probably talk about work, and thinking that he might offer me a really good job, I pinned my Komsomol badge to my lapel.

At nine o'clock I saw the black car through the window and went out. The colonel was standing on the pavement, and I saw anxiety in his eyes as he looked at me, as though he was worried I might not get in the car. When I did, he relaxed and told me we were going to pass the new University building which was just about to be opened. He said he'd helped to build it himself, and that it was thanks to 'that man' that there was a new University building in Moscow.

The car stopped by the low wall between the Moscow river and the University, and the colonel suggested that we get out.

'You saw who I was standing with,' he started again. 'That man very much wants to see you.'

'What then?' I asked.

The colonel started singing: 'You'll live in a wonderful apartment. You haven't a telephone? You'll have a telephone. Where does your mother work?'

'The Planning Institute. Look, we don't need anything. We have everything we want. I want to know why you need me.' And I repeated yet again Comrade Stalin's senseless warning to be vigilant. I could see I bored him terribly.

'We've been watching you for a long time. You're just the sort of needy, modest person "that man" likes to help. You'll get a good job.'

'What do I have to do?'

This question excited him; he evidently imagined I'd understood him, whereas of course I still hadn't understood a thing.

'We'll get in the car and go back to the building where we met. It's quite late – this will take some time.'

These words brought me to my senses a little. Mother would be anxiously waiting for me by now.

We got into the car and it shot off to Beria's villa. Inside, the colonel pushed me through a small door and quickly locked it behind me. I was alone in a vast, thickly carpeted room with a long table, high-backed leather chairs, and maroon blinds over the windows.

Beria entered like a cat, and, drawing up a leather chair for himself, he tugged at my arm and told me to sit down. He was old, much older than in the photographs, and he wore his usual *pince-nez*. He asked me my name and I told him, wondering why the colonel said they knew everything about me when they didn't even know my name.

'Has anyone in your family been arrested?'

'Yes.'

'Who?'

'The husband of Mother's sister. We live with my aunt now.'

He asked her name and frowned. 'I don't recall her. And where does your mother work?'

After questioning me about the other members of my family, he looked at me for a long time. 'Why did you change? The dress suited you. The suit's nice too, but a bit formal.'

'But we'll be talking formally!' I gabbled.

'Yes, of course. But first let's eat.' He pressed a button – the long table was covered in buttons – and a woman entered silently and was ordered to lay the table.

He opened a door on the left and we passed through a room filled with pieces of sculpture into a smaller room, where a table was laid for two with wine, fruit and pitta bread. He tucked into the food with gusto and poured me some wine. 'I don't drink,' I said. 'Stalin warns us to be vigilant.'

He looked at me dumbfounded. 'Just have a sip, then.'

I took a sip and wondered if it was drugged. The reasons why I had been brought here were starting to form in my mind, and I seemed to be developing defensive reactions. He questioned me again about my family and the Institute, again demanded why I had changed, and said he had been watching me for a long time. I wondered where. He got drunk. 'Teaching's no job for you – you need something better! You live in a shared flat? That's no good for a pretty girl . . .'

Just then a young man entered with a sheet of paper, then withdrew. I felt the goose flesh creep over my body when Beria said, 'Write, "Dear Mother, don't worry, I'm with friends and will be back in the morning." '

'No, no! I want to go home!' I cried, trying to pull away.

'That would be most inconvenient. How would you get back at this hour?'

The woman brought in tea. I drank, and my teeth chattered against the cup. I could see nothing, understand nothing, only that I must get away.

At last he said, 'Time for bed.' He took me to a bathroom, then left, and a huge peasant appeared. 'The bath's behind the screen,' he said. 'Wash yourself.'

'I'm not dirty. I don't need to wash!'

I went out of the bathroom into a bedroom containing a huge double bed, and amidst a chaos of thoughts and feelings I noticed that it was laid with dazzling white batiste sheets. A woman came in – I wasn't sure if it was the same one as before – and handing me a large linen nightshirt she said, 'Undress here, lie down here.'

She went out. I didn't put it on and lay hunched on the edge of the bed in my combinations. After about half an hour a concealed door opened and he entered the room wearing a long nightshirt. I shook with fear as he sat beside me on the bed. 'What are you afraid of? You're so pretty!' he murmured, and started to kiss my shoulders. I shook even more, and pushed him away. 'Don't be afraid, why are you trembling? Are you a virgin? Haven't you had a man before?'

'No!' I whispered.

'How old are you? Seventeen?'

'Twenty-one.'

'And you've not had a man yet?'

'No!'

He started murmuring about work again and kissing my shoulders, repeating, 'Is it true? Are you really a virgin?'

'Yes.'

Suddenly he stood up and went silently out of the room. Time passed. It grew light. As I lay there unsleeping, the colonel came in and told me that a car would be coming at six to take me home.

At five-thirty the woman came in, looked at me with undisguised contempt and ordered me to dress. I dressed in an instant and was driven home. Mother hadn't slept all night. She'd received the note, but she didn't know what to make of it. I told her everything.

When she realised I was still a virgin she stopped worrying, but I couldn't. Next morning I visited a friend whose father was a science professor and a very clever man and when he heard what had happened he lowered the blinds on his windows and said, 'Go away. Go home by a different route so they don't see where your friends live!'

He told me all about the women whose lives had been ruined by Beria, and about Kalinin and the operetta singers, and his words hit me like a thunderbolt, as I imagined the crystal-pure sitting in judgement above us and warning us to be vigilant. He said that I was lucky to have escaped so lightly, and that Beria had let me go because he was either tired or sexually inadequate. He also said that matters wouldn't stop there, and that I must go away for the whole summer, as far from Moscow as possible.

I spent the summer with my elder sister and her baby daughter in the Siberian town of Krasnoyarsk, and they returned with me to Moscow in the middle of August. My sister took the incident very seriously. Mother had also been away working over the summer, and the neighbours told us that a man had come several times, asking where I was. I had deliberately misinformed everyone as to where I was staying.

Two days after our return a youth appeared at the door, saying, 'So you're back from Kalyazan? The colonel wants to see you.'

The colonel instantly appeared, and, armed with a strange new courage, I demanded, 'What do you want?'

'You know – the Comrade wants to see you.'

'What Comrade? Why don't you say his name?'

At this, my sister appeared with the baby in her arms, and shouted, 'If you come here once more you'll be in trouble!'

We were ridiculous. Who were we to threaten them? Yet the colonel looked anxious. Did he think we might have connections? Was he scared by our decisiveness?

Suddenly the baby started to wail, and at this the colonel went to pieces, shouting, 'You listen to me! I'm working! I carry out orders! I do my duty!'

'So that's what you call duty!' my sister yelled. 'Get out of here! You say you know all about us – we weren't anywhere near Kalyazan! You've been playing tricks on us!'

We pushed the colonel out of the door, and as he left he said, 'We'll meet again. We won't forget you. That man still wants to see you.'

My sister went back home, and I started teaching in a school. All the time I felt I was being watched. A man kept following me. Once I turned round on him and shouted at him to go. He said nothing, of course. He was grey, like the rest of them. Another man immediately appeared behind him.

They followed me till November. Then one day I realised there was no one there, and although I was afraid they might start following me again, I felt easier in my mind. Then Stalin died and spring came. In the summer of 1953 I finished my first year as a schoolteacher and went off to work as a pioneer leader in a children's camp. There I learned that the trial of Beria had begun. I sighed with relief.

During Khrushchev's first days in office the vengeance of history returned to the corridors where Lavrenty Beria had worked, and Nina Teimurazovna fell into the very machine devised by her husband for others. By now he was no longer there, and new people – or rather the same old ones, Molotov, Kaganovich, Bulganin, Malenkov and Khrushchev, Beria's erstwhile friends and allies – had defeated him in the battle for power.

In 1953, as some went to prison and others returned, Nina Teimurazovna and her son Sergo were arrested.

I was imprisoned in various jails. They didn't touch Sergo's family – his wife Marfa and her three children remained at home. At first we thought there had been a government revolution or counter-revolution, and an anti-Communist clique had come to power. I was held at the Butyrki and questioned every day. The interrogator demanded that I testify against my husband. He told me that people were angry about the things Lavrenty had done. I answered categorically that I would give no evidence, good or bad, and after that they left me alone.

I spent over a year in the Butyrki. I was charged quite seriously with bringing a bucket of red earth back from a non-Black Earth region of Russia. When I was working at the Agricultural Academy doing research on different soil types, I had asked some people to bring me back a bucket of red earth by aeroplane, and since it was a government plane they claimed I was using state transport for my own personal use.

I was also charged with exploiting the labour of others. In Tbilisi there was a famous tailor by the name of Sasha who came to Moscow and made me a dress, which I paid for. This was called 'the labour of others'. Another charge was that I had ridden from Kutaisi to Tbilisi on horses with golden bells. I certainly rode horses, but never with golden bells on. People love to fantasise.

My time in jail was very hard. I spent over a year in a solitary confinement cell, where you can't sit or lie down.

This cell was the invention of her husband. To be sure, Nina Teimurazovna was not called an 'enemy of the people', they did not even dare to interrogate her. But by putting her in jail they made her one with all the other women who suffered for their husbands' struggle for power.

Many questions about Nina Teimurazovna remain unanswered. Was she Beria's victim or his ally? Did she really know nothing? Possibly. She was a naive woman surrounded by Cheka agents who forbade her to move a single step. She had several options, the most obvious being to throw it all up and leave – but that would have meant prison or the firing squad. Another was to follow the senseless example of Nadezhda Alliluyeva. But Nina Gegechkori was a very different person. She was a true Georgian girl, and her life of submission demonstrated to Josif Vissarionovich how right his mother had been in urging him to take a Georgian girl as his bride. The only choice left to her was to close her eyes and comfort herself with fairy-tales about the precious goal ahead, a goal in which people believed so readily in the first half of the twentieth century.

Having spent most of her life in cages – at first a gilded one, then prison – the naturally wise and intelligent Nina Teimurazovna had much to think about at the end of her long life. Maybe she could describe what happened. What reason would she have to lie? Yet I felt afraid to see her. Afraid not of the shadow of her husband, but of remembering again that beautiful woman in the theatre, and losing my sense of balance.

In the summer of 1991, still beautiful in old age, Nina Teimurazovna lived in the boundary between light and shade, guarding her devotion to her dead husband like the black-clothed widows of Georgia. She said:

> Stalin was a stern man with a harsh character. But who can say whether those times required a different character, and that harshness wasn't necessary? Stalin wanted to create a mighty state, and he succeeded. Of course, there had to be victims. But no politician then could see any other path which would lead us to our precious goal.

Stalin led us towards that precious goal squeezing us dry, regardless of how long it took. Khrushchev led us there saying nothing about how long it would take. The women of the Kremlin were slaves, who knew better than most that there was no such goal. These slaves had a particularly female talent for converting their fear of the Party machine into dedication to the working class. They did not doubt, because they had no choice.

Beria is said to have remarked, 'Where there's a woman there must be money.' He was lavish with government gifts, in other words his pleasures were paid for by the taxpayer.

To the end of her life, Nina Teimurazovna refused to accept the evidence of her husband's sexual crimes:

> The Prosecutor said that 760 women had described themselves as Beria's mistresses. When would Lavrenty have found time to make

these hordes of women his mistresses? He spent all day and night at work. No, it was something else. During the war and after, he did intelligence and counter-intelligence work, and all these women were secret agents and informers. He was their only contact. He had a phenomenal memory, and he kept all his contacts in his head. But when these women were asked about their relationship with their chief they could hardly say they were secret agents, so they said they were his mistresses.

At the end of Nina Teimurazovna's life, the chief cause of her suffering was quite different:

A man must never forget his own country. No other country will value his labour. Stalin, Ordzhokonidze, Chkheidze, Tseretelli, Gegechkori, Beria and the others all truly believed that they were fighting for the happiness of all the peoples on earth, for some common noble cause. But in the end they weren't good for anything, their country or their people. Other people rejected their labour, and when all these Georgians died they had no country.

The truth of these painful words is all too clear in the case of her husband's sexual abuse of little girls, which as a good wife she naturally denies. At home in Georgia his behaviour would not have been tolerated for a moment; the victim's grieving brother or father would have delivered a bullet to his head or a knife to the back. So why did Moscow put up with him?

Numerous memoirs have been written by Beria's mistresses, monotonous testimonies to the prizes awarded for eagerness in bed. People say how pretty young L. was, and how her baby used to play with the children of Beria's son. Yet I decided not to ask her to talk to me, for I think I know what she would have said. She would have spoken not of the delicious meals, the wonderful dresses and the luxurious living quarters, she would have said that Nina Teimurazovna had a great heart, that they all lived very simply, and that Beria was a good, generous man who loved children.

12

Nina Kukharchuk's Kitchen

Nikita Sergeevich Khrushchev (1894–1971). Born in the Ukraine, the son of a miner. As a small boy he worked as a shepherd, later training as a locksmith. Joining the Bolsheviks in 1918, he fought during the civil war in the Ukraine, where he attracted the attention of Lasar Kaganovich. Throughout the 1930s he worked his way up through the Party, joining war councils on various fronts during the Second World war, and taking part in the defence of Stalingrad. Subordinate to Stalin before his death, Khrushchev took over in 1953 as general secretary of the Party, and campaigned for liberalisation and peaceful coexistence with the West. These desires were expressed in his speech to the Twentieth Party Congress in 1956. In October 1964 he was toppled by colleagues, and he spent the next six years of his life in semi-disgrace, writing his memoirs.

One of the most striking features of the post-Stalin thaw was Nina Petrovna Khrushcheva. Preoccupied with the bread supply and the onslaught against Dudintsev's book *Not By Bread Alone*, people in Russia did not notice the significance of Khrushchev's wife as she modestly stepped through the oak doors of the Kremlin into the international arena. Yet people in the West noticed and were thrilled. Accustomed to their system, in which the smiling First Lady stands half a centimetre behind her husband, and to the Soviet system in which Stalin was surrounded by a gaping void, they welcomed her with open arms. 'Mother Nina!' 'What a lovely woman!' 'The soul of goodness!' 'She speaks English brilliantly!' 'She doesn't speak English so well, but what does it matter?'

Her appearance in America in 1959 made a great impression, and helped to offset Khrushchev's eccentric behaviour, as he banged his shoe on the table and threatened to bury the West. For the West, Nina Petrovna was an indication of important social changes in Russia, not because women in the West were finally gaining their equality, but because Western culture assumes that a woman standing beside a powerful man can have a civilising influence on him. People saw the sweet smile of this typical Soviet housewife in her black skirt and white blouse, devoid of make-up and with the shapeless figure of someone who lives on jam, bread and potatoes, and they were ecstatic. After long years in which the Leader had no wife, Nina Petrovna's homely face and her ability to hold a simple conversation in English reassured terrified Americans, as they saw that this vast empire was now ruled by a funny fat man and his provincial wife, clutching her handbag to her ample stomach. These were living people with whom one could do business.

After the Khrushchevs' visit to America and all the newspaper photographs of Nina Petrovna standing just behind Khrushchev's shoulder, she became the object of various well-founded rumours. Some said that Khrushchev was under her thumb, and that she had made him pull strings to get their son a job at the prestigious Chalomey Nuclear Research Institute. Others said that it was only because her sister Maria was married to Sholokhov that this writer carried such weight with Khrushchev. Yet America saw what it wanted to see, Russia did likewise, and few noticed what was before their eyes: the tight mouth and clenched lips, evidence of a humourless, inflexible, possibly malicious and definitely stubborn nature.

In the last years of Nina Petrovna's life she yielded to pressure from her daughter Rada to write her memoirs, and after her death Rada found this biographical sketch among her papers:

I was born on 14 April 1900 in the village of Vasilev, in Kholm province. The inhabitants of Kholm were Ukrainian and the villagers spoke Urainian, but the village administrators were all Russian and Russian was taught in the schools, even though no one spoke it at home. In the first class of the village infant school the teacher would hit our hands with a ruler for various crimes, including not understanding Russian, which none of us knew.

When my mother, Ekaterina Grigorevna Kukharchuk, married at sixteen she received for her dowry one and a quarter acres of land, a small oak forest and a trunk full of clothes and bedding. The villagers considered this very generous. Soon after the wedding, my father, Pyotr

Vasilevich Kukharchuk, went off to serve in the army. Father was from a poorer family than Mother's and owned part of a three-acre allotment, an old cottage, a small plum orchard and a cherry-tree in the garden. They had no horses. My father was the eldest in the family. When his mother died he inherited the land and had to pay his brothers and sisters a hundred roubles each, which was a large sum in those days. The 1914 war interrupted all their plans.

Vasilev was a poor village, and most of the villagers worked as day labourers for the landlord, who paid the women ten kopecks a day for picking beetroots, and the men twenty to thirty kopecks for scything hay. I remember cooking nettles and chopping them with a big knife for the pig, which we would fatten up for Easter or Christmas. The knife would often slip and cut my finger, and I still have a scar on the index finger of my left hand.

Mother and I lived with her family: Granny Ksenya had a large cottage and Grandfather was away on military service, first in Bessarabia then, in 1904, in Japan. We had no table so we all sat at a wide bench and ate from one bowl. The mothers held the babies in their arms, but there was no room for us bigger children so we had to reach over the grown-ups' shoulders for our food, and if we spilt some they would hit us on the forehead with a spoon. For some reason Uncle Anton was always laughing at me, and saying I would marry into a large family, my children would have runny noses, and I would have to reach over their heads for my food.

In 1912 Father put me in the cart, loaded it with a sack of potatoes and a side of wild boar, and drove to the town of Lublin, where his brother, Kondraty Vasilevich, was a conductor on the railways. Uncle Kondraty had arranged for me to study at the Lublin *progimnazium*. I had already done three years in the village school, and the village teacher had persuaded Father that I should be sent to school in the town.

I spent a year in Lublin, and when Uncle got a job as a watchman at the Kholm Treasury, I entered the second year of the *progimnazium* there. When the 1914 war broke out I was on holiday at home in Vasilev. I was fourteen then, and my brother was eleven. That autumn Austrian troops broke through to our village and went wild, looting houses and raping the girls. Mama hid me behind the stove, ordering me not to come out, and told the soldiers I had typhus. That sent them packing. Soon Russian soldiers drove the Austrians out, and we were ordered to evacuate the village. Mother, my brother and I grabbed as many bags as we could carry. We had no idea where we were going, and we had no horses. I remember Mama was carrying a primus-stove, the object of her housewifely pride, but there was no paraffin and she finally had to abandon it. For a long time we struggled on ahead of the advancing Austrians, until we finally reached the little railway station where my father was serving in a unit of Ukrainian auxiliaries.

Father informed his commander of our arrival and we were allowed to stay. Mother worked as a cook at the commander's headquarters, while my brother and I lived with his unit, helping as best we could.

During a lull in the fighting the commander gave Father a letter for Bishop Evlogia of Kholm, telling him to take me with him to Kiev. The bishop had started an organisation to help refugees in Kiev, and he arranged for me to enrol free of charge at the Marinsky women's school, which had been evacuated from Kholm to Odessa. I lived as a boarder in Odessa until 1919.

Bishop Evlogia was a bastion of the Russian autocracy in Poland and a fanatical agent of the government's Russification policies there, turning the children from the villages of the Western Ukraine into support troops for this policy. Without his intervention I would never have been educated at state expense at the school, for the children of peasants were not accepted, only those of priests and selected officials. After finishing school I worked for a while in the school office, writing testimonials and copying out documents (we had no typewriter).

At the beginning of 1920 I joined the Bolsheviks and worked for the Party in Odessa and the surrounding villages. In June all the Communists were mobilised, and I went off with a unit of soldiers to the Polish front. Since I knew the Ukrainian language, I travelled around the villages with a Red Army soldier, talking about Soviet power. When the central committee of the Ukrainian Communist Party was formed, I was elected to lead its women's section in Ternopol.

In the autumn of 1920 we were driven out of Poland, and, along with the central committee secretary and others, I left for Moscow, where I was assigned to enrol in a new six-month Party course at the Sverdlov Communist University.

In the summer of 1921 I was sent to Bakhmut in the Donbas, to teach the history of Western revolutionary movements at the regional Party school. Until the students arrived I was used by the regional Party commission to purge the ranks of unreliable elements. This was my second Party purge – the first was at the Ternopol front.

Requisitioning had been abolished after the Tenth Party Congress in 1921, the markets had opened, and all sorts of things appeared for those who had money. I and a couple of the other teachers would go to the market for bread, and all three of us caught typhus. One died, but the other girl and I survived. We didn't go to hospital, we just lay there at the school. The patients were nursed by Serafima Ilinichna Gopner, who was then conducting agitprop for the regional Party.

Nina Kukharchuk had ended up in the Party, and as she started working for a new life, straight roads opened up before her. It is appropriate that she should have been noticed by Serafima Gopner, who had so influenced Ekaterina Voroshilova sixteen years earlier.

This lost soul, who accidentally or by God's will raised herself to the highest rank in the land, acknowledged that without Bishop Evlogia she would have had no education, yet she could find not a single kind word for this 'bastion of the autocracy' and 'fanatical agent of Russification'. In the place to which he sent her she was an outsider, yet she took all that she could from it, and in the autumn of 1922 she was sent to teach political economy at the district Party school in Yuzovka (now Donetsk). Here she met Nikita Sergeevich Khrushchev, a student at the Yuzovka workers' college. At the end of 1923, she was sent by the regional Party committee to work as a propagandist in the mines near Rutchenkovka, where Krushchev's parents lived with the children from his previous marriage.[1]

In Rutchenkovka I lived in the guest-house, just over the road from the club. When it rained the road was impossible to cross and people's boots sank into the mud and had to be tied on in a special way. Before I left for Rutchenkovka I had been warned about the mud, and as I had no boots I had to find a private shoemaker to make me some.

At my lectures for the club there were always a lot of women who were interested in me as a woman and as the friend of Nikita Khrushchev. These were women he had met at the mines and elsewhere.

In those days there was a lot of unemployment, even among Communist miners. After the lectures my audience would follow me home, often complaining bitterly that I had a job and no children, while they had large families and no work. But gradually life settled down, and unemployment disappeared from the mines.

In 1924 Nikita Sergeevich and Nina Petrovna were married, and afterwards they worked together at the Petrovsk mine near Yuzovka. When Lenin died in January 1924 Nikita Sergeevich joined a delegation from Yuzovka at the funeral, and two years later

---

[1] Khrushchev had previously been married to Efrosinya Ivanovna, who died in 1918 of typhus, leaving their two children, Yulia and Leonid.

Nina Petrovna went to Moscow to improve her qualifications by studying political economy at the Krupskaya Communist Academy. After the course ended in 1927 she was sent back to the Kiev Party school to teach political economy, lecturing in Ukrainian to miners from the Western Ukraine.

By the autumn of 1927 Nikita Sergeevich was head of the organisation department of the Kiev district Party, and in 1929, shortly after the birth of their daughter, he left Kiev for Moscow to study at the Trade Academy. While he was finishing his studies his wife and baby moved to Moscow to join him:

> We lived at the Academy hostel, on Pokrovka Street. We had two rooms, at opposite ends of the corridor, Rada and I slept in one, and in the other slept Yulia, Lenya [Leonid] and Matryosha, the nanny Nikita Sergeevich had found for us.
>
> In Moscow the Party committee sent me to work at the electrical plant, where I set up a Party school. After a year I was elected to the Party committee, and led the agitation and propaganda department of the factory's central committee. There were three thousand Communists in the Party organisation and the factory worked three shifts, so I had a lot of work, leaving home at eight in the morning and coming back at ten at night.
>
> Then disaster struck and Radochka caught typhus. She went to the hospital attached to the factory, and I would run out every evening to look through the little window and see how she was doing. Once I saw the nurse feeding her a bowl of buckwheat porridge with a big spoon, then going off to chat with a friend. Rada was just over a year old and I saw her putting her feet in her bowl and sobbing, and the nurse didn't come, and I could do nothing. We took her home from the hospital early.
>
> I worked at the electrical plant until the middle of 1935, when Seryozha [Sergei] was born. I finished my first five-year assignment in two and a half years, and received a testimonial from the factory organisation. It was at the factory that the third purge of my Party life took place. I made contact with most of the active members there, including the old Bolsheviks, Party organisers, writers and pre-Revolutionary political prisoners who had been sent to work at the factory by their organisations and the collective-farm workers sponsoring them. I consider these years the most active of my political and personal life.
>
> Nikita Sergeevich did not finish his studies at the Trade Academy, but

was taken on by the Moscow Party as secretary of first the Baumann, then the Krasnopresnya district committees. There were terrible battles with the Right in the Party in those days.

Nikita Sergeevich was a delegate to the Fifteenth Party Congress. In 1932 he became secretary of the Moscow city committee, and in 1934 he was a delegate at the Seventeenth Party Congress and was voted onto the Party Central Committee. In 1935 he was elected first secretary of the Moscow city committee to replace Kaganovich, who became Commissar of Transport. He remained there until early 1938, when he left for Kiev as secretary of the central committee of the Ukrainian Communist Party.

In Moscow Nikita Sergeevich devoted much energy to building the first stage of the metro and the river quays and to the establishment of the bread industry. The entire economy of the capital had to be rebuilt – with bath-houses and toilets on the streets, electricity for Moscow's factories and government, and low-cost housing built to increase living space.

By then we had a four-room flat in Government House on Kamenny Bridge, and Nikita Sergeevich's parents were living with us. We had to buy food with ration cards in those days. My distribution centre was not far from the factory and Nikita Sergeevich's was on what is now Komsomol Street. His father, Sergei Nikanorovich, used to go there for potatoes and other things, and since we had no transport he would carry it home on his back; once he almost killed himself jumping off a moving tram with his load. He also had to carry Rada up to the kindergarten on the eleventh floor of our building, since the lift did not work. Rada adored her grandfather. Her granny, Ksenya Ivanovna, mainly sat in her room or would take her stool out to the main entrance and sit on the street. People always gathered around her, and she would gossip with them for hours. Nikita Sergeevich hated her sitting around like this, but she paid no attention to him.

One frequently observes comfortable Soviet wives worshipping at the shrine of their painful childhood, their unhappy youth, and the difficulties they experienced in struggling to bring up babies without adequate childcare. This is particularly noticeable in the memoirs of Nina Petrovna, who did indeed have a hard time both as a child, and later when trying to combine Party work with the care of a large family. Yet the reverence for such memories mainly seems intended to justify a standard of living achieved not by chance but fairly fought for and deserved.

The more one peers into the life of the Kremlin and the entire Soviet élite that underpins it, the clearer it becomes that without the privileges of the state apparatus, and the food and housing situation, the Party machine could not work.

Why should it so irritate Nikita Sergeevich to see his mother chatting with strangers outside the house? What could a simple peasant woman possibly pick up in a house where no secrets were ever repeated for fear that Stalin, in his office across the Moscow river, might pick them up on his secret cable? What Nikita Sergeevich surely objected to was the idea of his mother telling the neighbours about all the different foods available to the newly arrived provincial bosses and their families.

Nina Petrovna's memoirs – reproduced here almost in their entirety – are the only written testimony of a Soviet Kremlin wife to have seen the light of day. They contain no hint of any interpretation of what was happening in her country, no details of Kremlin life, no characteristics of any of her companions, or of her life. Why? Because Kremlin life is part of a complex system of distribution for the privileged and must always be kept secret. Although apparently written for her daughter, these memoirs read as though written for the Party. All personal details about those in the Kremlin are concealed, inessential. Only once does something of these details flash into Khrushcheva's memoirs:

When V. M. Molotov became Commissar of Foreign Affairs, I don't remember exactly when, they built him a specially designed dacha with large rooms for foreign receptions. One day it was announced that the government was throwing a reception there for commissars and leading officials of the Moscow Party.[2] The officials were invited to bring their wives, which is how I came to be there.

The women were asked into the reception room, and from where I sat, near the door, I could hear the conversations of the Moscow guests. All the women present worked, and they talked about various things, including their children.

We were called to the dining room, where the tables were laid out in a U-shape, and we were seated according to a pre-arranged plan. I sat next to Valeria Alexeevna Golubtsova-Malenkova, and facing the wife of Stanislav Kosior, who had just been promoted to the Soviet of

[2] Since Molotov was made minister of foreign affairs in 1939, and Khrushchev was then in the Ukraine, the events described are more likely to have taken place in early 1938.

People's Commissars. It was already known then that Nikita Sergeevich Khrushchev was to take over Kosior's old job as secretary of the Ukrainian central committee, and I asked Kosior's wife what kitchen-ware I should take with me. She was very surprised by my question and replied that our new house would have everything we could possibly want, and there was no need to bring anything. When I arrived in the Ukraine I discovered that everything was indeed supplied by the government – we collected our food from the store and settled up every month. There was a cook, all our furniture, plates and beds, and more pots and pans than I had ever seen in my life.

But to get back to Molotov's reception. After the guests were seated J. V. Stalin came through the door of the buffet room, followed by his Politburo members, and sat down at the top table. They were greeted with lengthy applause, of course. Stalin said that a lot of new commissariats had recently been set up and new leaders appointed, and the Politburo thought it would be a good idea to hold an informal meeting for everyone to get to know each other better.

After that a lot of people spoke and announced their job, and described how they viewed their work. The women were allowed to take the floor too, and Valeria Golubtsova-Malenkova spoke about her scientific work. A lot of the women did not like this. She was followed by the young wife of the Commissar for Higher Education, Kaftanov, who said she would do all she could to support her husband at his new post. Her speech was received with universal approval.

We may forgive Nina Petrovna all her caution, her silences and half-statements for this detail which identifies so clearly the changes taking place in Kremlin women's lives. All the women there that evening worked, yet they and their husbands greeted Malenkova's speech with open disapproval, while they applauded Kaftanova. The time had come in the Soviet Union to put women in their place. Stalin was victorious everywhere. He himself had suffered at the hands of his independent wife. Kremlin women had played at making revolution and building socialism, now it was time for them to return to the house and kitchen. Their reward was limitless material privileges; they had no cause to grumble.

The year 1937 had passed, the 'enemies of the people' were gone, and now a Kremlin wife could be a wife, and only a wife. Clearly the evening described by Nina Petrovna gave unofficial sanction to a crucial redefining of Kremlin wives' position in the second half of the thirties.

Nina Petrovna gives only a few hints as to how these changes affected her active and independent life in the years leading to the outbreak of war:

In 1939 the Germans occupied Poland and were approaching my parents' village of Vasilev. Our troops were meanwhile moving west and recapturing from the Nazis large areas of the Western Ukraine and Western Byelorussia, including the town of Lvov. Nikita Sergeevich telephoned me in Kiev and told me that since Vasilev and the surrounding area was about to fall to the Germans, I could travel to Lvov if I wanted, and be driven on to Vasilev to collect my parents. My trip was organised by the secretary of the Ukrainian Communist Party, Comrade Burmistenko, who informed me that I would be travelling with two women who were being sent by the central committee to work in Lvov. One of them, a young Komsomol member, was to work with Lvov's young people, and the other, a Party official, would be working with women. We were handed revolvers and told to wear army uniforms, so we wouldn't be stopped by army patrols on the way.

Our journey passed without incident, but not far from Lvov we were run into by an approaching lorry whose driver had not slept for three days and had fallen asleep at the wheel. The only one of us hurt was the Komsomol girl, who suffered some bruised ribs. A passing commander checked our documents and drove us the rest of the way to Lvov, where the girl was bandaged up in a hospital and soon recovered. The other girl and I stayed at the quarters of the General Command. Semyon Konstantinovich Timoshenko was commander of the Kiev military district then, and Nikita Sergeevich Khrushchev was a member of the Military Council. When they returned home and saw us with our revolvers and uniforms they roared with laughter, then Nikita Sergeevich became furious and ordered us to put on our dresses again. 'What are you thinking of?' he shouted. 'You want to tell the local people about Soviet power, and you turn up waving revolvers? Who will trust you? They've been told for the last thirty years that we're bandits – you'll just confirm it!'

I put my civilian clothes back on and set off for Vasilev with Bozhko, one of Nikita Sergeevich's guards, to collect my parents. We arrived safely at the cottage, and found Father and Mother at home. Crowds of people ran up to look at me and hear the latest news. No one believed that the village was about to fall to the Germans – even the junior officers knew nothing.

'Nobody could believe' might well mean that the villagers were waiting to welcome the Germans; there was certainly no shortage of such people. At any rate, the sight of this Soviet lady about to snatch her parents from the advancing bloodbath can have afforded them little joy.

> All night soldiers crowded into the cottage to warm themselves. Mother cooked for them, while Bozhko sat talking with them. Towards morning members of the newly organised local government arrived to arrest me as a spy and a *provocateur*, and Bozhko and the tank drivers had difficulty persuading them of their mistake. That morning my parents, my brother and his family loaded the cart with their possessions, and we drove to Lvov. I took my parents to the Lvov Palace of Fighters, where Nikita Sergeevich was staying, and they walked around the rooms marvelling at everything. My father turned on the water tap and shouted, 'Hey Mother, look at this – the water comes out of a pipe!' When he entered the room Nikita Sergeevich shared with Comrade Timoshenko, he pointed at Timoshenko and demanded, 'Is this our son-in-law?' But I didn't notice him looking too disappointed when I told him that his new son-in-law was in fact Nikita Sergeevich.

This last sentence softens the crudity of her father, who evidently would have preferred the more imposing of the two young men as his son-in-law, and in these words Nina Petrovna reveals herself as a woman in love.

Over the next ten years Nina Petrovna – the personification of Party spirit – gradually and almost guiltily turned herself into the wife of the leader, thus setting the pattern for a new type of Kremlin wife for whom kitchen and children are equated with Party membership and supersede the demands of Party work.

When I met Nina Petrovna's daughter Rada at her dacha outside Moscow recently, she said:

> When Mama was young, she stopped working. She started to believe it was her Party duty to look after her family properly, and she imposed Party order on the family. This wasn't easy for us children. Not only for us, but for her servants too. Father's salary was eight hundred roubles, and she kept a tight hold on it. When there was a reception at the house or the dacha, she made sure that not too many bottles were put out in case the guests drank too much or the servants got drunk afterwards. We children were never invited. We would sit separately and eat completely different food. Mother kept a strict eye on that. She never

threw anything away. After her death we found piles of darned old dresses and jumpers.

Mother was a strict disciplinarian, and very secretive. She never talked about herself. I was astonished when she accepted my advice and wrote her memoirs. I once asked her why they called me Rada, and she said, 'I was glad you were born.'[3] The two younger children, Seryozha and Lenochka, were often ill as children, and Lenochka caught tuberculosis and died in her twenties.

I was her second daughter. She had had another daughter named Nadya, who died. She had no time for her children. Until I was nine she spent almost no time at home with me, and I was looked after by nannies. She had strict Party principles, and I suffered from it – we always had a difficult relationship, even though we loved each other.

She was very strict about our schoolwork, especially with me. She wasn't so strict with the others; she didn't work then and looked after them herself, and she wasn't so tense. Yulia and Leonid, the two children from Father's previous marriage, were a lot older than us. Leonid's daughter, also called Yulia, was like a sister to us, and my parents adopted her when her stepfather died.

Leonid lived in Kiev, where he worked at the pilots' school. During the war he flew in several massive bombing raids over Germany and was seriously wounded. He spent a long time in hospital in Kuibyshev, where we were all evacuated as a family when Father was at the front. In hospital Leonid started to drink. One day when he was drunk he shot a man, and the court martial sent him to the front line.

At the beginning of the war his sister Yulia married the theatrical administrator of the Dumka choir. She worked but she was a very domestic woman at heart, more interested in sewing, cooking and washing.

Father hardly ever spent any time with us. He felt Mother should be in charge of the home, leaving him free to do his government work. He loved me, the house was always happy when he was around; when we went off to the dacha he would sing, read poems and take me skiing. It was almost impossible to ask Mother for anything; he was much easier.

Our children now ask us if we really knew nothing, and whether our parents ever said anything in front of us. The fact is that no one ever discussed politics at home. There were never any open displays of the Stalin cult, although I remember when guests came to celebrate the May Day holiday after the war Father would always propose the first toast to

[3]'Rada' means 'glad'.

Stalin. Even then it seemed false to me. But we were never allowed to say a word against Lenin or Stalin. Once I argued with my grandmother when she told me to listen to her because she was older and wiser.

'What, wiser than Stalin?' I demanded.

'Of course I am!' she retorted.

I was brought up not to ask questions. We children unconsciously knew what we could say and what we couldn't.

Mother was very hard-working and well organised. She had excellent handwriting; she was famous for it even at her high school. In our little factory settlement near Kuibyshev during the war she decided to take English lessons. I was shocked by this frivolity in the midst of war, but she soon collected a group of students, and an English teacher came to visit our flat. Father, who was rarely at home, was also amazed, but she cut him short saying it was time to strengthen relations with our allies. The lessons soon stopped, because of the difficulties of life at that time . . .

When Beria was shot, Nina Teimurazovna and her son Sergo wrote to Khrushchev complaining that her arrest was illegal. He was touched by their letter and believed them. After Beria's execution Mother felt very sorry for Nina Teimurazovna. She was glad that she and her son were allowed to live.

The memoirs of Rada's husband, Alexei Ivanovich Adzhubei, subsequently editor of *Izvestiya* and one of Khrushchev's closest associates, add their own colours to this portrait of Nina Petrovna:

Life was divided into two eras: before and after the death of Stalin. Afterwards, the entire Kremlin court seemed to empty.

I had been part of this world before I met Rada, since my mother, Nina Gopalo, was one of the best dressmakers in Moscow and made clothes for Svetlana Stalina, Molotov's wife, Nina Beria and later Nina Petrovna.

Nina Petrovna's unremarkable motherly figure required simple lines; anything grand or elegant would have looked ridiculous on her, and Gopalo realised this:

Both my mother and my mother-in-law were tough nuts. Nina Petrovna Khrushcheva hadn't been one of her customers until her visit to America in 1959, when Mother happily created for her a wardrobe which would show her off to her best advantage.

Nina Gopalo had joined the Bolshevik underground before the

Revolution, fought with the Red Army and was thoroughly trusted by the government, with her own workshop in Moscow. Yet when Adzhubei married Rada Khrushcheva, Nina Beria told his mother: 'It's bad that your Alexei has joined the Khrushchev family.' Nina Gopalo was upset, but Beria's wife proved to be right, for this was the time of Stalin's campaign against the children of leading officials, and shortly after the wedding an anonymous letter reached the government claiming that Rada and Alexei were leading a life of luxury.

> Nina Petrovna's character was guarded, to say the least. When Rada and I decided to marry she was the last to agree, and it was only after several years that her attitude toward me changed from distrust to sympathy, and at the end of her life, after all her misfortunes, she began to respect me.
>
> Kremlin families led a highly unusual life. We lived as tsars and died as paupers. We never had anything of our own, we were supported by the state, since it was contrary to Party principles to own anything. The Khrushchevs always had four portraits hanging in their dining room, of Marx, Engels, Lenin and Stalin.

Nobody obliged them to hang these portraits in their dining room. For Nina Petrovna and Nikita Sergeevich Khrushchev it was natural, for these were their teachers, the creators of their ideas. Yet the children felt uncomfortable with them, and the grandchildren found them ridiculous and now ask if their grandparents really believed it all. They most certainly did.

In 1956, when Nina Petrovna entered the place that had been occupied for the past two decades by the most powerful leader in the land, she did so as an experienced Kremlin wife, who had lived by its unwritten laws for almost two decades. Awaiting her in Stalin's Kremlin lay domestic desolation and the cold of the grave. If her husband was a reformer, it must be assumed that she was similarly inclined as she surveyed the apartments bequeathed to him as Russia's new head of state. Although she probably did not have the deciding vote in the move from the Kremlin to the Lenin Hills, it was probably she who first considered the idea and lodged it in the temperamental brain of Nikita Sergeevich, and in rejecting the Kremlin's blood-soaked legacy, her female instinct proved correct. The Soviet people naturally knew nothing of this, and the newspapers made no comment, so her decision appeared as a purely personal decision, which allowed the Politburo to open the Kremlin to the public.

The comfort and space of the leaders' living quarters on the Lenin Hills, south of the city, as in the Kremlin, corresponded strictly to rank, and the Khrushchevs had the best. Standard, stereotyped mini-palaces in the 'Stalin Empire' style, the new mansions and villas hastily constructed for the leaders and their families are visible today behind their high stone walls. The wives and children remember the inconveniences of the new life: the houses were built in a hurry, communications and plumbing were installed hastily, in winter the walls froze and pipes burst. There were no problems with private transport, since every wife had her own chauffeur-driven car, but they were still inconveniently far from central Moscow. In their cramped Kremlin quarters the government tags on the furniture had not been so obvious; against the bare expanses of new walls they caught the eye and reminded the inhabitants of the impermanence of their position. A few of the cleverer ones, knowing that they might be evicted at any moment, settled with their families in the centre of Moscow on Granovsky Street, but those hooked on power rarely think of impermanence.

When asked about Nina Petrovna's reaction to her husband's disgrace in 1964, Rada Nikitichna replies:

For many years Mother had suffered from a bone condition called osteochondrosis, for which she used to take the waters in the Crimea. After the war she started visiting Karlovy Vary in Czechoslovakia, and in October 1964 she was with Brezhnev's wife, Victoria Petrovna, when news of the government coup reached them. She could not immediately take in what had happened, and said to Victoria Petrovna, 'I suppose I won't be inviting you to receptions now, you'll invite me!'

When she returned to Moscow she was very ill, and refused to leave her villa on the Lenin Hills. They kept trying to get her out, but she insisted on staying another month. She was in a state of shock.

Rada and her husband had their own flat by then, as did Seryozha. Lenochka could find nowhere to live and stayed in her parents' new quarters on Starokonyushnyaya Street.

I don't think Father ever slept in Moscow, he lived at their dacha in Petrovo-Dalnoe. They were offered another dacha a hundred kilometres from Moscow, but they chose the nearer one.

After Father's fall my Kremlin friends all disppeared, as one might have predicted. That day in October I met Galina Satyukova, wife of the chief editor of *Pravda* and one of my father's closest associates. She knew nothing and was very friendly, insisting that we take a holiday together, and promising to phone me to arrange it. I never heard from her again. My university friends didn't abandon me, though, nor did my artist and actor friends, who continued to telephone and come around.

In fact Father and the intelligentsia never really understood each other – he loved them but they wrong-footed him. Mother had never made any friends amongst the government wives, and those who had hovered around soon disappeared. At the end of her life she used to be visited by her old friends from the Ukraine.

After Father's death she was moved from Petrovo-Dalnoe to a dacha at Zhukovka, the so-called 'widows' village'. She lived alone there and never locked the door, just put a stick across.

She received a monthly pension of two hundred roubles, half of Father's four hundred, plus, of course, access to the Kremlin's clinic, food supplies and the use of a car. She quickly grew used to living alone, and had an emergency telephone on her bedside table beside her medicines. When she was ill in hospital the nurses deliberately humiliated her and refused to give her a bedpan – but she just smiled at them and didn't say a word.

Nina Petrovna's strength of character is confirmed by all who knew her. In 1974, three years after Khrushchev's death, his youngest son, Sergei, was summoned to the KGB and was asked to denounce Khrushchev's memoirs, which had recently been published in the West as *Khrushchev Remembers: The Last Testament*. Sergei was even handed a letter written by the KGB, purportedly written by him, declaring the memoirs to be a forgery and clearly intending to create a scandal in the West and discredit the work. Sergei Khrushchev found the proposal highly irregular.

> I said I could make no decision on my own and would have to discuss it with my mother. When I told her, she asked me if I had read the memoirs. I said I hadn't even seen them. 'So how can you say it's a forgery if you don't know the text?' she demanded, logically. 'You can't make a statement about a book none of us has seen. It's as Father says: we don't know how the West got hold of it.'
>
> I told the KGB this at our next meeting. I knew the discussion wouldn't be easy, but I had an irrefutable argument: Mother had forbidden it.

The fact that even the KGB dared not approach Nina Petrovna is evidence that her strength of character remained unchanged. Yet she herself changed. It is curious that a correct Party functionary such as she should not regard the West's publication of Khrushchev's memoirs as an appalling security lapse requiring careful investigation. But in old age Nina Petrovna was of a different political generation, and her feelings as a wife and mother outweighed her feelings of Party duty. She still loved the Party and fondly recalled past purges, yet she would not sacrifice her life's companion to its gaping maw, even though he was no longer alive.

The memoirs proved genuine, as she must have known from the start. But she also knew the KGB and its tricks, and this is hardly surprising in one who lived for so many years by its rules.

13

Victoria for Victory

Leonid Ilich Brezhnev (1906–82). Born in Dneproderzhinsk, in the Ukraine. Joined the Party in 1931 and served as political commissar during the war. In 1950 he was made first secretary of the Moldavian Party. In early 1953 he became deputy chief of the political administration of the defence ministry. In 1954 he was secretary of the Kazakhstan central committee, and in 1960 he replaced Voroshilov as Soviet president. His ties with the military served him in the coup *against Khrushchev, whom he replaced in 1964 as the Party's General Secretary. His main priority was to roll back Khrushchev's domestic, foreign and administrative reforms, and intensify competition with the United States. His death came at the end of a long process of physical deterioration and senility.*

The scent of victory was keenly felt in Moscow during August 1991, when a group of politicians and military men attempted to depose Gorbachev. The blood of those who died during the *putsch* intoxicated the young and frightened the old. As ideals were trampled beneath the barricades, panic-stricken young men looked around them with drugged gaze, seeking a direction for this destructive unifying force.

One August day in 1991 I walked back into the past, to the world in which our late head of state, Leonid Ilich Brezhnev, had lived and worked. It was less than a mile from the barricades of the White House to his home in a large building on Kutuzov Prospect, where his eighty-three-year-old widow, Victoria Petrovna, now lives alone, seeing no one and rarely leaving the house.

I was accompanied by her daughter-in-law, Ludmilla Vladimirovna, wife of her son Yury. On the outside of the building a plaque bearing Brezhnev's name had recently been ripped down. In the hall was an intercom, a rug, an armchair, a bucket of flowers, an ordinary lift. Brezhnev had been given this flat many years back. He had had several opportunities to change it for another one. In the late seventies a splendid brick apartment building was erected on Shchusev Street, in one of the most prestigious districts of Moscow. Increasing numbers of such buildings were then appearing in the centre of Moscow for the new Party élite arriving from the provinces, but this building had several distinguishing features unnoticeable to the untrained eye: the third floor area was larger than the rest, as were its windows. This floor was designed especially for the Brezhnevs. It was said that Leonid Ilich participated in discussions about the project, and was the first to enter the new building, but that he refused to live there. According to his relatives, he had no discussions and gave no orders; his sycophants did it all without asking him, and when they invited the old people to move, they refused to leave their comfortable home, saying, 'We like it here. We must live modestly, we mustn't show off!'

Stopping before an ordinary door we ring the bell, and it is opened by Anya, a tall, elderly woman who has devotedly served the Brezhnevs for many years. As she goes off with Ludmilla Vladimirovna to tell Victoria Petrovna of my arrival, I sit alone in the spacious lobby, separated from distant rooms by two Corinthian pillars against the walls. Ahead of me is an open door into a large room with windows overlooking the noisy Kutuzov Prospect. There are two portraits of Leonid Ilich executed by a court painter such as Alexander Gerasimov; one is obviously taken from a well-known photograph, the other is an informal study of a youthful, handsome Brezhnev straining forward, his shirt unbuttoned and his hands in front of him. At one of the windows in this large room, evidently the former dining room, hang two elegant metal cages, containing some budgerigars; the General Secretary loved birds. The floor of the lobby is covered in linoleum. On the walls hang the heads of huge stuffed animals: a wild mountain ram with magnificent Ionic horns, and two stags, their vast antlers brushing the ceiling. A medieval castle would seem a more appropriate setting for the master's trophies, but as everyone knew, Brezhnev was passionate about hunting, and the family photographs I saw later included numerous hunting themes: Leonid Ilich with a gun slung over his shoulders, Leonid Ilich with a gun in his hands, Leonid Ilich with a dead boar at his feet.

In the mid-seventies people recounted how the General

Secretary's huntsmen would hobble these stags and rams, then lead Leonid Ilich through the forest for half an hour until he came upon a peacefully grazing animal, lifted his gun and was happy. Yury Gagarin was said to have protested at this deception when he went hunting with Leonid Ilich, but it evidently continued as Brezhnev became increasingly senile and unable to shoot.

Anya returns to tell me that Victoria Petrovna is dressing, and that she is not feeling well today. Finally Victoria Petrovna enters slowly, leaning on Anya. She is wearing a dark-green dressing-gown, her face is smooth, her grey hair is drawn back in a bun, and her watery blue eyes are veiled with blindness. She is radiant, tranquil, open to her unseen guest. She sits down. How can I harass this eighty-three-year-old woman with trite questions about her husband's womanising, her relatives' time-serving, her children's alcoholism, her son-in-law's embezzlement?

The Brezhnev family was not large, consisting of Victoria Petrovna, Leonid Ilich, their two children, Galina and Yury, Galina's daughter Victoria, and Yury's sons Leonid and Andrei. Galina had had three husbands: Evgeny Milaev, Igor Kio and Yury Churbanov. Yury Brezhnev had one wife, Ludmilla Vladimirovna, a very pleasant, intelligent woman.

Leonid Ilich and Victoria Petrovna did, however, have innumer-able brothers and sisters, and this produced a huge family clan, perpetually in need of help and support. Like all self-respecting clans, it was internally divided, and relations within it were complicated. The division occurred naturally, between his relatives and hers. Although submissive to her husband in all other respects, Victoria Petrovna maintained the defence of her family's interests within the larger Brezhnev clan, making sure that his relatives did not enjoy more privileges than hers.

There were always rumours about the Brezhnev family. The first I heard was in 1949, during a holiday in Dnepropetrovsk, where Leonid Ilich was first secretary of the regional Party committee, and people there would whisper the sad story of a four-year-old girl who had wandered unsupervised through the half-open gates of the Brezhnevs' mansion, where the guard dogs were off their chains and ripped her to pieces. Later I remember sitting with a crowd of people who had recently arrived in Moscow from Dnepropetrovsk, and a magnificent, loud-voiced blonde, generously revealing the vast range of her knowledge, said. 'Just ask us! We know things about the Brezhnevs they don't even know about themselves!'

During *perestroika* the press picked up and legitimised many Brezhnev rumours when they reported the arrest of Yury Churbanov, general of the Ministry of Internal Affairs and Galina Brezhneva's third husband. These rumours would make up a fat volume, but a single theme rings loud and clear through the factual confusions and inaccuracies: debauchery and drunkenness, nepotism and abuse of power.

What could there be to know about Victoria Petrovna? She just sat there quietly and handed it all to Leonid Ilich on a plate. He was a village boy, she was said to be from the Jewish intelligentsia, the daughter of an economics teacher named Olshevsky. Her family took Leonid Ilich in, educated him and did everything to help him rise in the world. And rise he did, like yeast. He was handsome, tall, elegant, always laughing; women fell at his feet. He betrayed her on their wedding day and innumerable affairs followed; local Party leaders were renowned for their wild orgies in bath-houses, with food, drink and a limitless supply of girls. Victoria Petrovna knew everything, of course, but decided that the wisest course was to say nothing, bearing him two children and quietly tying her husband to her, like a goat on a long string, who runs far away but always returns.

Everyone in Dnepropetrovsk knew of his affair with the beautiful T.R. He showered her with presents, and in the late 1940s they travelled to Germany together, bringing back with them some exquisite cut glass. Later, when he left to work in Moldavia, she married Brezhnev's best friend and he was said to have taken it hard, but in Moldavia he quickly found consolation with another woman, and back in Moscow he took up with an actress from the Moscow Arts Theatre. Victoria Petrovna sat and waited for his affairs to pass. The Moscow stories about Brezhnev quickly became stories with a political colouring, yet as ludicrous as Leonid Ilich himself, visibly decrepit and forced by his decrepit machine to push himself into view to stave off its final collapse.

Apart from hunting, his main hobby was his vast collection of foreign cars. Where did he acquire these cars? Did he buy them with foreign money? Was he given them by foreign heads of state? These are questions for the prosecutor. But here is an anecdote from the mid-seventies, when there were far fewer foreign cars on the road than there are now.

One evening in early summer, my husband and I were driving along Leningrad Prospect. Not far from the Sokolniki underground station he said, 'Who's that idiot in a foreign car breaking the speed limit and trying to overtake me?'

'Don't let him!' I replied. My husband moved out into the road, but the driver refused to give in.

'Strange car, no number-plates,' my husband said, finally allowing the 'foreigner' to flash past us.

Gripping the wheel and staring straight ahead at the empty highway sat Leonid Ilich Brezhnev. The seat beside him was empty, but behind him, crouching towards Leonid Ilich and shaking his fist at us in fury, sat Vladimir Medvedev, whose face has graced our televisions for many a year: personal adjutant first of Brezhnev, then of Gorbachev, Medvedev cut an odd sight during *perestroika*, and one was struck by the strangeness of a state machine which allowed Brezhnev to be judged guilty while his adjutant continued to guard the memory of all that he held dear.

The Mercedes was followed by a black Volga filled with military men, all angrily shaking their fists at us. I was grateful then that our adventure had no unpleasant consequences, but now I almost wish that we were crushed by the machine of state for criminal behaviour on the highway.

Eduard Gierek, general secretary of the Polish Communist Party, recalls Leonid Brezhnev in the early 1970s:

I don't think he had any friends ... After negotiations between the Czech, Soviet and Polish delegations there was always a friendly get-together. A huge quantity of Soviet cognac was consumed at such gatherings. Brezhnev was coarse, cheerful, but plainly irritated by the implications of the Prague Spring. He told a story: 'A bear invited a hare to visit, and made his guest a delicious meal. The hare felt at home, and after a drink he felt more than equal to the bear. Back home the hare's wife asked him: "Why do you smell so bad?" And the hare replied: "The bear was relaxing after dinner, so he took me by the ears and skinned me!" ' Brezhnev loved this story, as did the entire Soviet delegation, but members of the other delegations were outraged by his tactlessness and hurried to bring dinner to an end.

His office in the Kremlin was ten by five metres, with doors on either side. There was nothing special in it, just a bust and portrait of Lenin. I wondered why the General Secretary had such a modest office, and concluded there were two possible reasons. Next door Lenin's office had been carefully preserved, comfortable but simple; the office next to that of the founder of the state plainly could not be ostentatious. The other reason was that as ruler of one-sixth of the earth he could afford to be modest . . .

Brezhnev had no home. None of these people had what you would call a home. They were given flats and dachas 'for services rendered', but in fact these and all their other privileges depended upon the position they occupied. Each Party and government servant had his own specific privileges; falling from grace in the USSR meant losing everything, including, in the Stalin period, one's life. Under Stalin's successors an erring or banished politician would simply be evicted from his flat, and his living standards would drop in accordance with his new position. I must admit, we often compared our life in Poland to theirs, and none of us would have wished to change places with them. Although amongst us there were some clinging by their teeth to power for power's sake, over there it was a vital necessity for every member of government.

The most feverish of the Brezhnev rumours concern his daughter, Galina Brezhneva, an all-too-typical product of what came to be known as the stagnation era. This aging, heavy-drinking woman, with an insatiable appetite for jewels and limitless opportunities to gratify it, had a young husband, an even younger lover and a passion for diamonds. One would like to know how she acquired this vast store of jewels. Those living at government expense rarely have much money, and the mafia would not have wanted to part with such vast quantities of valuables for no money. Some said the precious stones were gifts from people who owed her favours, yet there were other, semi-official channels for this stream of jewels. People may remember how not so long ago it was impossible to sell diamonds from the family jewel-box. Dealers would only buy gold by weight, and gems fetched almost nothing. According to the director of the state jewellery company, many beautiful antique and contemporary pieces of jewellery in the shops were confiscated from criminals, but these jewels mainly bypassed the shops and went straight to women of a special government rank.

There are many 'diamond legends' about Galina Brezhneva. One involved the museum in the Georgian town of Zugdidi, which contained two relics, a death-mask of Napoleon and the diadem of the *tsaritsa* Tamara. The heavily-guarded diadem lies on velvet under a thick pane of glass in the centre of the hall, a limp old plate with some unexceptional stones. In 1975 Galina Brezhneva visited the museum, and was so enamoured of the diadem that she demanded that the noble Zugdidians give it to her as a present. The director of the museum, mad with grief, plucked up the courage to inform the first secretary of the Georgian Communist Party, Eduard Shevardnadze, who grabbed the government telephone and told Comrade Brezhnev that while Georgia deeply respected Galina Leonidovna they could not give away the national heritage as she wished. 'Send Galina home!' was her father's response.

Another 'diamond story' is set at the end of 1981, during a festival of the Moscow circus. Galina Brezhneva adored the circus, and used to take her husbands and lovers there. She and her friend, the wife of Internal Affairs Minister Shchelokov, were present, adorned with their best jewels. But the diamonds of lion-tamer Irina Bugrimova outshone the Brezhnev diamonds, and were clearly superior. A few days later Irina Bugrimova's entire collection was ransacked, and the evidence led to Boris Buryats, Galina Brezhneva's young lover. Several days later Buryats was apprehended at Sheremeteva airport with part of the Bugrimova diamonds.

These stories grieved and damaged the health of Leonid Ilich, who suffered greatly in his later years from his relatives' adventures. 'The world respects you, but your own family doesn't respect you and causes you shame,' he would grumble to his Party colleagues.

Rumours were turned by *perestroika* into half-facts. Many of these are flawed with inaccuracies, and details have often been invented to give Brezhnev's successors something to swear at. But there is no smoke without fire. As the friends of Galina Brezhneva were picked up and arrested, the flats of high-placed officials were searched, and millions of roubles, together with gold and valuables, were confiscated, and Galina stopped appearing in public. At Brezhnev's funeral in November 1982, two burly guards were constantly by her side and people sat glued to their television sets as the funeral was broadcast and Andropov was seen to embrace Brezhnev's wife and turn his back on Galina.

Andropov ruled for fifteen months, during which time the investigations continued, and Galina Leonidovna's lover, Boris Buryats, was sentenced to five years in prison, where he died in mysterious circumstances. After Andropov's death, during the leadership of Chernenko, the rumours surrounding Galina weakened somewhat and she started to appear in public again. At a large reception held in 1948 in the Lenin Hills to commemorate International Women's Day, she was dressed in a severe blue suit.

Pinned to her bosom was a single piece of jewellery: the Order of Lenin, awarded to her in 1978 by Foreign Minister Gromyko on the occasion of her fiftieth birthday.

Yet the KGB continued to unearth more and more crimes, and as the investigation went on, criminal charges were brought against Andrei Shchelokov, former Minister of Internal Affairs, who in 1984 dressed himself in his army general's uniform and shot himself in the head.

Chernenko died, Gorbachev arrived, and Galina's husband, Yury Churbanov, was finally arrested, along with Brezhnev's son Yury, formerly deputy Minister of Foreign Trade. Searches of Galina's homes failed to yield results; some said Churbanov had hidden the diamonds, others that he had given them to friends. Galina Leonidovna's rooms were regularly searched in her presence, and she was habitually drunk, signing statements without reading them, taking a friendly interest in the police, and proposing that they all drink together.

It is a striking fact that amidst the mountain of gossip about the Brezhnevs and their wickedness there is nothing about Victoria Petrovna. Rumour simply runs off her.

As I sit with her in her apartment, where the recently destroyed past is still alive, she talks to me about her life. One of five children, she was born in Kursk, where her father, Pyotr Nikanorovich Denisov, was an engine driver. Her mother did not work. After leaving school she studied nursing at technical college, and it was at a dance there in 1935 that she met Leonid Ilich, then an agronomy student at Kursk technical college.

> He asked my best friend to go out with him, and she refused. He asked her out again, and again she refused him, because he couldn't dance. 'Coming, Vitya?' he said to me, so I went with him. Next day he asked my friend out again, and again she refused to go dancing with him. So once again I went with him. I taught him to dance, and he began seeing me home. I started looking at him seriously. He was solid, well educated. I can't say if he was handsome. He wore his hair with a side parting then and it didn't suit him; I persuaded him to change it, and he wore it that way ever since.

They married in 1938. Victoria Petrovna worked as a midwife until the birth of their two children. He qualified as a land surveyor, then studied at the metallurgy institute. There followed Party work, the war, and his steady rise up the Party ladder, crowned in 1964 by his appointment as General Secretary of the Party.

> He almost never saw the children, he was always at work. He loved it when the family got together, but when we were all sitting around the table on Sundays, the phone would invariably ring and he would be called out.
>
> At first I couldn't cook, but I was keen to learn, and it turned out I had a talent for it. Leonid Ilich, the children and our guests would praise my meals. Leonid Ilich had a splendid appetite, he loved my cooking, especially my borshch. 'No one cooks like Vitya,' he used to say. There are several types of Ukrainian borshch, you know – cold or hot, vegetarian or meat. Cutlets too; the secret of good cutlets is to beat the stuffing thoroughly before you fry them. I adore markets. When Leonid Ilich was first secretary in Dnepropetrovsk during the late forties, I always went to the market and bought everything myself. In markets the chickens are always in cages. I always bought a live chicken, the best. Saturdays and Sundays were lovely. I would take my time choosing, then say, 'Give me that one!' Then there were the fish. Dnepropetrovsk is on the river Dnepr. What perch and salmon there were! I'm on a special diet now, everything is boiled and tasteless. Only the memory remains.

When asked about the few occasions on which she travelled abroad with her husband, she says:

> I never liked those trips much, I always avoided them whenever possible. You never saw anything, just sat in the car listening to the guide.
>
> Once we flew to Paris for a magnificent reception, but in the distance people were demonstrating with banners which read, 'Victoria Petrovna, you are a Jew! Help your people leave for their homeland!' I felt uncomfortable. I'm not a Jew, you see, although people say I look like one, but I felt awkward saying I wasn't one, in case people thought I was denying my people.

Ludmilla Vladimirovna joins us at this point, and Victoria Petrovna asks her about the shopping.

Galina Kravchenko, Nadezhda Voroshilova, Ludmilla Vladimirovna – the daughters-in-law in this book – belong to a special category. Living in the Kremlin, submitting to its rules and accepting its privileges, all discovered the reverse side of Kremlin life when these privileges were withdrawn. A warm, youthful woman, Ludmilla Vladimirovna too has been bypassed by the rumours, because there is so obviously nothing to be said about this level-headed woman forced by circumstances to understand more than necessary and unable to do anything about it.

When I married Yury Leonidovich and moved in with the Brezhnevs they welcomed me into their family. I got on with Leonid Ilich, with his expansive character, from the start. He said I was to call them 'Papa' and 'Mama'. I couldn't right away as my own parents were alive, and Leonid Ilich said to Victoria Petrovna, 'Hey, Vitya, our daughter-in-law doesn't respect us – she won't call us Mama and Papa!' So after that I did so.

Victoria Petrovna is a good person, but difficult. The two of them got on wonderfully together. When he was young he was very lively, handsome and outgoing – he loved poetry and used to recite Merezhkovsky and Esenin from memory. Beside him she seemed less successful. She was just an engine driver's daughter, shy and ordinary. When I grew more comfortable with them I used to say to her, 'Your mother must have been courted by an educated Jew while your father was driving his train!' and she would laugh.

They both had large families, and family feelings were in their blood and maybe brought them together. Vitya would never start dinner without him, and he never did anything in the house without her permission; all domestic questions hung on his phrase: 'Ask Vitya, Vitya knows everything.'

Victoria Petrovna looked after not only her own children but her nieces and nephews too. When they went on holiday they would be accompanied by the entire family clan – nieces, nephews, his brothers' wives.

With people she was quiet and uncommunicative. It was hard to start a conversation with her. Receptions of any sort, even International Women's Day, were a torment for her. She would say, 'You go, Lusya, you speak.' And I would say, 'It's you they want to hear, not me!'

The servants especially loved Leonid Ilich, and she cherished her husband's authority in the home. When we were on holiday in the south, after swimming and eating we would want to sleep, but she would insist we stay at the table until he came, and he would invariably arrive with a bunch of flowers for her. Vitya and Lenya were like a pair of doves together.

Sitting at the table generally were not just Leonid Ilich's family but also his doctor, his nurse and the maid. There were two cooks, Slava and Valera, who worked for the Brezhnevs for twenty years. Victoria Petrovna always watched them work, and would say, 'It's good to see you've studied cooking, but that's restaurant food. For food to be special you must put a piece of your soul into it.'

She was always cooking: pepper with apples, home-smoked sausage, black pudding with buckwheat. She knitted clothes for Galina and Galina's daughter, and she brought up her granddaughter from the start; the child was named Victoria in her honour. She loved her nephews and her brothers and sisters too, and often seemed to favour them over Leonid Ilich. She gave no sign of suffering during the last stages of her life. But her voice trembled when she told me she had to leave her dacha. And later, when she was being criticised for something, she said in a breaking voice, 'It had to be like this – they blame me for the war in Afghanistan!' The fact was, she was totally uninterested in politics. Picking out a nice piece of lamb or some pigs' trotters was another matter, or whipping up a cherry pie, or beating cream for his mother, Natalya Denisovna, or peeling apples for the pudding.

She seemed to have a natural talent for cooking. She bustled around the house from morning to night, making jam, bottling cucumbers and tomatoes, pickling, drying herbs, making ravioli and cherry pies. Victoria Petrovna had several special recipes, including gooseberry jam. She would labour for hours over it, and it always tasted marvellous. People loved talking about food in the house, even at mealtimes.

She hated going out, he always invited people around to see them instead. If she told him Andryusha Gromyko had invited them over for dinner, he would say, 'Fine, but why should we go to them? Let them come here!'

Gromyko, Ustinov and Andropov were always visiting. It was all so inconsistent: set against the house and all the comforts of the flesh was an ostentatious show of modesty, with the grandsons forbidden to wear jeans for fear of what people might say. I wanted to dress well but I had to dress plainly to avoid gossip, so I would buy the cheapest earrings, and brooches that wouldn't fasten properly.

They had a four-hundred-rouble food allowance. Victoria Petrovna never let anything be thrown away, even an old battery, in case it came in useful later on. She kept all his old shirts and had them endlessly darned and mended. She and the two servants would work in the house for days on end without sitting down.

She wasn't an easy person. If she didn't like something she would be silent and her whole figure would be filled with reproach. I never saw her in tears. When he was in power in Dnepropetrovsk, Moldavia and finally Moscow, she had to keep moving from dacha to dacha, and her first question was always, 'Is there a cellar?' When she was moved on she never complained, she just said, 'All right, I'll go.' She had no women friends. But the wives of Mazurov, Kulakov, Gromyko and Ustinov often visited, and they would dine together and play cards.

Leonid Ilich shone so much more brightly than she did. He had an attractive personality and unlimited oportunities for love affairs. But they never quarrelled. She accepted their differences right from the start. She took care of the domestic side, and he appreciated her ability to create a homely atmosphere. In the morning she would sit beside him as he ate his breakfast. It calmed him to have her sitting there without eating. When he had his insulin injection for his diabetes she always had to be there. At night she would sit dozing until past midnight, waiting for him, and you never knew if she suspected anything. Her most striking feature was her patience and endurance.

The victory of Victoria Petrovna was the final victory of the Kremlin family woman over Nadezhda Krupskaya and the women of action who followed her. Yet her family triumphs yielded sad results, and as she herself says, 'The children gave me much happiness when I was young, but as they grew up they brought me much grief.'

The path from Krupskaya to Brezhneva defined the various stages of development in Soviet society, from a mighty explosion to stagnation, from the birth of an epoch through degeneration and on to rebirth. As this blind woman faces the advancing winter of 1991, her needs are few, she will survive, yet she is hurt because she has to worry about the shopping, and when the old *Kremlyovka*[1] is finally closed we can be sure that Raisa Gorbacheva and Naina Yeltsina will not be standing in line for bread. But these questions are not for her. As Anya slowly leads her out she smiles at me and we say goodbye. She is so simple, so ordinary, that I imagine I have understood nothing about her.

Victoria Brezhneva's experiences leave many questions unanswered, but they do provide us with the following excellent recipe:

Victoria Petrovna's gooseberry jam

Choose green, unripe gooseberries. Cut off the stems and extract the insides with a fork, exercising great care. Finely chop two or three walnuts, blanched and peeled. Add some finely minced lemon, and

[1]The special Kremlin foodstore.

insert the mixture into the skins of the fruit. To the extracted gooseberry pulp add two glasses of sugar for every kilo of fruit. Lay out the stuffed fruits in a flat dish, keeping them apart so the stuffing remains in place. Add sugar to the pulp mixture, bring to the boil, remove from the stove and sieve. Pour this liquid over the gooseberries and allow to stand for three to four hours. Pour off. Leave the gooseberries in the dish, boil the liquid five more times and pour it back in the dish. Place the gooseberries in a jar with the liquid, with two or three cherry leaves and one or two currant leaves. The jam should be a pinkish-green colour.

14

The Mystery of Tatyana

Yury Vladimirovich Andropov (1914–84). Born in a small railway town in the Northern Caucasus, son of a station master. Leaving school at sixteen, he entered the Rybinsk Water Transport College, but gained his chief education at Moscow's Higher Party School. In 1953 he joined the diplomatic service and went to Hungary, where he played a significant role during the 1956 uprising. In 1957 he was responsible for liaison with foreign communist parties, and in 1963 he became head of the KGB. A strong supporter of détente *with the West, he beat Chernenko to succeed Brezhnev as Party Secretary after the latter's death in 1982. He himself died within two years of a chronic kidney condition.*

Yury Andropov held power for over a year and was active for all but three months in this period; the rest of the time he was ill. Yet in these three months people felt that a mighty hand had pulled a lever and they could relax a little. Determined to preserve their illusions, people felt that this KGB man would provide the strong hand that was needed. He also issued a cheap new brand of vodka, popularly known as 'Andropovka'. In one working family, the poor wife, tormented beyond endurance by her drunken husband, called the police, told them he had been drinking 'Andropovka' and asked them to lock him in the cooler. Ignoring the drunkard, the policeman arrested the woman and threw her in prison for two weeks for insulting the government.

There was always a fearful, deferential attitude surrounding the new General Secretary, and although his official biography is contained in the Large Soviet Encyclopaedia, almost nothing is known about his personal life. Despite the sense of relaxation, it was under his leadership that the dissident movement was quietly trampled into the ground. Andropov could not be compared with Beria, of course; dissidents were no longer shot in the courtyard of the Lubyanka. Instead they were deposited in psychiatric hospitals or deported to the West, where they were welcomed with open arms. Yet Andropov was rumoured to be a widely-educated man who collected icons and loved poetry, and after his death his own poems were published, and reveal an aesthetic view of the world although little innate poetry or fire.

If Andropov was an enigma, his wife, Tatyana Fillipovna, was a total mystery. No word of her ever filtered through to the press, her face never appeared on our television screens, and her only public appearance was on the day of her husband's funeral, a large weeping woman dressed in black. While writing this book I attempted to meet her, but her telephone was never answered, and since it seems wrong to talk to someone's children and grand-children while they are still alive, I did not pursue it. And then, at the end of 1992, she died.

If I did not try too hard to meet Tatyana Fillipovna while she was alive, this was because of what I already knew from people who worked closely with Andropov and knew his family. This is how one of them described it:

Tatyana Fillipovna was Yury Vladimirovich's second wife. He had been married before and had a daughter, who lived with her mother. Tatyana Fillipovna and Yury Vladimirovich met in Karelia, where they both worked, and a great love grew between them. Yury Vladimirovich had a subtle, delicate nature and he knew how to love and respect people.

The tragedy occurred in Hungary during 1956, when Andropov was ambassador there. The Soviet wives were imprisoned in the Soviet embassy and their children were used as hostages. Tatyana Fillipovna behaved heroically, helping to evacuate the women and children, and leaving with her children in a tank. After this she became seriously ill, and one might say her life never recovered from the Hungarian earthquake.

In every battle, every clash of systems, there is no more horrifying sight than the suffering of women and children. I wished to know nothing more about this woman, who bore the tragedy of Hungarian-Soviet relations within her to the end of her days, but many people still testify to the fact that she remained to the last a sweet and delicate person.

15

Anna of Three Hundred Days

Konstanin Ustinovich Chernenko (1911–85). Born into a poor family in a remote Siberian village. Served with the border guards in Kazakhstan in the 1930s, then became Party secretary in Krasnoyarsk and stayed on in Siberia throughout the war. His move to Moldavia in 1948 was the start of his association with Brezhnev, who made him his propaganda chief. Brezhnev took him with him to Moscow to work on the Central Committee. After Andropov's death in 1984, Chernenko was the Central Committee's cautious choice of successor. Frail and wheezing, the new General Secretary held power for just a year, and died in March 1985.

One day in 1986, as *perestroika* proceeded apace, an elderly male voice spoke to me on the telephone and invited me to read my poems to a house management meeting of the Party Central Committee. He had been asked to contact me, he said, by Anna Dmitrevna Chernenko. A minute later, Anna Dmitrevna rang herself. I was leaving for Leningrad that evening and was reluctant to change my plans. But it proved impossible to refuse the widow of the former General Secretary, and I accepted.

Later Anna Dmitrevna and I talk in her spacious flat. She strikes one as a tall, elegant, middle-aged woman of severe Party demeanour, but when she speaks one realises she is actually small, with bright-blue eyes, a shy smile and a hint of sadness in her eyes. As director of the University of Culture at the building which houses Central Committee officials, this woman, who was briefly First Lady of State, has been responsible for a wealth of lively cultural events in the building's small lecture hall, with visits from actors and writers, distinguished scientists, cosmonauts and touring theatre productions. Governments may change, but Anna Dmitrevna remains the cultural director of the house on Kutuzov Prospect, and her husband's position has given her access to a wide range of interesting speakers.

Why did she work for thirty years to promote culture for others? What was her role beside the shadowy figure of her grey, slow-moving husband? In her flat we sit surrounded by numerous cut-glass vases, some pictures and a variety of gifts from organisations and governments: the typically impersonal accessories of a high-placed official's life; nobody wants them, there is nowhere to put them, but it would be wrong to throw them away. As Anna Dmitrevna reviews her past, she is alternately agitated and laughing: 'There's nothing especially interesting about my life. First came work, then family, then it was family and work.'

Despite her passion for political activity, she has always been a shy, modest person, who has spent her life battling with her nature. She was first politicised during the collectivisation of the thirties, when children and teenagers were recruited to the Party's Pioneer and Komsomol organisations, and masses of children were drawn into local departments of the universal-enlightenment machine. With adults and on their own, children flocked to villages, stations and farms to search out hidden grain for the hungry towns, and monuments went up thoughout Russia to young pioneer Pavlik Morozov, who lost his life after informing on his father for refusing to hand over bread. It was at this time that a notice entitled 'Lenin's Grandchildren' announced in a Rostov newspaper: 'Pioneer Anya Lyubimova has brought to the town a Red convoy bearing 1,046 *puds* of bread!'[1]

Anya and her girlfriends were proud. None of them had suffered Pavlik Morozov's fate as their convoy journeyed through the villages of the Don; people had gladly shared their grain with them, and she recalls how, as they were passing through one village, an old Cossack said, 'What are they thinking of, sending children! How can you refuse children?'

Born into a large and illiterate family, the best Komsomol in her class and the best science student, Anna Dmitrevna Lyubimova was a living example of Nadezhda Krupskaya's educational aspirations. She dreamed of building electric locomotives and studying at Moscow's Electro-mechanical Institute of Transport Engineers, but

---

[1] A *pud* is 16.5 kilograms.

her friends persuaded her to study at Saratov's Institute of Agricultural Engineering instead, and she ended up designing machines for sowing, winnowing and mowing. At first she did not like this, but she soon grew used to it, and her socially active temperament brought her a mass of new responsibilities as she climbed the ladder from Komsomol organiser to secretary of the Komsomol committee, and had to deal with applications for Party membership and process recommendations.

At the Institute there was a very popular lecturer in Marxism named Josif Kassil, brother of the children's writer Lev Kassil, and the halls were generally packed for his lectures. But Kassil had written a book entitled *The Steep Step*, in which those who wished to could trace sympathies with Trotsky. In 1936, during Stalin's campaign against the 'Trotsky–Zinoviev bloc', Josif Kassil was sent to the camps, and Anna Dmitrevna's hostel room-mate was expelled from the Komsomol for reading the book. Anna herself was attacked for 'sheltering' her friend, the Institute dealt her a severe reprimand for not exposing her teacher as an enemy of the people, and the man who had written her recommendation for Party membership hastily withdrew it, not wishing to compromise his career. The reprimand was lifted three years later, and she was again selected for Komsomol work, but she was a very anxious Komsomolka and suffered badly.

Anna Dmitrevna's experiences with the Red convoy served her well in her subsequent work in the villages around Moscow, supervising the transportation of agricultural goods. Her natural organisational abilities threw her into the thick of so-called 'dirty' village problems, such as raising the mileage-tonnage coefficient of agricultural machines, and exploiting motor-transport; she even wrote a pamphlet on the subject.

She did her work well, and she loved it. She often used to drive a tractor, and could repair one as well as any man. The only problem was the roughness of the company. She could not bear the drivers' cursing, and would frequently appoint someone else to replace her, for she was excellent at delegating. It was a long time before she married, for no one took her fancy, and she found all the men around her too coarse.

During the war she worked without respite. In 1944, as the war was ending, she and three men were sent off to the Volga to organise the State grain procurement. One of these men was kind and gentle, and in the evenings after work they would stroll along the river

Volga and watch the steamers. As she boarded the train back to Moscow, he thrust a note through the window, telling her to read it when the train was moving. In the note he wrote that he hoped to see her again in Moscow, and begged her to write to him. She wrote, and several months later they were married. They lived together in love and friendship for forty-two years with their three children, Elena, Vera and Vladimir, as well as his daughter from a previous marriage.

Anna Dmitrevna says:

Konstantin Ustinovich was a good, sensitive man. When he graduated from the Higher Party School after the war he was sent to do propaganda work in Penza, where our two daughters were born. He worked very hard. The light was always switched off last in his study, and he was never home before two or three in the morning. I always waited up for him. When he came in he would wash, I would give him something to eat, and afterwards we would sit chatting on the porch and wait for the sun to come up. Sometimes I would become silent, and he would say, 'What are you thinking about? Think aloud. We must think together!'

Sometimes he was very tense when he came home, and I could see he was miles away. I would keep quiet and not call him to dinner, and he would lie on the bed and close his eyes.

He always knew what people were thinking. He hated cunning and couldn't bear it when people tried to curry favour with him, but he quickly forgot about it if they didn't do it again.

When he was at home on Sundays it was like a holiday. He was witty and cheerful, and his reactions were quick. He didn't have much general culture, of course; I always regretted that and tried to help him, but I didn't know how. It was impossible to drag him to the theatre. 'I don't have time,' he would say. He was from a large peasant family. His mother died in 1919 of typhus, when he was eight, and his father remarried, to a very cruel woman who made the children's lives hell. Their village was flooded when a new dam was built, and all the people who lived there were evacuated to Novoselovo.

When we lived in Penza I worked until the children arrived. When we went to Kishinev I wanted to start work immediately, but Konstantin Ustinovich's sister, Valentina, a woman with a strong, domineering character, said to me, 'Don't be selfish, think about your husband and children! He has a good job! You should be looking after him instead of putting your own interests first. He has weak lungs!' So I didn't work, and I regretted it, of course. Our third son, Konstantin, was born in Kishinev. My husband rarely saw the baby, he was at work for days on end. Once he returned at five in the morning. I was in an agony of jealousy all night watching for him at the window, and when I saw him appear at the end of the street my nerves snapped. He came into the house, and I said to him, 'I don't know why you bothered coming home – you should have stayed where you were!' And he replied, 'Zhdanov has died. We've been writing the obituaries.'[2]

Later, when Brezhnev left Moldavia and gathered in Moscow all his most trusted officials, we moved into this building on Kutuzov Prospect. The building's management committee set up a 'University of Culture', and they chose me to be president. I felt that my old-fashioned organisational abilities could be useful to people, you see. The audience at our university were all old people, the children of peasants and workers, who had worked all their lives for the Party and the Komsomol, fulfilling Five-Year Plans, and culture had passed them by. They were happy to attend lectures, and said their studies helped them find their feet in the new life and gave them something to talk about with their grandchildren.

The day Konstantin Ustinovich was appointed General Secretary of the Party he stood at the door and said, 'They've confirmed it!'

'Confirmed what?' I said. 'The funeral?'

He explained that it had been discussed at great length, and it had been decided that he had the necessary experience and efficiency for the job. He was indeed an outstanding organiser, and he established a high level of record keeping. He organised the Politburo's work, and under his leadership all paperwork was dealt with promptly.

The last year of his life is terrible to remember. Everyone could see that he was dying and had not the strength to continue, but what could I do? When a person falls into the system he ceases to belong to himself and his loved ones. How often I would run beside his escort, grabbing their jacket and saying, 'Where are you going? Look at him – he shouldn't be getting out of bed!' But they'd say, 'We have to, Anna Dmitrevna, people are waiting for him, he's the head of state!'

As soon as he became General Secretary the red government telephone appeared beside his bed. I was so afraid. Of course I tried to protect him, and put the telephone beside me so when it rang I could pick up the receiver, ask who it was, and decide whether it was worth waking him or not. But when the phone rang in the middle of the night my heart would be pounding!

[2]Andrei Zhdanov, Stalin's most prominent lieutenant from 1946 until his sudden death in 1948, which was possibly engineered by Stalin himself.

When asked what privileges remained to her, Anna Dmitrevna replied that to begin with she had briefly enjoyed the use of a free motorcar, but that now she had to pay a prohibitive fifteen roubles an hour for the hire of one. Recently she received a plot of land, on which she and the children were building a dacha. She and her children are all friends, and it is this which makes her more happy than anything else, and reconciles her to the sacrifices she has made in her life for them and for Konstantin Ustinovich.

16

The Raissa Phenomenon

Mikhail Sergeevich Gorbachev (b.1931), born in a village near Stavropol in the Northern Caucasus, the son and grandson of prominent collective-farm workers. A star pupil, he left Stavropol in 1950 to study law at Moscow University, where he joined the Party and met Raissa; it was said to be under her influence that he became a reformer. After graduating he spent over twenty years in Stavropol, working for the Party and becoming first secretary there in 1970. In 1978 he was elected secretary of the Party Central Committee, and after the death of Chernenko in 1985 he was elected General Secretary on the basis of his grassroots Party experience.

As Mikhail Gorbachev revolutionised the Soviet power machine, with his wife by his side, Russian people's reactions to Raissa Maximovna were sharply divided. Many felt it was high time that Russia had a real First Lady, smart, elegant and clever, who travelled everywhere with the leader and whom we could be proud to show abroad. Others accused her of vulgarity, of stealing Gorbachev's publicity, of dressing like royalty at the state's expense and speaking out instead of staying in the background and sticking to official speeches.

Proponents of the second view evidently prevailed over the defenders of civilised values, yet I think that most Russians were behind Raissa. Like Mikhail Sergeevich, she was a child of her times. Born during the war into a poor family, she was a star pupil who had left school with a gold medal, a woman of the Khrushchev thaw, and the provincial wife of a Party worker as he rose irresistibly up the ladder of state power.

Since our frozen press regarded the personal as having no political significance, almost nothing was written about Gorbachev's domestic life when he became General Secretary in 1985. Yet millions throughout Russia were switching on their television sets to see Raissa Maximovna's sweet, smiling face, her trim figure and her large wardrobe of well-tailored suits. The Gorbachevs lent credibility to illusions of a new rapport between the people and this new, unusually pleasant-looking government. Mikhail Sergeevich was elected leader for his 'Party approach to people', and Raissa was the same; they were both of the people.

I had my own experience of this new spirit of *glasnost* (openness) in February 1987, when *Pravda* invited me to write something for International Women's Day. Since I have never been a member of the Party, I was astonished to be offered total journalistic freedom. Then I recalled Gorbachev's recent speech, in which he had said, 'We must draw women into ever wider echelons of power . . .' Oh, those echelons! I wrote my article, 'The Living Female Soul', in a fury of passion, demanding that women be allowed to achieve their social equality without being saddled with ever more social and political burdens.

The article prompted over eight thousand replies, the vast majority of them favourable, and the following March I was invited by Raissa Maximovna to a Women's Day celebration in the Lenin Hills. In November 1988 I joined the Gorbachevs' press corps on their visit to Italy. There I saw crowds thronging Raissa Maximovna's car, and in the evenings we talked together about *perestroika*'s implications for women. Nothing would come of Gorbachev's reforms, we agreed, unless women were allowed to take their proper place at every level of society, not merely to help men to fight, spoil and divide the world. We even discussed the possibility of a special parliament for women in Russia.

Of course Raissa Maximovna did not please everyone. Men were irritated not so much by Raissa herself as by the spectacle of a man taking his wife around with him when she should be at home watching television. Women were irritated by Raissa herself, and felt that anyone could look young and talk knowledgeably about art if they did not have to work and stand in queues all day. There were even dire hints that her thinness was the result of some unspecified internal disease. Yet we learned to live with these love–hate feelings, and we felt bereft when she failed to appear at her husband's side during several of his trips around Russia. Shortly after she disappeared, her autobiography, *I Hope*, appeared with a smiling picture of her on the cover.

Raissa Maximovna Titarenko was born of peasant stock in Siberia. Her mother had spun and ploughed from the age of eight, and learned to read and write only in her twenties. Her father was born in the Ukraine, but moved to Siberia in 1929 to work on the construction of a new railway line in the Altai region of Western Siberia, and worked for the rest of his life on the railways. He never joined the Party. Their first child, Raissa, was born in 1932 and christened in the Orthodox tradition.

In the 1930s her parents were denounced as '*kulaks*', their property was confiscated, and her grandfather disappeared in the camps, leaving his wife to die of grief and starvation. From then on the family was constantly on the move, and when the Second World War broke out Raissa's father went to fight at the front. She and her younger brother and sister attended a succession of schools, but their mother was determined to give her children the education she had never had, and her elder daughter became an avid reader. In 1949, seventeen-year-old Raissa spent her last year of school in the small Urals town of Sterlitamak, in Bashkiria. There she was awarded a gold medal for 'excellent results and exemplary conduct', and the 'right to enter institutes of higher education in the USSR without entry examination'. She chose to enter the philosophical faculty at the Lomonosov State University in Moscow.

In her book she describes the slow, cramped train journey to Moscow, and her pride and anxiety as she entered the old university buildings on Herzen Street in the city centre. There was a rich ethnic mix among the students at that time, and a large number of mature students whose education had been disrupted by war and who brought a special diligence to their studies in logic, philosophy and psychology. She recalls the optimism of student life in these years leading up to the Khrushchev thaw:

> I still find myself unable to explain how people achieved what they did in those unforgettable years. Where did they draw the strength? Factories, electric power stations, towns and villages were rebuilt, and the land, devastated by war, was restored to life. Lord, what joy we took in everything, how proud we were!

She writes of the student societies, the excited discussions on Hegel at Komsomol meetings, the passionate defence of student rights, the eminent lecturers and the radical, creative teaching. But she writes too of people who had overcome disaster at the cost of unbelievable sacrifices at the front, and were further humiliated by the last convulsions of Stalinism. And she describes her gradual disillusionment with the dogmatic teaching methods which replaced world culture with rote learning of Stalinist texts.

Like most of her fellow students, Raissa Maximovna lived in the forbidding four-storey university hostel in the Sokolniki district, near the Yauza river. Each room housed eight to fourteen students, kitchens and toilets were communal, and lacking the money to buy enough food or warm winter clothes she tried when possible to dodge paying her train fares. But unlike the Moscow girls, who had more interesting things to occupy them, she was a hard worker, studying in the library most of the day and delivering her final-year lecture on 'Sleep and Dreaming in the Teaching of I. P. Pavlov'. She lived her own life, she was popular, and all the boys wanted to dance with her.

It was at a student dance at the hostel that she and Mikhail Sergeevich Gorbachev first met. It is not known if she had any previous boyfriends, but all university girls of her generation were under great pressure to marry before graduating. Various cat-egories of men were considered eligible. First came diplomats and journalists who had the opportunity to work abroad. (The bolder girls even considered foreign students.) Next came postgraduate students in any subject. (There were rather few of these at the time.) The third group were professionals – scientists, teachers – provided they were from Moscow and of a good family. If all else failed there were always one's fellow students, preferably someone older and reliable. Boys in one's own year were chosen only in cases of passionate love, or fear that the exams were approaching, time was running out and one would have to leave Moscow.

Raissa Titarenko was one of those beautiful, romantic girls who married boys of their own year out of love. Long walks with Mikhail around Moscow were followed by outings to the cinema and the skating rink. In 1953 they parted for three months while he went off to the provinces to do his practical training as a lawyer, writing back to her of his disgust at the arrogance of the bosses and the passivity and conservatism of the masses. That summer he went back to his village near Stavropol in the Caucasus, where he worked as a combine driver, harvesting wheat to pay for the wedding. The parents were informed only days before the ceremony took place that autumn at the Sokolniki registry office. The celebration was attended by their student friends, and shortly afterwards the Gorbachevs travelled back to his village. Raissa Maximovna writes: 'We could have stayed on in Moscow after the wedding to do postgraduate work, but we didn't, and time proved this to be the right decision.'

Proud and independent by nature, she might secretly have dreamed of marrying into a rich family, but she could not have endured being patronised for her humble origins, and Gorbachev was the same. They were perfectly matched: hard-working, scrupulous, intelligent provincials, who had started from nothing and dreamed of achieving everything together. Had he married a girl from a comfortable Moscow family, and had she married a Moscow boy, they would have been less strong.

In the Caucasus, Raissa Maximovna taught philosophy at the Stavropol agricultural institute and the nearby farms, lecturing on logic, ethics, sociological concepts, contemporary philosophical trends, and the views of Kant and Lenin. She also taught the history of religion and atheism, and in the 1960s she discovered the Bible, the Koran and the Gospels.

As the focus of her studies and the subject of her doctoral thesis, however, she chose the family life, relationships and material conditions of the peasantry. For several years she tramped around the villages in rubber boots, drinking tea with old women and war widows, visiting medical centres, nurseries and old people's homes, and speaking at regional Party meetings. She gathered statistics, documents, archives, interviews and over three thousand questionnaires, in which women were asked if they would give up work if their husband could earn enough; the vast majority of them replied that they would not. She later described the importance of peasant life in shaping her attitudes: 'The Russian village is where we all have our roots, the source of all our strengths and perhaps our weaknesses too.'

Shortly after the birth of the Gorbachevs' daughter, Irina, in January 1957, Raissa Maximovna was again probing the depths of village life for her thesis, entitled 'The Development of New Features in the Life of the Peasantry in Collective Farms'. But her thesis was never completed. As she ascended the professional ladder as a teacher, Mikhail Sergeevich was rising up through the Stavropol Party organisation, and it quickly became apparent that he was overtaking her. Couples embarking on their professional lives together often find that one quickly takes the lead and the other has to choose. Generally, of course, it is the man who takes the lead; when it is the other way round the family often breaks up, with the man unable to forgive his wife's 'strength', and the woman her husband's 'weakness'.

Raissa Maximovna evidently had no desire to compete with Mikhail Sergeevich. There was even talk that she was offered the directorship of the Stavropol philosophy faculty, but that she turned it down. She had chosen to adopt the role of the 'weak' woman, and she apparently saw this as her strength.

For twenty years of her adult life she lived as a privileged provincial wife, who had to defer to the wife of the Stavropol Party boss. This could not have been easy for one with her independent temperament, but her own professional life as a teacher protected her from such humiliations. She always sought harmony, and she could find it in any situation. And when she became wife of the leader, and the other wives had to defer to her, she was once again protected by her teaching work and her relationship with her pupils.

The wife of one of Gorbachev's Stavropol subordinates did not find Raissa Maximovna easy to get along with:

> Her didactic tone and her unspoken assumption of her own infallibility grated on people's nerves. It was impossible to criticise her narrow-minded Party correctness, as this might reflect on her husband.

This arrogance with her subordinates and desire to please her superiors is a typical trait of those who come to power, and although not an inherent part of Raissa's nature, it became identified with her. She was a kind and generous woman, who cared for orphans and gave her money to children in the best traditions of her Kremlin predecessors. Yet she naively imagined that her kindness would be reciprocated, whereas paradoxically the more she gave, the more she irritated people. 'So what if she gives her money away? She has nothing else to do with it!' they said. Or, 'She lords it over people – it's vulgar!'

After Mikhail Sergeevich's election to the Central Committee in 1978 the Gorbachevs moved to the capital. Despite the improved housing and increased privileges in Moscow, she was repelled by the cold, hierarchical nature of her new life, and by the wives' narrow views and their incessant talk of home and family.

When Mikhail Sergeevich became General Secretary, his wife

inherited just one tradition, which had been established in Stalin's day: the absence of any right to a public, official existence. This is why her appearance as First Lady caused such a sensation. With no experience of diplomatic protocol, she had to pick up as she went along the etiquette surrounding seating, clothing and dining when she accompanied Gorbachev to his meetings with Presidents Reagan and Bush, Mrs Thatcher and the Queen of England. On her travels around Russia with her husband, she talked to women about jobs and pensions, schools and children's homes. In Moscow she threw herself into a variety of public works, and helped to promote the Soviet Fund for Culture. But her chief priority was the welfare of children, visiting those crippled and orphaned by the Armenian earthquake and the Chernobyl disaster, and acting as patron of a Moscow children's hospital and of the Moscow-based Haematologists for Children. Although deluged with requests concerning children, health, education and culture, she dealt single-handed with all correspondence, without any office or secretarial assistance.

After the publication of her autobiography and her reappearance by her husband's side, discussions about her flared up again, jokes and rhymes circulated about the Gorbachevs, and their hold over the popular imagination seemed assured. Yet she once said to me, 'I fear we won't last four years.' Did she fear that *perestroika* would not last? Surely she must have realised that the process would take decades. Whatever her words meant, they show her personal involvement in the political process. No wonder the boorish Yeltsin's reaction to her in the early days of *perestroika* was so inadequate, evidently assuming that a woman should function as some sort of fifth wheel, servicing men's domestic and physical needs.

While hiding behind conventionally female acts of charity, Raissa Maximovna played a far greater role in Russian politics than had any other Kremlin wife before her, even perhaps Nadezhda Krupskaya. Krupskaya had served Lenin as the personification of her all-consuming ideal. Raissa Maximovna's ideal was Gorbachev, and he was always right. She went further even than Victoria Brezhneva in subordinating herself to her husband. Aided by the television cameras and her famous charm, she transformed Soviet socialism into a more welcoming, stylish place with a subtle hint of capitalism. Yet when told that her appearance on television enlivened the tedium of Soviet life, and that if she were not there people would not listen to Gorbachev, she would invariably protest, 'That's terrible! You *must* listen to him!'

Mikhail Gorbachev had the choice of repairing the system or destroying it, and in trying to repair it by harnessing socialism to capitalism he destroyed it. Raissa Maximovna's conduct was most remarkable during the *putsch* of 1991, when she behaved like a woman afraid for her family. Her fear spoke in gentle, female words, but it taught the victors nothing and she fell ill.

*

For centuries Russia has been a field of battle for land, water, spheres of influence, the soul. Nowhere else in the world did these battles cover such vast and inaccessible dimensions of territory. Now, as innumerable doors open up to reveal the secrets of the past, Russian people gulp down a flood of information, seeking in it some explanation for the failures of the present. Some see these failures as a distortion of the socialist path. Others see nothing remotely socialist in this path. Some cite Stalin's terror, Brezhnev's stagnation, or Gorbachev's inconsistency. Yet few have thought to explore the role of those who bore and nurtured our leaders.

From Lenin on, the women of the Kremlin had complemented their male partners to an astonishing degree, whether as their allies or their polar opposites. The quiet spirit of rebellion lived within all of them, from Nadezhda Alliluyeva to Victoria Brezhneva, but all were ultimately prisoners of the male power machine. Princesses in their own domestic realm, their political power was notional, and they differed from other woman in Russia only in the material privileges which Kremlin life temporarily offered them. Women who refused to serve the machine faced the same fates as awaited Nadezhda Alliluyeva, Olga Budyonnaya and Ekaterina Kalinina.

The Kremlin wives appear as but the pale shadows of frighteningly great men, yet the men too were afraid, even Stalin. These men forced their people to go hungry, as food rotted in freight trains and those capable of unloading them sat in committees and fought for power. Had men linked their fates not with every passing '—ism' but with the women who shared their lives, then perhaps they would have renounced their bloodthirsty instincts. Had the leaders' wives been forced to queue for meat like ordinary mortals, and wait interminably to see the doctor at the local clinic, and travel to work by underground, changing twice, then wait for a crowded bus and pack into it like sardines – then perhaps they might have forced their husbands to forswear political heroics and our beautiful country would not have known such queues.

As always throughout our history, Russia's leaders have failed to foresee the bloody retribution which will inexorably follow. As the men now in power dance on their predecessors' graves, it is time for the women of Russia to cry: 'Enough! Stop the killing! Men and women together must build a new world, and a strong, secure Russia for our children!'

Chronology

1861 Tsar Alexander II emancipates the serfs and introduces reforms.

1860s and 1870s Radical men and women discuss ways of abolishing the autocracy. Some are drawn to the non-violent ideas of Tolstoy. Others, the populists, travel to the villages to urge the peasants to rise up against their masters. Many are arrested. Women's schools and further education courses are established, including the Bestuzhev courses for women.

1870 First factory strikes in St Petersburg.

1877–8 Two great show-trials of populist revolutionaries.

1878 Populist revolutionaries adopt terror tactics; numerous assassinations and attempted assassinations of prominent government officials.

1881 Revolutionary terrorists assassinate Alexander II. Six leading terrorists, including one woman, Sofia Perovskaya, are hanged.

1890s Revolutionaries abandon terror tactics and turn to the ideas of Karl Marx, who called on workers to use their industrial power to overthrow the class system.

1895 Marxist groups in St Petersburg united by Vladimir Lenin into the League of Struggle for the Emancipation of the Working Class. Lenin arrested.

1896 Large-scale textile-workers' strikes in St Petersburg. Many women workers involved.

1900 Lenin leaves Russia for Switzerland, to escape arrest.

1901 Formation in Russia of the Socialist Revolutionary Party, heirs to the terrorists of the 1870s.

1904 Outbreak of the Russo-Japanese war. Strikes and demonstrations throughout Russia.

1905 Russia's first revolution. *January*: thousands killed by police in peaceful demonstration outside Tsar Nicholas II's Winter Palace. Russia's towns and villages hit by waves of strikes, riots and demonstrations. Revolutionaries urge on the turmoil by conducting propaganda meetings and addressing strike gatherings. *October*: formation of the St Petersburg Soviet, or Council of Workers' Deputies, to co-ordinate the strike movement. Tsar Nicholas II issues Manifesto promising reforms. *December*: mass uprising in Moscow is suppressed. Revolutionaries rounded up and sent to prison and exile. Many escape abroad.

1906 The Tsar establishes the *Duma*, a legislative body with limited representation and powers.

1906–8 Suppression of the revolution: strikes banned, revolutionaries arrested. Alexandra Kollontai urges her fellow revolutionaries to turn their attention to the needs of women, calling on factory women to join the revolutionary movement and writing a book outlining a socialist approach to women.

1911 Lenin and his wife, Nadezhda Krupskaya, now based in Paris, become the focus of the future Bolshevik leadership. Inessa Armand, Alexandra Kollontai and other exiled revolutionaries in Paris write articles and address meetings to spread socialist ideas and recruit men and women to the revolution.

1914 *August*: start of the First World War. St Petersburg renamed Petrograd.

1915–17 Strikes and food riots throughout Russia. Lenin and the Bolsheviks in Switzerland urge Russian soldiers to turn their weapons against those in power at home, and turn the imperialist war into revolutionary war.

1917 *March:* women storm the streets of Petrograd. The riots spread, the capital is brought to a standstill. Tsar Nicholas II abdicates and a new Provisional Government takes power. *April:* Lenin and other exiled revolutionaries are allowed by the German government to pass through Germany in a sealed train and return to

Russia. In Petrograd they agitate in factories, military garrisons and warships for Bolshevik power. Riots and demonstrations throughout Russia. *July*: revolutionary sailors attempt to storm the Winter Palace and are crushed. Bolshevik leaders go underground and in September institute the *Cheka*, the Extraordinary Commission for the Struggle against Sabotage and Counter-Revolution, under the leadership of Felix Dzerzhinsky. *October 25–6:* at the second All-Russian Congress of Soviets the Bolsheviks declare themselves in power, and workers and sailors storm the Winter Palace and oust the Provisional Government. The Bolsheviks form a new government, the Soviet of People's Commissars, with Lenin as its president, Lev Trotsky as Commissar of Foreign Affairs, Alexandra Kollontai as Commissar of Social Welfare, Yakov Sverdlov as head of the Central Committee, and Anatoly Lunacharsky as Commissar of Enlightenment. *November:* First Congress of Petrograd Working Women.

1918 *March*: the capital moves from Petrograd to Moscow in anticipation of a German invasion of Russia. Brest Litovsk peace treaty signed with Germany. Armies of fourteen states, including the White Czech Legions, attack Bolshevik Russia as the civil war begins in earnest. Leading Bolsheviks tour the front in agit-trains, urging people to fight the Whites. *July:* Tsar Nicholas II and his family shot in Ekaterinburg. *August:* Lenin shot and seriously wounded by a terrorist woman in Moscow. Beginning of the Red Terror, in response to the White Terror. Numerous purges of the Party and the army. *November:* First All-Russian Congress of Working and Peasant Women held in Moscow.

1919 Establishment of special women's department of the Party, the *Zhenotdel*.

1920 Eighth Party Congress creates a Political Bureau (*Politburo*), a small group within the Central Committee, and the Organisational Bureau (*Orgburo*), to check Party records and staff. Kollontai appointed director of the *Zhenotdel*.

1921 Adoption of the New Economic Policy, favouring a limited return to private enterprise.

1922 The *Cheka* is replaced by the GPU, the Government Political Administration, later known as OGPU. *April:* as Lenin's health deteriorates Josif Stalin replaces him as acting Party Secretary.

1923–4 The Party organises discussions on ethics and the family.

1924 Lenin dies. Petrograd is renamed Leningrad.

1927 Trotsky and Grigory Zinoviev expelled from the Party.

1928 More oppositionists to Stalin arrested and imprisoned.

1929 Trotsky is exiled to Turkey, and Nikolai Bukharin, Alexei Rykov and other prominent Bolsheviks are arrested by Stalin. *April:* first Five-Year Plan. *December:* Stalin calls for accelerated collectivisation of the peasantry.

1934 The OGPU comes under the adminstration of the People's Commissariat for the Interior (the Ministry for Internal Affairs), the NKVD, under which name it is now known. *December:* the assassination in Leningrad of government member and loyalist Stalinist Sergei Kirov is the signal for savage new Party purges.

1936 The first public show trials, of Grigory Zinoviev and Lev Kamenev. Adoption of the 'Stalin Constitution'. Execution of hundreds of Red Army leaders.

1937 Stalin's terror starts in earnest.

1937–8 The second show trial, of old Bolsheviks Karl Radek and Yury Pyatakov.

1938 *March:* the purges continue with the execution of Bukharin and fifteen others. *December:* Lavrenty Beria takes over from Ezhov as head of the secret police, the NKVD.

1939 *August:* Russia signs non-aggression pact with Germany. Two weeks later Hitler invades Poland.

1940 Trotsky assassinated in Mexico.

1941 *June:* Nazi troops invade Russia. Moscow threatened.

1943 *February:* Soviet troops defeat Nazis in the battle of Stalingrad.

1945 *May:* victory over Germany.

1946 Mounting post-war terror, with campaigns against the Jews.

1952 *December:* anti-Semitic campaign culminates in the Doctors' Plot, in which Kremlin doctors are accused of poisoning Soviet leaders at the behest of international Zionism and the CIA.

Formation of the KGB, the Committee for State Security, under the Ministry for Internal Affairs.

1953 *March:* Stalin dies. *June:* arrest and execution of Beria. End of the Stalinist terror. Nikita Khrushchev emerges from the ensuing power struggle as new Party Secretary.

1956 *February:* the high-point of post-Stalin liberalisation, the 'Thaw', comes with Khrushchev's 'secret speech' on Stalin at the Twentieth Party Congress. Prisoners released *en masse* and disgraced intellectuals rehabilitated. *October–November:* uprisings in Poland and Hungary cause panic in the Soviet government, and 'liberalisation' is halted.

1964 *October:* Khrushchev ousted from power and replaced by Alexei Kosygin and Leonid Brezhnev.

1966–7 Stalin partially rehabilitated. Dissidents arrested and forced to leave Russia.

1968 Soviet invasion of Czechoslovakia.

1969 Clashes between Soviet and Chinese border troops.

1979 *December:* Soviet invasion of Afghanistan.

1980 *Summer:* Olympic Games staged in Moscow.

1981 Martial law imposed in Poland. Brezhnev's health in decline.

1982 The country suffers severe food shortages. Growing pressure on the ailing Brezhnev to resign. *November:* Brezhnev dies of a heart attack. Andropov becomes Party Secretary. Talks with China open and relations with the US become warmer. Hints that Soviet troops will be withdrawn from Afghanistan.

1983 Andropov pursues his campaign against corruption, profiteering and bureaucracy with raids on bars, cinemas and shops. Arms talks with the US government continue in Geneva. *September:* Korean Airline plane carrying 269 people, including many Americans, shot down by Soviet fighter aircraft.

1984 *January:* Andropov launches his 'limited industrial experiment', designed to give increased economic powers to factory managers. *February:* Andropov dies and is succeeded by Konstantin Chernenko.

1985 *March:* Chernenko dies, to be succeeded by Mikhail Gorbachev, whose efforts to modernise and liberalise the country are summarised in the concepts of *perestroika* and *glasnost*, reconstruction and openness.

1989 Communism in Eastern Europe is swept away by revolutions in Hungary, Czechoslovakia, Poland and Eastern Germany. Mounting ethnic and political crises in Georgia, Baku and the Baltic states.

1990 The Soviet Communist Party is undermined by Russia's new parliament, the Congress of People's Deputies. Mounting economic and political chaos; mass demonstrations in Moscow for the new Congress President, Boris Yeltsin.

1991 *February:* Yeltsin calls for Gorbachev's resignation. *June:* Yeltsin is elected President of the Russian Federation and makes his power base in the White House. *August 19:* while Gorbachev is on holiday at the Black Sea former members of his staff order him to stand down or be deposed. Yeltsin leads the opposition to the *putsch.* Gorbachev is brought to the White House, where he publicly renounces the Communist Party and resigns as its General Secretary. As Soviet President, Gorbachev works with Yeltsin to negotiate a new Union treaty, but as the Soviet Union disintegrates, Gorbachev resigns under pressure from nationalist movements and Yeltsin assumes power.

Select Bibliography

Books and articles

Two publications widely quoted will be given in abbreviated form. These are *Novy zhurnal* (New Journal), represented here as *NJ*, and *Sovershenno sekretno* (Top Secret), *SS*.

Adzhubei, A, 'Te desyat let' (Those ten years), *Sovietskaya Rossiya*, 1989.
Alexandrova, V, 'Pervaya voennaya zima v Rossii' (Russia's first winter of war), *NJ*, 1943, no. 4.
Alexinskaya, T. '1917 god' (The year 1917), *NJ*, 1968, nos 90–4.
Alliluyev S, *Proidyonny Put* (The path covered), Moscow, 1946.
Alliluyeva, N. S, obituaries, *Pravda*, 10, 12, 16 November 1932.
Anin, D, 'Perspektivy i vnutrennie protivorechiya bolshevisma' (The prospects and internal contradictions of Bolshevism), *NJ*, 1954, no. 36.
Annenkov, Y, *Dnevnik moikh vstrech* (Diary of my meetings), vols 1 and 2, Moscow, 1966.
—, 'Vospominaniya o Lenine' (Memories of Lenin), *NJ*, 1961, no. 65.
Antonov-Ovseenko, A, *Stalin bez maska* (Stalin without mask), Moscow, 1990.
Arbatov, Z, *Ekaterinoslav 1917–1944*, vol. 12, Berlin. Archive of the Russian revolution.
Armand, I, *Stati, rechi pisma* (Articles, speeches and letters), Moscow, 1975.
Arsenidze, R, 'Iz vospominanii o Staline' (Memories of Stalin) *NJ*, 1963, no. 72.
Avtorkhanov, A, 'Koba i Kamo' (Koba and Kamo), *NJ*, 1973, no. 110.
— 'Lenin i Ts.K. v oktyabrskom perevorote' (Lenin and the Central Committee in the October revolution), *NJ*, 1970, no. 100.
— 'Ts.K. protiv planov Lenina o vosstanii' (The Central Committee against Lenin's plans for the uprising), *NJ*, 1971, no. 101.
Berberova, N, *Zheleznaya zhenshchina* (Iron woman), Russica publishers, New York, 1982.

Berdyaev, N, *Istoki russkogo komunizma* (The sources of Russian Communism), Moscow, 1990.

Berter, I, 'E. D. Stasova', *NJ*, 1971, no. 103.

Bocharnikova, M, 'Boi v zimnem dvortse' (The battles at the Winter Palace), *NJ*, 1962, no. 68.

Bonch-Bruevich, M, *Vsya vlast sovetam* (All power to the soviets), Moscow, 1958.

Borev, Y, *Staliniada* (Staliniad), Moscow, 1990.

Breshkovskaya, E, '1917 god' (The year 1917), *NJ*, 1954, no. 38.

Bunin, I, *Pod serpom i molotom* (Under the hammer and sickle), London/Canada, 1975.

—, *Okayannye dni* (Cursed days), Moscow, 1990.

Buranov, Y, 'Poedinok s gensekom' (Duel with the General Secretary), *SS*, 1991, no. 7.

Burt, V, 'Zinochka iz 1917-ogo' (Zinochka from 1917), *SS*, 1990, no. 8.

Chernov, V, *Pered burei* (Before the storm), New York, 1953.

Chernova, O, 'Kholodnaya zima: Moskva 1919–1920' (A cold winter: Moscow 1919–1920), *NJ*, 1975, no. 121.

Chuev, F, *Sto sorok besed s Molotovym* (One hundred and forty conversations with Molotov), Moscow, 1990.

Dan, 'Bukharin o Staline' (Bukharin on Stalin) *NJ*, 1964, no. 75.

Domontovich, A, *Zhenshchina na perelome* (Woman at the turning-point), Moscow-Petrograd, 1923.

Dopolev, E, 'Taina zolotykh byustov' (The secret of the golden busts), *SS*, 1991, no. 3.

Drabkina, E, 'Zimnii pereval' (Winter crossing), *Novy Mir*, 1968, no. 10.

Dridzo, V, *Nadezhda Konstantinovna*, Moscow, 1969.

Druzhnikov, Y, 'Blizhnyaya dacha' (The next-door dacha), *SS*, 1991, no. 4.

Dumova, N, *Konchilos vashe vremya* (Your time is over), Moscow, 1990.

Essen, *Inessa Armand*, Moscow, 1925.

Feikhtvanger, L, *Moskva 1937* (Moscow 1937), Moscow, 1990.

Geller, M, *Mashina i vintiki* (The machine and the cogs), London, 1985.

Gins, G, 'Perevopolshchenie Peterburga' (The reincarnation of St Petersburg), *NJ*, 1952, no. 58.

Gippius, Z, 'Dnevnik. 1938 g.' (Diary for 1938), *NJ*, 1968, no. 92.

Gorky, M, *Vladimir Ilich Lenin*, Moscow, 1924.

Gul, R, 'Krasnye marshaly' (The Red Marshals), Moscow, 1990.

—, 'Ya unes Rossiyu' (I took Russia away), *NJ*, 1978–79, nos 132–8.

Gurvich, A, 'Artisticheskaya Moskva 1917–1920' (Artistic Moscow 1917–1920), *NJ*, 1977, no. 129.

Guseinov, E, 'Syn partii' (Son of the Party), *Izvestiya*, 14 November 1982.

Kerensky, A, 'O revolyutsii 1917 goda' (The revolution of 1917), *NJ*, 1947, no. 15.

—, 'Dva Oktyabrya' (Two Octobers), *NJ*, 1947, no. 17.

—, 'Kak eto sluchilos?' (How did it happen?) *NJ*, 1953, no. 34.

Kheraskov, M, 'Obshchestvo blagorodnykh' (Noble company), *NJ*, 1946, no. 14.

Khodasevich, V, *Literaturnye stati i vospominaniya* (Literary articles and memoirs), New York, 1954.

Kolesnik, A, *Mify i pravda o seme Stalina* (Myths and truth about Stalin's family), Moscow, 1991.

Koltsov, P, *Diplomat Fyodor Raskolnikov* (The diplomat Fyodor Raskolnikov), Moscow, 1990.

Koridze, T, 'Intervyu N. T. Beria' (Interview with N. T. Beria), *SS*, 1990, no. 9.

Kozhenova, T, 'Budni sovetskoi zhenshchiny' (Everyday life of the Soviet woman), *NJ*, 1953, no. 34.

Kramov, I, *Utrennii veter* (Morning Wind), Moscow.

—, *Literaturnye portrety* (Literary portraits), Moscow, 1962.

Krasnopolskaya, I, 'Komandarm' (Army Commander), *Moscow Pravda*, 2 August 1987.

Kravchenko, G, *Mozaika minuvshego* (Mosaic of the past), Moscow, 1975.

Kreidlina, L, *Bolshevik dragotsennoi proby* (A Bolshevik of precious worth), Moscow, 1990.

Krivorotov, V. and Chernyshev, S, 'Zagadka Lenina' (The mystery of Lenin), *Literaturnaya gazeta*, 17 April 1991.

Krotkov, Y, 'KGB v deistvii' (The KGB in action), NJ, 1973, nos 108–12.

Krupskaya, N, *Pedagogicheskie sochineniya* (Pedagogical writings), 11 vols, Moscow, 1957–63.

Kunetskaya, L. and Mashtakova K, *Krupskaya*, Moscow, 1985.

Kuskova, E, 'Davno minuvshee' (The distant past), *NJ*, 1958, no. 54.

Larina-Bukharina, A, *Nezabyvaemoe* (The unforgotten), Moscow, 1989.

Lenin, V. I, *Pisma k rodnym. 1893–1922*, vol. 37 of his Complete Collected Works, Moscow, 1957.

Lukomsky, A, *Vospominaniya* (Memoirs), vols 1 and 2, Berlin, 1922.

Manukhin, I, 'Vospominaniya o 1917–1918' (Memories of 1917 and 1918), *NJ*, 1958, no. 54.

Medvedev, R, *Oni okruzhali Stalina* (They surrounded Stalin), Moscow, 1990.

—, 'Konets "sladkoi zhizni" dlya Galiny Brezhnevoi' (The end of the 'sweet life' for Galina Brezhneva), *SS*, 1990, no. 2.

—, *Stalin i Stalinizm* (Stalin and Stalinism), Moscow, 1990.

Melgunov, S, *Krasny terror* (The red terror), Moscow, 1990.

—, 'Osada zimnego dvortsa' (The siege of the Winter Palace), *NJ*, 1947, no. 17.

Naglovsky, A. D. (signed A.N.), 'Lenin', *NJ*, 1967, no. 88.

Kremlin Wives

—, 'Vospominaniya' (Memoirs), *NJ*, 1968, no. 90.

Nikolaevsky, B, 'Porazhenie Khrushcheva' (The defeat of Khrushchev), *NJ*, 1951, no. 25.

Nord, L, *Marshal Tukhachevsky*, Paris, 1978.

Olesin, M, *Pervaya v mire: Biograficheskii ocherk ob A. M. Kollontai* (First in the world: a biographical essay on A. M. Kollontai), Moscow, 1990.

Oskotsky, V, 'Glavny ideolog' (The chief ideologue), *SS*, 1991, no. 5.

Pestkovsky, S, 'Vospominaniya o rabote v Narkomnatse' (Memories of work in the Commissariat of Nationalities), *Proletarskaya revolyutsiya*, 1930, no. 6.

Pilnyak, B, *Ubiistvo komandarma* (Death of a commander), London, 1965.

Pleshakov, L, 'I styla krov pri imeni ego' (The blood froze at his name), *SS*, 1990, no. 3.

Popov, I, *Odin den s Leninym* (A day with Lenin), Moscow, 1963.

Pribytkov, V, 'Pomoshchnik genseka' (The General Secretary's assistant), *SS*, 1990, no. 7.

Prushinsky, K, 'Noch v Kremle' (Night in the Kremlin), *SS*, 1990, no. 7.

Pushkarev, S, 'Oktyabrsky perevorot 1917 g. bez legend' (The October 1917 revolution without legends), *NJ*, 1967, no. 89.

Reisner, L, *Izbrannye proizvedeniya* (Selected works), Moscow/Leningrad, 1956.

Rolitsky, Y, 'Bolshoi brat' (Big brother), *SS*, 1991, no. 5.

Rotin, I, *Proidem za rytsaryami revolyutsii i lyubvi* (Let us follow the knights of revolution and love), Moscow, 1978.

Rubanov, S. and Netinsky, S, *Krupskaya v Peterburge* (Krupskaya in Petersburg), Leningrad, 1975.

Satina, S, 'Obrazovanie zhenshchin v dorevolyutsionnoi Rossii' (The education of women in pre-Revolutionary Russia), *NJ*, 1964, no. 76.

Semyonov, Y, 'Taina Kutuzovskogo prospekta' (The secret of Kutuzov Prospect), *SS*, 1989, nos 6–7.

Shelest, P, 'Kak eto bylo' (How it was), *SS*, 1990, no. 6.

Shturman, D, *V. I. Lenin*, Paris, 1989.

Shub, D, 'Tri biografii Lenina' (Three biographies of Lenin), *NJ*, 1964, no. 77.

—, 'Kupets revolyutsii' (The merchant of the revolution), *NJ*, 1967, no. 87.

—, 'Iz davnikh let' (From bygone years), *NJ*, 1970–3, nos 99–110.

Simonov, K, 'Glazami cheloveka moego pokoleniya' (With the eyes of a man of my generation), *Znamya*, 1988, nos 6–7.

Tolstaya, A, *Probleski vo tme* (Glimmers in the dark), Washington, 1965.

Tolstaya, O, 'Dozhd i solntse' (Rain and sun), *NJ*, 1979, no. 132.

Turov, N, 'Vstrecha s Abbakumovym v tyurme NKVD' (A meeting with Abbakumov in the NKVD jail), *NJ*, 1970, no. 98.

Tyrkova-Williams, N, *To, chego bolshe ne budet* (What will not be again), Paris, 1953.

Valentinov, N, *Vstrechi s Leninym* (Meetings with Lenin), New York, 1953.

—, *NEP i krizis partii posle smerti Lenina* (The New Economic Policy and the crisis of the Party after Lenin's death), Hoover Institutions Press, 1971.

—, 'Chernyshevsky i Lenin' (Chernyshevsky and Lenin), *NJ*, 1951, nos 26–27.

—, 'Lenin v Simbirske' (Lenin in Simbirsk), *NJ*, 1954, no. 37.

—, 'Vydumki o rannei revolyutsionosti Lenina' (Fabrications about Lenin's early life as a revolutionary), *NJ*, 1954, no. 39.

—, 'Rannie gody Lenina' (Lenin's early years), *NJ*, 1955, nos 40–41.

—, 'Vstrecha Lenina s marxismom' (Lenin's encounter with Marxism), *NJ*, 1957, no. 53.

—, 'O lyudyakh revolutsionnogo podpolya' (People of the revolutionary underground), *NJ*, 1963, no. 63.

Vasetsky, N, *Likvidatsiya* (Liquidation), Moscow, 1989.

Vishnevskaya, G, *Istoriya zhizni* (History of a life), Moscow, 1991.

Volkonogov, D, *Triumf i tragediya* (Triumph and tragedy), vols 1 and 2, 1989.

Voslensky, M, *Nomenklatura* (Nomenclature), London, 1990.

Vulf, B, 'Krupskaya chistit biblioteki' (Krupskaya purges the libraries), *NJ*, 1970, no. 99.

Zemtsov, I, *Chernenko: Sovetsky soyuz v kontse perestroiki* (Chernenko: the Soviet Union at the end of *perestroika*), London, 1989.

Zenzinov, V, *Perezhitoe* (Experiences), New York, 1953.

Zhid, A, *Vozvrashchenie iz SSSR* (Return from the USSR), Moscow, 1990.

Zykina, L, 'V moei zhizni vse bylo krasivo' (Everything in my life was lovely), *SS*, 1991, no. 3.

Anthologies

Dodnes tyagoteet (A burden to this day), Moscow, 1989.

Larisa Reisner v vospominaniyakh sovremennikov (Reisner remembered by her contemporaries), Moscow, 1969.

Ot ottepeli do zastoya (From thaw to stagnation), Moscow, 1990.

'Partiinaya etika': Diskussii 20-x godov (Party 'ethics': discussions of the 1920s), Moscow, 1989.

Reabilitatsiya (Rehabilitation), Moscow, 1991.

Reabilitirovan posmertno (Posthumously rehabilitated), Moscow, 1989.

Vozhd, diktator, khozyain (Leader, dictator, master), Moscow, 1990.

Vozvrashchennye imena (Returned names), Moscow, 1989.

Odinadtsatyi sezd RKP(b). Stenograficheskii otchet (The Eleventh Party Congress, a stenographic record), Moscow, 1922.

Trinadtsatyi sezd RKP(b). Stenograficheskii otchet (The Thirteenth Party Congress, a stenographic record), Moscow, 1924.

Chetyrnadtsatyi sezd RKP(b). Stenograficheskii otchet (The Fourteenth Party Congress, a stenographic record), Moscow-Leningrad, 1926.

Shestnadtsaty sezd RKP(b). Stenograficheskii otchet (The Sixteenth Party Congress, a stenographic record), Moscow, 1950.

Books in English

(English translations of Russian books are cited wherever possible)

Alliluyeva, S, *Letters to a Friend*, trans. Priscilla Johnson, Hutchinson, London, 1967.

—, *Only One Year*, trans. Paul Chavchavadze, Hutchinson, London, 1969.

Clark, W, *The Man Behind the Mask*, Faber and Faber, London, 1988.

Conquest, R, *The Great Terror*, Macmillan, New York, 1968.

Engels, F, *The Origins of the Family, Private Property and the State*, Pathfinder Press, New York, 1972.

Fisher, L, *The Life of Lenin*, London, 1964.

Gorbacheva, R, *I Hope*, trans. David Floyd, Harper Collins, London, 1991.

Krupskaya, N, *Memoirs of Lenin*, London, 1930.

Mandelstam, N, *Hope Against Hope*, trans. Max Hayward, Penguin, 1970.

—, *Hope Abandoned*, trans. Max Hayward, Penguin, 1974.

Rayne, R, *The Rise and Fall of Stalin*, W. H. Allen, London, 1965.

Trotsky, L, *My Life*, Penguin, London, 1975.

—, *History of the Russian Revolution*, New York/London, 1932.

—, *Stalin*, Harper, New York/London, 1941.

Tucker, R, *Stalin as Revolutionary, 1879–1929*, Chatto & Windus, 1974.

Wittlin, T, *Commissar*, Angus and Robertson, Sydney, London, 1973.

Index

Index

Happy Flight (film), 52
Hart-Maxin, Doris, 130
Hegel, G.W.F., 214
Hitler, Adolf, 75, 127
Hot Days (film), 158

International Women's Conferences:
  1920, 22; 1921, 127, 138–9
Ioffe, Adolfe, 65
Ivan Susanin (opera), 91
Ivan the Great (building), 18
Ivanov, 124
Izvestia (newspaper), 43, 69

Jewish Anti-Fascist Committee, 135,
  140–1
Jews (Russian), 132, 140–3

K (prisoner), 102–3
Kaftanova, 181
Kaganovich, Lasar, 36, 68, 127, 157,
  170, 173
Kaganovich, Maria, 68, 113, 132
Kalinin Museum, 125
Kalinin, Mikhail Ivanovich: and
  Nadezhda Stalina, 68; background,
  113; and Ekaterina Ivanovna, 114,
  118–19, 124; presidency, 115; on
  power, 123; and the operetta
  singers, 168
Kalinin, Valerian, 114
Kalnina, Ekaterina Ivanovna (*née*
  Lorberg): background, 113; and
  Kalinin, 114, 119; and the
  Trotskys, 115; in Altai, 116–18;
  interrogations, 120–3; letter to
  Rudenko, 124–5; and Valentina
  Ostroumova, 126; files on, 160;
  and Kremlin wives, 219; *The
  Glorious Path of the Komsomol*,
  119
Kalinina, Ekaterina Valerianovna,
  116, 123, 125
Kalinina, Maria Vasilevna, 114
Kamenev, Alexander Lvovich
  (Lyutik), 47–53
Kamenev, Lev Borisovich (*born
  Rosenfeld*): and the Lenins, 25, 27;
  and Nadezhda Stalina, 29, 64;
  families, 33, 49; background, 46;
  and Galina Sergeevna, 48, 52;

food, 50; arrest, 51; death, 53; at
  Adolfe Ioffe's funeral, 65;
  marriage, 78
Kamenev, Vitalik Alexandrovich
  Kravchenko, 50–3
Kamenev, Yura Lvovich, 49, 51, 53,
  115
Kameneva, Galina Sergeevna (*née*
  Kravchenko): background, 47;
  marriage, 48; family life, 49–50;
  Lyutik's arrest, 51
Kameneva, Olga Davidovna, 46–53,
  55, 76
Kant, Immanuel, 22
Kaplan, Fanya, 22
Karpovskaya, Pearl Semyonovna, *see*
  Molotova, Paulina Semyonovna
Kartashov, 40
Kassil, Josif, 208
Kassil, Lev: *The Steep Step*, 208
Katukov, Marshal, 131
Katukova, Ekaterina Sergeevna, 92,
  131, 153, 157
Khazan, Dora, 68
Khodasevich, Vyacheslav, 22, 46–7
Khoroshkevich, 124
Khromchenko, 136
Khrushchev, Leonid, 177–8, 184
Khrushchev, Nikita Sergeevich: and
  the Palace of Congress, 18; on
  Nadezhda Stalina, 66, 71;
  marriage, 78; and the Voroshilovs,
  80; and Ekaterina Kalinina, 125;
  and Molotov, 127; at Stalin's
  funeral, 145; and the Molotovs,
  146; and Beria, 170; compared
  with Stalin, 171; background, 173;
  visit to America, 174; meets Nina
  Petrovna, 177; career, 178–9; Nina
  Petrovna on, 180–3; Rada
  Khrushcheva on, 184–5; Alexei
  Adzhubei on, 186; and Brezhnev,
  190; Raissa Gorbacheva on, 214;
  *Khrushchev remembers: The Last
  Testament*, 188–9
Khrushchev, Sergei Nikanorovich,
  179, 188
Khrushchev, Seryozha, 178, 184, 187
Khrushcheva, Efrosinya Ivanovna,
  177
Khrushcheva, Lenochka, 187

Index

Index

/